JAILBAIT

JAILBAIT

The Politics of Statutory Rape Laws
in the United States

Carolyn Cocca

State University of New York Press

Published by
State University of New York Press, Albany

For information, address State University of New York Press,
90 State Street, Suite 700, Albany, NY 12207

Production by Kelli Williams
Marketing by Michael Campochiaro

Library of Congress Cataloging-in-Publication Data

Cocca, Carolyn, 1971–
    Jailbait : the politics of statutory rape laws in the United States / Carolyn E. Cocca.
        p. cm.
    Includes bibliographical references and index.
    ISBN 0-7914-5905-5 (hardcopy : alk. paper) — ISBN 0-7914-5906-3 (pbk : alk. paper)
        1. Statutory rape—United States. 2. Teenagers—Sexual behavior—Government
    policy—United States. 3. Marriage—Government policy—United States. I. Title.
    KF9329.C63 2004
    345.73'02532—dc22

                                                                          2003060148

                        10 9 8 7 6 5 4 3 2 1

For my mother,
Anne McCallen Swinton

Contents

Illustrations

Preface

"Are you saying it's OK for a 45-year-old to have sex with a 5-year-old?"

"Did you go out with someone older while you were in high school?"

These two questions, and variations on them, have been asked of me repeatedly as I worked on this research. The assumption was, apparently, that if I were studying statutory rape I must either have a prurient interest in young children or as a teen I must have been in a relationship with someone much older than myself. I shouldn't continue to be so surprised by this. A colleague who studied fascist parties was often asked if he was fascist himself; those colleagues who even mention queer theory are assumed to be gay. For studies of sexuality in particular, though, these assumptions serve to marginalize work that is no less rigorous, and has no less to say about political, economic, social, and cultural conditions   particularly about inequalities and hierarchies that in some measure are maintained through the regulation of sexuality.

What no one has ever asked me is why I am so interested in the subject of single-parent households. This is probably because, despite what every apocalyptic set of statistics constantly linked to growing up in such a household might purport to predict was my fate—propensity toward juvenile delinquency and violent crime, less likely to finish high school, more likely to become dependent on public assistance—many people don't know that I grew up in one of "those" homes; indeed, they probably assume I did not. But as I often point out in this volume, correlation and causation are not the same thing. Perhaps, I have always thought, being brought up by a woman by herself is not the root of all evil in the world.

How does this link to studying sexuality and studying marriage? A conservative agenda seeking to shift debate away from structural problems, and inequalities of gender, race, and class in particular, has repeatedly sought to moralize and individualize every ill in the United States. Why is there poverty? Not because of a capitalist system, or unequal pay, or a neoliberal ideology that does not provide for but rather stigmatizes a lack of economic success, but because of an amoral nonwhite underclass that has sex and has children outside of marriage and depends on the state for handouts. Why is there crime? Not because of systemic poverty, lack of access to quality education, or discrimination, but because that same dysfunctional group of people must have grown up without a father figure and therefore has not been socialized properly into what it supposedly means to be a good man or good woman or good American. These types of assumptions, that place blame on those who do not conform to socially constructed notions of a "traditional" sexuality or family structure, must be interrogated if there is to be any transformative change in this country.

This book is dedicated to my mother, Anne McCallen Swinton. Had I two parents or twenty-seven parents rather than one, I can't imagine that there could have been a more extraordinary role model for me or for anyone else who has ever had the privilege of knowing her.

Having said this, there are a number of other people who assisted my work on this book; some of them know it and others do not.

I first wrote a paper about statutory rape laws at the New York University Law School for Judith Resnik in the spring of 1997. She encouraged me to look further into the subject (and when I did, I discovered there were no books about it) and she told me that my paper was publishable, although I didn't believe her at the time. Beginning that fall and throughout my time at NYU, Lisa Duggan in the Departments of American Studies and History was enormously enthusiastic about this subject matter, especially when no one else was, and was incredibly generous with her time and assistance in applying for grants and for jobs. She provided me with a number of opportunities I would not otherwise have had, and it was in her courses that I continued to write about the subject and receive excellent feedback both from her and from my fellow students. The Institute for Law and Society, the Women's Studies Program/Center for the Study of Gender and Sexuality, and the "Marriage, Women, and the Law" Project at the NYU Law Library (thanks especially to Carol Alpert at the library) all provided financial support from 1997 to 1999, as well as providing me with all kinds of resources I would not otherwise have had had I not reached beyond my own department of politics.

On the political science side, Anna Harvey took on this project when no one else would, and kept me pointed toward theoretical rigor. Rich Fleisher was always willing to talk about the quantitative analysis and the data, and Larry Mead reinforced the importance of the qualitative case study research. These three made my research, especially in its dissertation stage, much stronger than it could have possibly been without them. The Bradley Foundation, through the NYU Politics Department, also provided financial support from 1995 to

1997. John Entelis in the Department of Political Science and the Middle East Studies Program at Fordham University read countless drafts of this work with great interest, enthusiasm, and care, and was instrumental in providing research and teaching opportunities for me throughout my graduate school career. He also provided plenty of outrage, good humor, and beer when I was discouraged by criticisms of the interdisciplinary nature and subject matter of my research; for his tremendous support of and confidence in me, I will always be grateful.

At the State University of New York, College at Old Westbury, my colleagues—particularly, Tom DelGiudice—have been very encouraging and helpful, as have the Presidential Development Grants program and the United University Professions' Professional Development Grants program.

Along the way, I interviewed numerous people who participated in amending or implementing (or were threatened by arrest under) statutory rape laws around the country. In particular, Leigh Bienen, Steve Langford, J. Tom Morgan, and Matt Towery were very generous with their time and their insights. Anne Schulte kindly granted me permission to reprint the photograph she took of a billboard about statutory rape. It is on the cover, "If your sex partner is under 16, they [sic] won't be when you get out of prison."

Portions of chapters 2, 3, and 4 originally appeared as articles in *Polity*, *Michigan Feminist Studies*, and the *National Women's Studies Association Journal*, respectively, in 2002. The editors (and anonymous readers) at each were invaluable in asking questions and helping to streamline the prose. In particular, Trish Bachand and Claudia van der Heuvel at *Polity*, Carole Lee at *MFS*, and Amy Ruth and Amy Hudnall at *NWSA Journal* had numerous suggestions for improving those articles.

Khalen Gloeckner, Stratton Danes, and Matthew Wilkening merit special mention for their moral support throughout the writing of this book. Margaret Genden read and commented on drafts of this research in both article and book form. Her other contributions to my well-being are related to discussions of *Buffy the Vampire Slayer* at Burritoville and Bleecker Street Bar and are equally as important. Steve Goodman also read the final drafts. He both writes about and works with teens, and is praxis personified. I benefit greatly from our daily conversations about agency, critical literacy, social change, bad traffic, good music, and Mimi and Theo.

Lastly, my parents, Anne and Steve Swinton, are unfailingly supportive of me in everything that I do. I am extremely thankful to have their love. Everyone should be so lucky.

Introduction

Seventeen-year-old Delia was two months pregnant when she went to her doctor for a checkup. The doctor, knowing that Delia's fiancé was 22, called the police. Her fiancé's public defender noted, "The couple is happy together. He is working and supporting the child and they intend to be married and live with the girl's parents. What purpose does this serve?" The two were married by the time they went to court, where he was sentenced to time served. Delia was frustrated and scared, "Loving somebody is not a crime" (Rendon 1997).

Sixteen-year-old Sharon did not want to have sex with Michael, 17. She recounts, "I said no, and I was trying to get up and he hit me back down on the bench and then I just said to myself forget it and I let him do what he wanted to do." One justice's opinion characterized Sharon as a not "unwilling participant" in "their foreplay . . . which she seems to have encouraged" and concluded that these facts together with the "closeness of their ages are factors that should make this case an unattractive one to prosecute at all" (*Michael M. v. Superior Court of Sonoma County* 1981: 484–486 fn* and 483–485).

Twenty-one-year-old Summer gave birth to her baby and was immediately reported to the Department of Family and Children's Services by a hospital worker. Shortly thereafter, she married the baby's father, Tony, 14. Although the couple was allowed under the state's law to marry because they were parents,[1] it was illegal for them to have had sex when they were unmarried the previous year. Summer said, "He's my husband. I just don't understand" (Jones 2000).

Statutory Rape

These three cases are all examples of statutory rape. Statutory rape laws prohibit sexual activity with an unmarried person under a certain age. Those "under age" are deemed incapable of giving valid consent to such activity. The

1

laws therefore protect young people from engaging in potentially coercive sex, that may not be recognized as meeting a legal definition or popular perception of forcible rape, before they are physically or emotionally ready. Protecting the very young and the vulnerable from unequal, manipulative, or predatory relationships is unquestionably a laudable goal. But statutory rape laws are more complicated than that: They also proscribe and punish sexual activity that may be consensual in nature simply because the two parties are not married to one another, thus giving legal force to a particular construction of what type of relationship is "moral" and what type is not.

Further, while the subject of statutory rape appears to be only a moral issue, it is also an economically based one. Debate over the laws has focused on fundamental values rather than financial interests, although economic concerns have historically been interwoven into the laws and the discourses surrounding them. These laws have indeed been contested repeatedly throughout the history of the United States, and have been constructed as having different purposes at different points in time. For instance, in colonial times, comments regarding the laws show less of a concern with the age of the victim and more of a concern with preserving a female's virginity as a precious commodity that would make her more marriageable. In the late 1800s, many of those engaged in the subject felt that the laws were a beneficial tool with which to protect young females from older "lecherous" males, but at the same time to protect young females from themselves and their own potentially "loose" morals that might later reduce their marriage prospects. One hundred years later in the late 1900s, left and right on the political spectrum clashed over whether the laws could or should reduce the growing numbers of young people (principally those who were impoverished) engaged in nonmarital sexual activity, particularly when that activity was not abusive, and especially when that activity resulted in out-of-wedlock births.

Following a concentrated campaign at the turn of the twentieth century, statutory rape laws became basically uniform in every state: They prohibited a male of any age from having sexual intercourse with a female not his wife under the age of 16 or 18. But at present, the laws are different in virtually every state. The age of consent to sexual activity varies, the mandatory age difference between perpetrator and victim varies, the delineations of whom can be prosecuted varies, the penalties vary, and the means of discovering the illegal activity varies.

Why such variation? What can this variation tell us about policymaking in the 50 states? And what can a closer examination of this variation tell us about the ways in which gender, sexuality, class, race, and ethnicity are implicated in public policy? I explore these questions through detailed case studies, supplemented by quantitative analysis of all 50 states, of three sets of changes to statutory rape laws that occurred from the 1970s through the 1990s.

In analyzing discourses about statutory rape in addition to tracking the "nuts and bolts" of policy adoption, I am approaching law as not merely an independent body of rules, separate from society, that is to be followed. Rather, I examine how statutory rape laws reflect, or contribute to shaping, or constitute cultural narratives of gender and sexuality. These narratives circulate, through repetition and resonance ringing as commonsensical in tone, and are embedded in material practices.[2] Their unstable and changing nature reveal that the crime of statutory rape has served as a site for multiple constructions of gender and sexuality, as well as a site for the playing out of historically specific and historically contingent policy issues. Examining only policy outcomes would miss the nuances of language on this subject, and the ways in which the subject of statutory rape has been shaped and reshaped to act as a symbol of various American cultural anxieties.

Exploring Morality Politics

As noted, statutory rape can be considered a morality policy. Many scholars of state politics have concluded that morality policies are different from other types of policies that seem purely redistributive or regulatory or economic in nature.[3] But morality politics are always redistributive although they redistribute values rather than goods; they always have a regulatory component as they are intended to regulate behavior; and they always have an economic component because they require state monies for enforcement, as well as because they often construct categories of criminality that disproportionately impact those with fewer resources. Statutory rape laws in particular intertwine moral and economic concerns, especially through their links to marriage. Therefore, I expect that while morality policies appear distinctive because of their high emotional content and salience to the public, the policymaking process is basically the same as with other policies.

The distinction that previous writers have drawn between policy types has divided policies into smaller and smaller subsets, leading us to results that are not generalizable. In addition, the conclusions drawn about different types of politics have been based in large part on the question that researchers have asked; namely, What forces *correlate* with policy outcomes in this given policy area? With this orientation, one might ask Which states have which types of statutory rape laws? I ask a different question. What forces can actually *cause* policy change? Who or what caused particular types of statutory rape laws to be adopted in particular states?

I argue that interest group activity upon reelection-minded partisan public officials is crucial to policy change, regardless of the type of policy. This orientation differentiates this research from a number of works in the morality politics subfield which have claimed that the adoption of morality policies is simply "different" because of strong demonstrated effects for the leanings of public opinion. I would suggest that mass public opinion is a latent force that does not cause policy change directly, in and of itself, even though it may correlate strongly with a particular policy outcome. Given extremely low voter turnout, and with little likelihood that a voter's preference is based on a candidate's support for or opposition to a single issue, there is little incentive for a public official to cater to mass public opinion. On the other hand, interest group members represent a segment of the electorate that is aware and concerned, and probably more likely to vote. Groups are also able to provide a host of much-needed resources to a public official, both as candidate and as policymaker. In this way, groups can both channel and filter public opinion so that public opinion may have an indirect effect on policy change; or they may stand opposite of public opinion. Such a finding has broader implications about inequalities of resources, power, and "who gets what when how" in the United States.

While I follow scholars of state politics in modeling policymaking across the 50 states and over time,[4] I also address two other layers of inquiry neglected in the state politics subfield: broader theories of policymaking and comparative case studies. Rather than examining a host of political, economic, social, and demographic forces previously analyzed in the state politics literature to discover if they apply to yet another policy area, I am guided in the chapters that follow by incorporating theories of national-level policymaking to explore the influence of groups, public opinion, and policymakers themselves on the adoption of particular types of statutory rape laws.[5]

There are excellent detailed case studies in the subfield, particularly of single states, but this contributes little to more general explanations of policy change. To this end, I undertake comparative historical case studies of three states.[6] In detailing the configurations and activities of specific interest groups and state and party officials in particular states and therefore better capturing the nuances of policymaking in a particular place at a particular time, this material supplements, expands on, and better grounds the large-scale quantitative work, as well as compensating for the nuance and specificity that the latter misses. This entailed analyzing legislative debates, introduced bills (both rejected and accepted), session laws, letters of support from within the government as well as from outside interested parties, testimonies at committee hearings and committee notes, and other supplementary material in the relevant bill jackets. At the same time, I examined local, national, and international press accounts of statutory rape, as well as news and newsmagazine programs and internet sites. Interviews with the relevant parties were conducted whenever possible.

Within the broader theoretical framework outlined above that seeks to unify researchers' approaches to the study of policymaking, using more than one methodological approach has the advantage of compensating at least somewhat for the oversights and biases of each approach as used in isolation. The combination of qualitative and quantitative methods can present a richer picture of policy adoption and policy change in the states and allows us to draw more general conclusions about those processes.

Exploring Statutory Rape Politics

Why statutory rape laws? The history of the laws has been one of constant tension between protection and proscription, safeguarding and social control, and the tenuous and fine line between the two.[7] They have been a battleground for questions about sexuality, marriage, and reproduction and have continuously implicated a cultural uneasiness about class, race, and ethnicity. At the site of statutory rape, opposing groups have clashed over the meanings of the right to privacy and state regulation of the body, gender differences, patriarchal power, sexual consent, homosexuality, abortion and childbearing, and the role of sexuality in maintaining social hierarchies. But while law can be a resource for groups seeking change, it can also play a role in supporting such hierarchies (McCann 1994); while law can be protective, it can also be patriarchal. As such, the subject has never divided opposing groups into two neat sides: Feminists, liberals, and conservatives have argued among themselves over the laws as well as occasionally forming strange-bedfellow alliances across the political spectrum.

Undergoing a number of incarnations over the past 200 years, statutory rape has been discursively constructed and reconstructed as a symptom, or symbol, of larger social, cultural, political, and economic issues: changes in women's power within the home and in the workforce; growing tolerance of nonmarital relationships and sexualities; the threat of child sexual abuse, now often linked to fears about the medium of the Internet and its chat rooms; an uneasiness about immigration that combines diffuse economic and ethnic insecurities; and a backlash against the seeming overgenerosity of a welfare state that would give economic assistance to women in poverty who have borne children out of wedlock. These connections allow the subject of statutory rape to serve as a prism that can illuminate not only policymaking processes on a hot-button issue, but also cultural narratives of gender, sexuality, race, ethnicity, class, and nation.

There is no full-length treatment of the subject of present-day statutory rape laws. Four fields of study contribute to this examination of the politics of statutory rape, but do not explore those specific politics in depth themselves. Feminist theorists, while providing a framework for examining the deployment of particular constructions of gender and sexuality in cultural and legal contexts, have concentrated more on issues that affect "all" women, such as abortion, rape, sexual harassment, and social and economic inequalities. Feminist legal theorists have written about the ramifications of the one Supreme Court–level statutory rape case,[8] but have been more focused on forcible rape law and have not explored the historical and social contexts within which statutory rape occurs. Social and cultural historians have touched on statutory rape in research on the "purity campaigns" of the Victorian and Progressive eras and have enriched our understanding of morality-based movements and their objects of reform, but do not cover the postwar period. Political scientists have focused on the participation and behaviors of adult women in the political sphere vis-à-vis policymaking in general, and on the impacts of particular policies on women, but have not focused on young women and the politics of adolescent sexuality.

In short, modern debates about and lawmaking processes surrounding statutory rape have not yet been examined in depth in any field although a number of fields contribute to an exploration of the topic. It also is a divisive issue implicated in a number of seemingly unrelated policy initiatives, giving it unique characteristics not only as an interesting object of study in its own right, but also as one that can inform discussions of policymaking in general.

Plan of the Book

Chapter 1 reviews the specifics of the politics of statutory rape laws, with a historical overview of the origins of and debates around them. This broader context of the construction of the crime of statutory rape as it has been contested over hundreds of years illuminates each of the following chapters. Through detailed case studies of three states as well as quantitative analysis, chapters 2, 3, and 4 explore the influence of public opinion, interest groups, and legislators vis-à-vis three sets of amendments to statutory rape laws that have been enacted over the past 30 years: (1) age-span provisions in which one partner must be a certain number of years older for the crime to be prosecuted at the felony level; (2) gender-neutral language to include females as perpetrators and males as victims; and (3) prosecuting the partners of pregnant female teens as a means to lower welfare rolls. While the first two sets of changes were spearheaded by feminists as part of a broader program of rape law reform in the 1970s and 1980s, the third set of changes in the 1990s was pushed by religious conservatives and others located more to the right on the political spectrum.

Each of these three chapters also discusses the implementation of the different facets of statutory rape laws, through brief case studies of prosecutions under the laws. It is through the discourses surrounding such prosecutions, as well as through the language used by the above groups in pressuring legislators for change, that the double-edged nature of statutory rape laws reveals itself— the laws both protect and proscribe unmarried adolescent sexuality, and are used for different purposes by different interests. Finally, the last chapter draws some conclusions about statutory rape laws and their implications, as well as about morality politics and policymaking in general.

Chapter 1

Statutory Rape Laws in Historical Context

Introduction

Today's statutory rape laws prohibit sexual intercourse with an unmarried person under the age of consent, which varies depending on the state.[1] That is, if the victim is under that certain age and not married to the perpetrator,[2] he or she is presumed incapable of giving informed and valid consent to sexual activity; therefore, consensuality is not permitted as a defense to the crime. Yet almost all states allow those under their jurisdictional age of consent to marry with judicial and/or parental approval. In other words, sex between a married couple in which at least one party is under the age of consent cannot be prosecuted under the law, even if it is the same sexual activity as that taking place between an unmarried couple in which at least one party is under the age of consent. Several states allow marriage at any age if the female is pregnant or if the two prospective spouses are already parents of an out-of-wedlock child. Of all brides in 1970, 13% were under 18; in 1980, 8.2%; and in 1990, 3.7%. Of all grooms in 1970, 2.1% were under 18; in 1980, 1.3%; and in 1990, 0.6% (Clarke 1995: 14). In 1998, 137,000 15–17-year-olds had ever been married; more than half were already separated or divorced (U.S. Census Bureau 1998).[3]

The laws originally were gender-specific: They punished a male who had sexual intercourse with a female, who was not his wife, under the age of consent; today, they are gender-neutral so as to cover both females and males. When the activity is heterosexual, it is usually the male who is charged; for instance, in

9

cases in which a female becomes pregnant, she is assumed to be the victim. There is also some evidence that prosecutions under the laws have disproportionately targeted homosexual relationships.[4] In many states, the perpetrator may be the same age as the victim and still be charged with a felony; in most of the states mandating that the perpetrator be a certain number of years older then the victim, a same-age perpetrator can still be charged with a misdemeanor. The perpetrator, regardless of age, will most likely have to register as a sex offender. Some jurisdictions still allow perpetrators the "mistake-of-age" defense, and to escape prosecution by claiming that they had thought the victim to be older than the age of consent.

Considering the marital exemption, the use of the laws against homosexual activity even as most states had decriminalized sodomy of their own accord before the Supreme Court ruling in *Lawrence v. Texas* (539 US ___, 2003), the prosecutions of same-age perpetrators (usually males), and the mistake of age defense, one wonders if "age" is really the operative category in statutory rape laws. Indeed, the categories of victim and perpetrator have proved to be quite fluid as they have been drawn and redrawn throughout the history of the United States. Rather, it appears that such laws are based on proscribing sex outside of marriage, and serve to police and reinforce cultural narratives of gender and sexuality.

This historical contextualization of statutory rape laws and the various amendments made to them is crucial to an understanding of the ways in which such laws have served as a site for the playing out of multiple and historically contingent policy initiatives by particular groups and public officials. Given the more recent public policy attention to the topic, the past three decades will receive greater emphasis and more detailed treatment than previous decades. The three sets of changes to the laws in the 1970s, 1980s, and 1990s are the focus of this research and are detailed in chapters 2, 3, and 4.

English Common Law through the 1800s

Under early English common law, a male could not be convicted of rape if the female had consented to the activity (Fuentes 1994: 139; McCollum 1982: 341; Miller 1994: 289). But as England codified its statutory rape law in the Statute of Westminster of 1275, "The King prohibiteth that none do ravish . . . any Maiden within age."[5] This newly drafted law constructed the crime as sexual intercourse with a female under 12, who was regarded as unable to consent. The offense was made a capital one in 1285,[6] and the age was lowered to 10 in 1576, "if any person shall unlawfully and carnally know and abuse any woman-child under the age of ten years, every such unlawful and carnal knowledge shall be a felony."[7]

Colonial American statutory rape law basically imported this language. Some states chose 10 as the age of consent, while others chose 12.[8] The idea behind such laws at the time was less about the ability or lack thereof to consent to such activity on the part of the female, and more about protecting white females and their premarital chastity—a commodity—as property (Fuentes 1994: 141; Eidson 1980: 760). The laws thus stated, as they still do today, that no crime has been committed if the female is the wife of the perpetrator. Justice Brennan noted in *Michael M. v. Superior Court of Sonoma County*, the only Supreme Court case having to do with statutory rape law, that "because their chastity was considered particularly precious, those young women were felt to be uniquely in need of the state's protection" (450 US 464 [1981] at 494–495). Females, in other words, were seen as "special property in need of special protection" (McCollum 1982: 355) and thus "statutory rape was a property crime" (Eidson 1980: 767).

This, in practice, only applied to white females. Black females were generally formally enslaved, and for a variety of political, economic, social, and cultural reasons their sexuality was not deemed to be in need of legal protection. This manifested itself in several myths about the "natural" state of black female sexuality as being the opposite of the "natural" state of white female sexuality. While the latter were "chaste [and] pure" and on a "moral pedestal," the black female was promiscuous, impure, and lascivious. "This construct of the licentious temptress served to justify white men's sexual abuse of black women" (Roberts 1997: 11).[9] While black female bodies were commodified, along with their childbearing capacity, their chastity was not.

At first in the United States, the crime was one of strict liability and allowed no defenses if the prosecution could prove that sexual activity occurred with an unmarried underage female. The penalties in all states for statutory rape were harsher than those for fornication—sex between unmarried people regardless of the age of the parties.[10] Two defenses thus entered into statutory rape law: claiming that one was mistaken as to the victim's age, and claiming that the victim was sexually experienced. The former was not often accepted until midway through the twentieth century. The latter, however, was codified in every state much earlier on: If the young female in question were "impure," statutory rape had not been committed and thus both the perpetrator and the victim would probably be charged with fornication. This defense was manifested by language requiring that the victim be an "unmarried female of previously chaste character." To summarize the intent and effect of the law at this time, "Thus by extending legal protection only to virgins, early statutory rape law served as a tool through which to preserve the common morality rather than to penalize men for violating the law" (Oberman 1994: 26).

Indeed, in both of these defenses, the concern seemed to be less about the age of the victim than about her marital or virginal status. About a dozen states retain the mistake of age defense today. The "previously chaste character" requirement remained in effect in some states until as recently as the 1990s. As of Mississippi's code revision in 1998, no state now retains this language.[11]

The First Wave: Reforming the Laws
at the Turn of the Twentieth Century

In the 1890s, statutory rape laws were changed in virtually every state. A coalition of feminists, religious conservatives, and white working-class men's organizations lobbied together to raise the age of consent. Workingmen joined in this cause generally because the crime was constructed as one of middle-class men preying on working-class women; indeed, the federal Mann Act of 1910 was also known as the White Slave Traffic Act and was based on hysteria about middle-class businessmen kidnapping working-class girls from the street and forcing them into a life of prostitution (Langum 1994). One could also argue that workingmen were also concerned about the public morality of working-women, and joined the age of consent movement out of social conservatism along with protectionist instincts. That this coalition was uneasy in nature is vital to understanding the ways in which the laws were constructed prior to, and implemented after, their amendment.

Background to Raising the Age of Consent

The end of the nineteenth century saw numerous crucial social, economic, and political dislocations; for instance, increasing immigration; imperialistic notions of expansion and of civilizing those deemed more primitive, along with fears of "race suicide" due to the numbers of white, middle-class women having abortions; women securing dominance over the "private" sphere and using that leverage to gain some power in the "public"; and perhaps most important, urbanization and industrialization. These last transformations drew young women to work in the cities, gave them a small measure of economic power, and fostered unchaperoned heterosocial activities.

Of great concern to middle-class women were working-class mores, and the public and therefore quite visible nature of the latter's leisure time activities in the cities.[12] These strange new activities and their customs, undertaken by "the other," in the seemingly foreign city, were symbols of disorder and moral decay. The reformers sought to portray a hearth-oriented married life as the ultimate goal to which a decent and moral woman would aspire. This, they thought, would help save working-class girls from their own apparently degraded or perverse moralities. Unmarried female sexuality was viewed as being akin to prostitution, as young urban women who dated were often "treated" to dinner, dancing, or a movie and then had sex with their dates (Peiss 1986; Larson 1997). Reformers felt that this was one step removed from a female being overtly given money for sex. They therefore fashioned the "language of virtue and vice into a code of class" (Stansell 1987: 66).[13] They focused more on the moral than on the economic component—the concern was with young women having sex in exchange for commodities they could not purchase, rather than with the fact that young women earned such unequal and meager wages that they could not purchase goods or entertainment for themselves. They also were unable or unwilling to accept that some of these young women may have chosen to engage in sexual activities and perhaps experienced pleasure through them. Thus, they sought to "uplift" the working girls' morals so that they might aspire to take on middle-class values.

At the same time, as "Victorians," these social purity reformers were concerned with the potential for young, vulnerable, and supposedly passionless and passive females to be abused by predatory males, both within and outside of one's family. Like casual dating, this could lead to one's becoming a "fallen woman" looked down on by society, unable to marry, perhaps having to become an actual prostitute.[14] Thus, the reformers' second major concern was with the sexual double standard that demanded female chastity before marriage yet allowed men access to those above age 10 or 12 without much fear of repercussion. As such, they fashioned a particular narrative in which "men of status and wealth took advantage of poor, innocent young women, using various forms of trickery and deception, and force if necessary" (Odem 1995: 16). They wanted society at large to acknowledge sexual coercion and sexual danger, at least that facing white women.

It was this image of the passive white victim that drew the support of more conservative religious elements; indeed, these forces became dominant. But they did not share the feminists' interest in a single moral standard to uplift women. They were more concerned with proscribing premarital sexuality, and particularly female sexuality (Walkowitz 1980; Odem 1995; Olsen 1984; Kunzel 1993).

Black women's groups did support the idea of a single moral standard. But they worried that more stringent age of consent laws within a racist society would be used to target black males, who were stereotyped as uncontrollable rapists of white women and therefore as deserving of being lynched in order to protect the white race.[15]

Second, black women were concerned that the white middle-class feminists did not take into account the kind of sexual danger faced by black women. Namely, that if raped by a white man, black women could scarcely make a legal claim: The laws described black women as property and as not deserving of the same legal rights as whites. The laws of the southern states generally did not allow blacks to testify against whites; some rape laws specifically excluded black women (Roberts 1997). At the same time, cultural narratives constructed black females as promiscuous and as devious and thus undeserving of protection.

Third, violence within black communities, if reported at all, was generally ignored by the mostly white legal establishment. If the parties were slaves, their activity was deemed outside the criminal code and under the jurisdiction of the master. Later, some black women became reluctant to subject black men to the discrimination of the legal system and often did not report if black men had harmed them.[16]

In short, black women's groups did not support the white reformers' campaign. They conducted their own program of moral uplift in their communities which included the idea of racial uplift as well (Odem 1995: 26–30). White women reformers went forward without them in the campaign to change statutory rape laws.

Implementing the Changes

In 1885 in England, conservative purity reformers and feminists together successfully lobbied Parliament to raise the age of consent to 16. This prompted American reformers to act. That same year the New York Committee for the Prevention of State Regulation of Vice, a group dedicated to a single moral standard for men and women as well as to abolishing prostitution, began its lobbying (Odem 1995: 13; Larson 1997: 27). The national Women's Christian Temperance Union (WCTU) revived its Department for the Suppression of Social Evil and in the 1890s broadened its efforts from temperance in alcohol consumption to combating "depraved appetite in every form" (Larson 1997: 22, 24).[17] Using a narrative of sexual danger to female virtue, feminist movements and suffragists, religious leaders, and white workingmen's organizations led by the WCTU agitated at the state level to have "the age at which a girl can legally consent to her own ruin be raised to at least eighteen years" (Odem 1995: 15, 16; Larson 1997: 38, 46). All states did raise the age, to 16 or 18; at one point, Tennessee raised it to 21. The changes occurred most quickly in those states in which women could vote at the state level (Larson 1997: 44).

The male legislators did not give in without a fight. "In incidents in several states, legislators proposed dilatory amendments to mock the proposed reform, such as proposing that the age of consent be raised to eighty-one years, that all girls be required to wear a chastity belt, or to mandate that all women must consent to sex after the age of eighteen years" (Larson 1997: 41–42).[18] In short, they did not take the protectionist ideals very seriously. As early as the 1890s, many states considered measures to roll back the age of consent to their pre-reform levels although in most cases the women's groups were able to halt those efforts (Larson 1997: 57–58; Pivar 1973: 144–145).

The men had two basic concerns: that young men in particular would be denied sexual access to young women in an era in which marriage in one's teens was extremely common, and that men of any age who were expressing their "natural" sexual desires would be punished for engaging in activity with willing and sexually mature young women. Legislators in a few states graded the penalties so that underage males would have more lenient sentences; for instance, bills regarding the District of Columbia mandated a 5-year maximum for a male under 18 and a 15-year maximum for a male 18 and older, with no minimum sentences (Larson 1997: 56).

This was the point at which the requirement that female victims be "of previously chaste character" began to be codified. A Kansas legislator protested that because the age had been raised to 18, "'several young men from highly respectable families' had been sent to the penitentiaries by 'immoral young women'" (Odem 1995: 33). A representative from Kentucky noted, "We see at once what a terrible weapon for evil the elevating of the age of consent would be when placed in the hands of a lecherous, sensual, negro woman, who for the sake of blackmail or revenge would not hesitate to bring criminal action even though she had been a prostitute since her eleventh year!" (Odem 1995: 33). This was exactly the kind of characterization of a young black female that the black women's clubs feared—highly sexualized, promiscuous, dishonest, and undeserving of the law's protection regardless of her age.

In effect, the raising of the age of consent and the codification of the "chaste character" defense made what was a crime about taking the virginity of a female of 10 or 12 into a crime about taking the virginity of a female of 16 or 18. The amended laws became almost identical to the traditional crime of "seduction," which punished sexual activity with a woman of previously chaste character, generally under promise of marriage (Bienen 1980a: 191). Seduction laws presumed nonforcible sexual activity involving an unmarried female, who was generally a teenager, although they did not assume she was incapable of consent. Rather, they assumed she had been tricked, or defrauded by promise of marriage, into having sex. The new statutory rape laws covered the same "crime," but also codified a young female's incapacity vis-à-vis decisions concerning sexuality. Yet marriage laws presumed that "underage" females could decide to marry—and sex within marriage was and continues to be an ironclad defense to a statutory rape charge.

Thus began an interesting anomaly in which one could be of age to choose to marry and thus have sexual intercourse legally, but not of age to consent to unmarried sex. Indeed, today, tens of thousands of underage teens marry each year because although in most states one must be 18 to marry on one's own, one can do so at a younger age with parental or judicial permission; and in some states the couple does not need such permission if the female is pregnant or has already given birth. But in the Victorian period in particular, many young women were married and had children before they reached the age of consent.

Activity centered around statutory rape laws began to take a more conservative and punitive turn in the Progressive Era, when reformer women joined forces with the male establishment to create juvenile courts and reformatories to better serve the needs of youth. But the feminists did not have quite as much control over the implementation of the laws as did their former allies. This had three major implications for statutory rape prosecutions: (1) Middle-class women reformers had begun to discover that many working-class females were willing participants in sexual activity and sought to repress and "rehabilitate" those instincts through reformatories and maternity homes; (2) families began to use the laws to try to control their "incorrigible" and "delinquent" daughters, and young females were unable to stop the prosecutions; and (3) male police, prosecutors, and judges were more prone to subscribe to the notion of female as temptress rather than victim and would often sentence the male defendant to probation while sentencing the female on delinquency charges and sending them to the above-mentioned reformatories. These young women were far more often than not poor and of immigrant descent or status.[19] At this point, classed notions about female sexuality appeared to triumph over the desire to protect young women from harm. As a result, "[s]ometimes the supposed beneficiaries of such efforts often [found] their lives overly regulated and controlled by legal definitions that fail[ed] to reflect their circumstances" (Fineman 1995: 193).

The workings of statutory rape law at the turn of the century are vital to understanding the ways in which the laws operate today. First, codes of class, and of race and ethnicity, continue to operate as a strong undercurrent to contemporary statutory rape laws. Second, even though many states have gender-neutral laws, the idea of male as aggressor and female as victim pervades the discourse as well as the prosecutions. Third, the laws as implemented at the turn of the nineteenth and the turn of the twentieth centuries are a double-edged sword—they both protect and punish adolescent sexual activity. Lastly, a feminist–liberal–conservative coalition is still in evidence on this issue, and has had repercussions for the ways in which the laws have been debated, amended, and implemented.[20] These points, and present-day conflicts over statutory rape laws, will be discussed further in chapters 2, 3, and 4 and are outlined below.

The Second Wave: Feminist Reforms of the 1970s and 1980s

Second-wave feminists sought and secured two sets of changes to statutory rape laws beginning in the 1970s.[21] In most states, one of the participants in the sexual activity now must be a certain number of years older than the other for that person to be prosecuted at the felony level. Second, in all states the laws are now gender neutral—that is, both males and females can be victims of the crime, and both males and females can be charged as perpetrators of the crime.

Background to Age-Span Provisions and Gender-Neutral Language

Statutory rape reform was part of a larger program of forcible rape reform begun in Michigan in 1973. The goals for forcible rape reform included:

1. redefining "rape" as "sexual assault" or "sexual battery" to emphasize the violent nature of the crime and to take away the emphasis on "consent";
2. grading the offenses based on the seriousness or severity of the conduct;
3. broadening the offenses beyond penile–vaginal penetration to include other penetration, touching, and oral/genital activity;
4. lowering and grading the penalties for fear that the traditionally high penalties for rape of 25 years to life in prison to the death penalty deterred juries from convicting;
5. eliminating the "marital exemption" in forcible rape law that excluded husbands from prosecution;
6. eliminating corroboration requirements and proof of resistance requirements;
7. implementing rape shield laws so that the victim's sexual past could not be brought into evidence;
8. implementing gender-neutral language.

The feminists hoped that reform would symbolize a rejection of the patriarchal and stereotypical view of what sex crimes consisted of, increase the number of reports by women through the removal of antiquated notions of consent and resistance, and increase the number of arrests and, hopefully, prosecutions and convictions. To accomplish this, the reformers had to ally with law-and-order forces, such as police and prosecutors, who wanted rape reform that would encourage women to report the crime and cooperate with authorities so that convictions were easier to obtain.[22]

At the same time, the reformers decided to redraft statutory rape laws, seeing them less as protective and more as punitive, less as empowering and more as infantilizing. They felt that the nineteenth-century feminists had served in some measure to reinscribe patriarchal notions of female sexuality and mental (in)capacity into law and to reinforce stereotypes of gender by prohibiting sex with an underage female only. They were also concerned with the discourses used by the first-wave feminists who advocated for passivity and chastity, and implied that sexuality be confined to heterosexual marriage.

But second-wave feminists also felt that the shortcomings of forcible rape law proved the necessity of statutory rape law to "catch" coerced or manipulated sex with the underage that fell short of the legal definitions and cultural conceptions of rape. For instance, while today "date rape" has been defined as a crime and has been prosecuted with varying degrees of success, in the 1970s juries were even more likely to feel that the crime of rape required an armed male stranger as the perpetrator. Further, most states required that a victim resist the force of her attacker to her utmost ability and to prove that that resistance had occurred. In a statutory rape case, the prosecution has to prove only that the victim was underage and that the two people were not married when the sexual act occurred.[23] Statutory rape is simply easier to prosecute than is forcible rape.

Liberal feminists thus sought to restore some agency and formal equality to young women while also retaining the ability to safeguard them from sexual coercion. Specifically, they lobbied for gender-neutral language, which would include young males as part of the protected class and enable females to be charged as perpetrators, and age-span provisions, which mandate that the perpetrator be a certain number of years older than the victim. These two reforms are the subject of chapters 2 and 3. Along with gender-neutral language and age spans, their other goals for statutory rape laws (similar but not identical to their goals for forcible rape reform) included:

1. redefining the crime as "sexual assault" or "sexual battery" to emphasize coercion;
2. grading the offenses based on the age of the victim;
3. broadening the offenses to include touching and oral/genital activity; this was particularly important for cases having to do with very young children;
4. lowering and grading the penalties;
5. eliminating corroboration requirements;
6. eliminating the "promiscuity" clause that dismissed cases if the young female was not a virgin;
7. eliminating the mistake-of-age defense in which the perpetrator could claim he thought the victim was above the age of consent.[24]

The liberal feminists felt that the gender-specific laws inscribed the stereotypes of male-as-aggressor and female-as-victim in the realm of sexuality, and phrased their argument in terms of an inequality of the rights granted to males and females: "If sex is viewed as a privilege, for a state to say that a girl of a certain age is neither legally nor factually capable of consenting to that act while boys are able to consent to sex at any age with any women, that girl has been deprived of a right that her male counterpart has been allowed to engage in" (Fuentes 1994: 151). Second, they argued, the gender-specific language neglected young males as victims.

The age-span, or age-differential, provisions required that one partner be a certain number of years older than the other for the crime of statutory rape to occur. Such a provision was intended by the liberal feminists to allow conduct that was more likely to be consensual, between teenagers of similar ages, to go unprosecuted.[25] Age acts as a proxy for a power differential that is suspect of coercion. The idea here is that being the less powerful party in heterosexual relationships because of one's youth, added to the well-catalogued vulnerability of the teen years in which one's (and particularly, young women's) self-esteem tends to decline, could be easily taken advantage of by someone who was older and thus more experienced in manipulating sexual situations.

But this is not to say that all feminists were united in their support of statutory rape laws. Their views on the issue were somewhat reflective of the virtually simultaneous debates over sexuality, sexual consent, and pornography. Radical feminists in particular critiqued the legal construct that sex fell into two categories: consensual sex or rape. They argued that for socially constructed reasons, men and women were simply not similarly situated in modern society and that females were always already inside a power relationship with males in which they were the less powerful party; some extended that argument to suggest that the idea of a woman being able to give true consent was untenable (see, e.g., Chamallas 1988). As such, pornography reflected the degraded status of women and should be regulated as a means of pursuing equal protection for women. In this environment, radical feminists were concerned that gender-neutral statutory rape laws could not acknowledge that adolescent males and females in particular were not similarly situated in regard to psychological needs and sexual power. The problem was one of "social inequality, of sex aggravated by age" (MacKinnon 1991: 1281), and that a young female's nonconsent may manifest itself in a way not recognized in forcible rape laws.

In other words, gender-neutral laws would not serve to advance the substantive equality of females in the law and in real life, but instead would grant females only formal equality, which would do them a disservice. "Boys and girls may both be harmed by early sexual activity, but they are harmed differently and we gain nothing by pretending the harm is the same" (Olsen 1984: 426). A number of studies recount that adolescent females have low self-esteem, are uncomfortable with speaking their minds for fear of appearing unfeminine or intellectually threatening to their male counterparts, and are insecure and willing to please (see, e.g., Oberman 1994). Adding to the potential for pregnancy, disease, pain, and shame, a young female might engage in sex before she is ready, and then regret having made that decision—but socialized as she is to believe that sex and love go together, still see such an encounter as consensual because she was not physically forced (but perhaps felt coerced) to do so. In this line of argument, age-span provisions can be useful to targeting older males who would take advantage of young females, but they also presume that males and females close in age are engaged in consensual activity when they may not be. Therefore, these feminists would worry, statutory rape reform might actually worsen the situation by allowing public officials, and feminists, to claim credit for advancements in the cause of gender equality, thus causing any fervor for change to be undercut with no progress made on the underlying structures of gender inequality that pervade (adolescent) heterosexual relationships.

Feminist sex radicals (sometimes referred to as pro-sex feminists or sexual libertarians) were on the opposite side of the sexuality and pornography debate from the radical feminists. They felt that the latter essentialized all females as victims and all pornography as problematic, rather than acknowledge that many women were actively confronting inequalities and that pornography in and of itself could be received differently by different audiences—perhaps even reconstructed in a feminist fashion (see, e.g., Duggan and Hunter 1995). Worse, they worried, the radical feminist position that women are different (for socially constructed reasons) could play right into the hands of conservative censorial forces, who were all too willing to agree with that notion (for biological reasons); indeed, these two groups joined forces to pass antipornography ordinances in the midwest (Ind. Code §16-1 to 16-28, 1984).

While they acknowledged that statutory rape laws had a protective function, sex radicals were concerned that their patriarchal and proscriptive roots punished potentially consensual unmarried sex, painted young people and particularly young females as a monolithic group unable to make decisions about their own bodies, and sent a message that nonmarital sex and female sexual agency in and of themselves were wrong and harmful (see, e.g., Rubin 1984). Therefore, they saw the laws as violating rights of privacy and personal autonomy in sexual matters.

Sex radicals also argued that the laws' marital exemption which allowed those under the age of consent and married to be free from prosecution showed that the laws had little to do with one's age and everything to do with one's marital status. Along the same lines, the gender-neutral language would enable the prosecution of homosexual couples already suffering from other forms of legalized discrimination based on their sexuality. Indeed, in the battle over pornography, many sex radicals were appalled but not surprised that one of the arguments used to win over male judges was to tell them that in gay porn, males were just as degraded as females (Duggan and Hunter 1995: 10). The intertwining of sex and violence in statutory rape laws might only serve to further marginalize, rather than protect, homosexuals.

The problem, then, was and is the following:

> Every effort to protect young women against private oppression
> by individual men risks subjecting women to state oppression, and
> every effort to protect them against state oppression undermines
> their power to resist individual oppression. Further, any acknowl-
> edgment of the actual difference between the present situation of
> males and females stigmatizes females and perpetuates discrimi-
> nation. But if we ignore power differences and pretend that
> women are similarly situated, we perpetuate discrimination by dis-
> empowering ourselves from instituting effective change. (Olsen
> 1984: 411)

Implementing the Changes

With these problems in mind, the reformers moved forward. One participant
described the dual-pronged approach to statutory rape reform:

> Rather than focus on a gendered notion of power in sexual rela-
> tions, they decided to isolate and criminalize sexual conduct which
> they felt raised a presumption of concern. This conduct was then
> incorporated into [the revised statute] using gender-neutral lan-
> guage which penalized sexual conduct according to varying de-
> grees of severity, depending on the age range between the victim
> and the accused. (Oberman 1994: 31)[26]

They also designed the penalty structure to reflect the age of the victim. With
both of these provisions in place, reformers sought to better protect young children while exempting similarly aged teenagers from felony-level prosecution:

> These goals are potentially contradictory, as increasing protection
> for children requires relatively high statutory ages, while permit-
> ting consensual sexual contact requires somewhat lower ages. Fem-
> inist reformers are divided on how to translate these goals into law,
> although a common approach is to identify a series of two or more
> graded offenses that prohibit sexual activity with youths below
> specific ages (e.g., first degree sexual assault if less than twelve
> years, but second degree assault if greater than twelve but less than
> sixteen). (Searles and Berger 1987: 26)

But while one can look at the gradation of offenses through the lens of preventing sexual abuse rather than through the lens of protecting virginity, the new language viewed sexual activity with a person under 10 or 12 and with a person under 16 or 18 as two manifestations of the same crime. The problem in making the offenses parallel in language and in offense lies in their implementation. The teenage boyfriend or girlfriend of a 15-year-old and the adult stranger who molests a 5-year-old both may be required to register as sex offenders under Megan's Law provisions; both may be subject to confinement and/or psychiatric treatment to "cure" such urges as part of their prison term, parole, or probation. Both are perpetrators of statutory rape. By redefining the offenses as sexual assault or sexual battery, the reformers purposely made no room for the notion of consent or for stereotypes of gender to be considered. But in practice, what is clearly child abuse and what may be a consensual sexual relationship can both be prosecuted as sexual abuse under statutes titled "statutory rape," "child molestation," "sexual assault," or "sexual battery."[27]

This problem is similar to that encountered after the raising of the age of consent by nineteenth-century feminists, which made statutory rape more akin to the traditional crime of "seduction," sexual activity with a woman of previously chaste character under promise of marriage (Bienen 1980a: 191). Seduction laws presumed nonforcible sexual activity involving an unmarried female, who was generally a teenager, although they did not assume she was incapable of consent. The revised statutory rape laws combined traditional statutory rape laws (which criminalized sexual activity with a female under 12 or 10) with seduction laws, and thus treated all underage females as equally incapable of consent in matters of nonmarital sexuality.[28] In some sense, then, the modern gradation of offenses solidifies the duality of statutory rape laws—they may prevent abuse, but may also punish consensual nonmarital conduct and label it "abuse."

The drive for gender-neutral language was successful in all states by 2000. The laws now read that "any person" who has sex with "any person" under the age of consent has committed a criminal act. Age-span provisions were adopted by all but seven states by 1999, and the spans themselves vary wildly, as shown in table 1.1.

Those at the forefront of the reform movement, successful in agitating for both age spans and gender-neutral language, hoped that those reforms would speak to the concerns about adolescent sexuality cited above. But as the underlying gendered inequalities could not be changed overnight as could the formal language of the law, and as feminist reformers have had little control over the implementation of the laws (as was true in the nineteenth century), the gains made have been noteworthy but incomplete. These two sets of amendments to statutory rape laws are discussed in detail in chapters 2 and 3.

TABLE 1.1   Ages of Consent 1885–1999, and Age Spans in the Fifty States, 1999

State	1885	1890	1920	1999	Age Span in Years
Alabama	10	10	16	16	2
Alaska	NA	NA	16*	16	3
Arizona	12	14	18	18	2
Arkansas	10	10	16	16	5
California	10	14	18	18	3
Colorado	10	10	18	15	4
Connecticut	10	14	16	16	2
Delaware	7	15	16	16	4
Florida	10	10	18	18	6
Georgia	10	10	14	16	3
Hawaii	10*	NA	NA	14	0
Idaho	10	10	18	18	5
Illinois	10	14	16	17	5
Indiana	12*	NA	16	16	3
Iowa	10	13	16	16	5
Kansas	10	10	18	16	0
Kentucky	12	12	16	16	6
Louisiana	12	12	18	17	2
Maine	10	14	16	16	5
Maryland	10	10	16	16	6
Massachusetts	10	14	16	16	0
Michigan	10	14	16	16	0
Minnesota	10	10	18	16	2
Mississippi	10	10	18	16	3
Missouri	12	14	18	17	5
Montana	10	15	18	16	3
Nebraska	10	15	18	16	4
Nevada	12	14	18	16	6
New Hampshire	10	10	16	16	0
New Jersey	10	16	16	16	4
New Mexico	10	10	16	17	4
New York	10	16	18	17	5
North Carolina	10	10	16	16	4
North Dakota	10	14	18	18	5
Ohio	10	10	16	16	4
Oklahoma	NA	14*	NA	16	3
Oregon	10*	NA	16	16	3
Pennsylvania	10	16	16	16	4

(continued)

TABLE 1.1   Ages of Consent 1885–1999, and Age Spans in the Fifty
States, 1999 *(continued)*

State	1885	1890	1920	1999	Age Span in Years
Rhode Island	10	13	16	16	3
South Carolina	10	10	16	15	0
South Dakota	10	14	18	16	3
Tennessee	10	10	18	18	4
Texas	10	10	18	17	3
Utah	10	13	18	16	4
Vermont	10	14	16	16	0
Virginia	12	12	16	15	3
Washington	12	12	18	16	4
West Virginia	12	12	16	16	4
Wisconsin	10	14	16	16	0
Wyoming	10	14	16	16	4

NA = not available.

*Data drawn from Bienen (1980a: 190).

Note: Compare these ages and their variety across the states to those of some European countries: Austria 14, Belgium 16, Denmark 15, Finland 16, France 15, Germany 16, Great Britain 16 (except Northern Ireland 17), Greece 15, Ireland 17, Italy 14, Luxembourg 16, Netherlands 16, Portugal 16, Spain 12, Sweden 15. Data from Levy (1999).

Sources: Adapted by the author from state statutes, current through 1999 sessions. For 1885, 1890, and 1920, data are drawn from Odem (1995: 14–15, 30, 199).

The Third Wave: Conservative Reforms of the 1990s

In the late 1990s, statutory rape laws were amended in ten states in order to target males whose underage female partners become pregnant. This was a move supported at first by some feminists and liberals who felt that young, abused, impoverished women deserved protection and predatory males deserved punishment. But, different from the other two sets of amendments to statutory rape laws in this century, this was a policy initiative most pursued by conservative forces, who as in the nineteenth century were able to exert more control over the policy's implementation.

Background to Targeting Pregnancy

Reacting to longer-term changes in the social structure and mores of the United States that had begun in the 1960s and 1970s, conservative forces in the 1980s became focused on the rising numbers of nonmarital sexual relationships and out-of-wedlock births and on the concurrently rising percentage of women and children in poverty who required public assistance. The 1980s saw a dual backlash: against moral and sexual permissiveness as well as against the perceived overexpansion of the welfare state that gave incentives to the poor to receive economic assistance but seemed to require little from them in return.[29] Indeed, the two became tied together in a cultural argument: The lax morals and single-parent families of the poor, particularly people of color, were responsible for the rising number of such families requiring welfare and the rising cost of supplying that welfare.

In 1981, the Supreme Court heard its only case dealing with statutory rape laws, *Michael M. v. Superior Court of Sonoma County*,[30] which considered whether gender-specific statutory rape laws violated the equal protection clause of the Fourteenth Amendment of the U.S. Constitution. The majority opinion held that such laws, in which only males were considered perpetrators, were constitutional because they served to deter the "epidemic" of teenage pregnancy. Young females were, or should be, deterred from sex by the threat of pregnancy, and young males would be deterred from sex by the fear of prosecution. In making this much-criticized argument, the court explicitly linked teen pregnancy, statutory rape, and adolescent sexuality. This judicial support dovetailed with the movement described above vis-à-vis sexuality, pregnancy, and the economy, making the 1980s and 1990s ripe for a new policy initiative aimed at reclaiming "traditional" American economics and morality.

Implementing the Changes

Both the discourse about and the activities around statutory rape vis-à-vis teen pregnancy and teen births intensified beginning in 1995, when the non-partisan Alan Guttmacher Institute released a study on teen pregnancy.[31] It found that 65% of teen mothers had children by men who were 20 or older; and that often the younger the mother, the larger the age gap between her and the baby's father. While subsequent studies showed that about two-thirds of these teen mothers were 18 or 19 with partners of 20 or 21, and more than one-fourth of the 15–17-year-old mothers had a same-age partner,[32] calls for stemming the tide of teen pregnancy grew louder. Vital to doing so, according to this view, would be to get tough on statutory rape. This would deter the behavior of predators whom one sociologist described as engaging in "hit and run . . . sex without commitment and babies without responsibility" (Goodman 1995).[33] Further, some argued, severe punishment for violating statutory rape laws would result in fewer unmarried teen births and thus reduce the public assistance rolls.

Just one year after the statistics appeared, the newly Republican-controlled Congress was debating welfare reform. The Personal Responsibility and Work Opportunity Reconciliation Act (PRWORA) of 1996[34] established Temporary Assistance to Needy Families (TANF), a block grant to the states that replaced Aid to Families with Dependent Children. The first line of the PRWORA is "Marriage is the foundation of a successful society." Shortly thereafter, it says, "The increase in the number of children receiving public assistance is closely related to the increase in births to unmarried women." Here, directly stated, is a cultural concern that had been underlying contestations over the meaning of statutory rape since the eighteenth century when female chastity was a commodity with which to bargain for a spouse, and since the nineteenth century when working girls in the cities seemingly exchanged sex for being treated to dinner, thus potentially harming their marriage prospects. In these two time periods as well as in the 1990s, the focus was on the morals of an individual rather than on social, political, or economic structures. Here, the number of people in poverty is caused solely by unmarried females giving birth.

Focusing on the high economic and social costs of out-of-wedlock childbearing, the welfare reform act has as an integral part a section on teen pregnancy and statutory rape that links the two and challenges states to put that link into action. Each state must submit plans on how it will "prevent and reduce the incidence of out-of-wedlock pregnancies, with special emphasis on teen pregnancies, and establish numerical goals for reducing the illegitimacy ratio of the State . . . [and provide] education and training on the problem of statutory rape so that teenage pregnancy prevention programs may be expanded in scope to include men."[35] Up to five states each year can receive bonuses of up to $100 million if they have the highest rates of decrease in both illegitimate births and abortions. By merging the nineteenth-century image of the seduced and/or abused teen with the twentieth-century impoverished teen mother, the Congress was able to attack nonmarital sex as well as the perceived lax morals and economic handouts of the welfare state.

With TANF resources to back them, and in response to conservative lobbying, some states began to dust off their statutory rape laws to target men for the impregnation of young impoverished women (Navarro 1996). Ten states quickly allotted millions of dollars to targeting the partners of pregnant teens, explicitly intertwining the moral and economic bases of statutory rape laws.[36]

While some feminists and liberals supported the targeting at first as a means by which to collect child support and protect young women from exploitative relationships, they became wary of the fervent support from some from the Religious Right, and backed away from the issue (Maynard 1999). Groups such as the National Organization for Women protested the welfare reform bill; Planned Parenthood and the American Civil Liberties Union, among others, testified repeatedly at the state level against the new construction of the crime. While little noted in the media,[37] these groups expressed a number of concerns about the potentially adverse effects of the implementation of the laws:

1. A pregnant teen in a consensual relationship could be deterred from seeking prenatal care for fear that her partner might be incarcerated during his child's infancy or have to register as a sex offender if he were convicted at the felony level, even if he intended to support the child and remain in a relationship with the mother.
2. A pregnant teen in a nonconsensual relationship could similarly be deterred because she would fear physical or other retribution from the father.
3. A pregnant teen wishing to receive an abortion might be more prone to seek an illegal one so as to avoid a judicial bypass requirement[38] in which she might have to name the father.
4. The law would tell males that coercive relationships would go unpunished as long as they did not result in pregnancy.

In other words, these groups argued, same-age relationships that do not result in pregnancy might be nonconsensual, and age-differentiated relationships that do result in pregnancy might be consensual and long-term—but the newly revised laws would not catch the first instance and would punish the second.[39]

The link forged between statutory rape, the number of births to teen mothers, and public assistance expenditures served to reinvigorate funding and prosecutorial efforts toward the crime, while also undermining the gender-neutral language of the laws by focusing on young women as victims. But as in the nineteenth century, the implementation of the laws has tended to have mixed results that have pleased few and have not served to deter adolescent sexuality—they remain both protective (if indeed a young female is being abused) and punitive (if the relationship is a consensual one).

Conclusion

Statutory rape laws have undergone numerous constructions and reconstructions over the past one hundred years in particular. This history of revisions to the laws and the discourses surrounding them has served to illustrate their unsettled nature as both safeguarding and punishing adolescent sexuality.

The laws also serve to marginalize adolescent sexuality and pregnancy. As they specifically state that the perpetrator and the female be unmarried to one another, and as homosexual couples have been charged disproportionately, they reveal themselves to be more about marriage and sexuality than about age. Statutory rape laws purport to be about protecting those under a certain age from sexual intercourse, but marriage laws allow those under the age of consent to marry. This leaves married males and females of the same age as their unmarried counterparts unprotected, simply by virtue of their being married. Married teens in coercive relationships will go unprosecuted, while unmarried teens cannot prevent prosecutions of their sex partners. Indeed, "marriage laws and practices [operate] as linchpins at the intersection of economic and political institutions regulating race and reproduction, and defining the American nation" (Duggan 2000: 187). In the 1800s, statutory rape laws were focused on preserving the chastity of white females for marriage, but black and Native American women were not so safeguarded; in the 1900s, the laws centered on reforming the sexual behavior of immigrant working-class girls in the cities so that they would aspire to middle-class values and family structures; in 2000, the laws targeted a population coded as nonwhite and as immoral: teens who give birth out of wedlock and require public assistance.

Rather than consider structural problems, institutional failures, or ideological contradictions, blame for societal ills is placed on individuals—in this case, teens and their sex partners, especially those of low income. While individual behavior can be contained much more readily than, say, the economic dislocations wrought by urbanization or globalization or the political implications of the civil rights and feminist movements, neither poverty nor the changing nature of the family are likely to be stemmed by regulating the female body. The debate over statutory rape laws has focused on individual private morality, rather than delving into cultural assumptions about gender roles and gender equality, marriage and the family, sexuality and sexual violence, and poverty and capitalism.[40] The next three chapters will detail various facets of statutory rape laws, and their adoption and implementation in the United States.

Chapter 2

Robbing the Cradle
Age-Span Provisions
Decriminalize Teen Sex

Rob the cradle and find yourself a brand new crib.
    —*Billboard sponsored by the Connecticut Department of Social Services*

Introduction

Statutory rape laws had formerly criminalized sexual activity by a person (generally male) of any age with a person (generally female) under the age of consent. In other words, if the male were the same age as the female, or even younger than the female, he would still be prosecuted for the crime.[1] Age spans, however, mandate that the perpetrator be a certain number of years older than the victim; some require that the perpetrator be at least of a certain age, such as 18. A law that formerly read, "It is a felony for any person to commit an act of sexual penetration with any person under the age of 16," would be changed to "It is a felony for any person to commit an act of sexual penetration with any person under the age of 16, provided that the actor is at least four years older than the victim." An age span effectively decriminalizes sexual activity between similar-aged teens at the felony level. Many states retain statutes making such activity a misdemeanor.

Portions of this chapter were originally published in *Polity* 35, no. 1 (fall 2002).

Three questions arise when looking at the adoption of these provisions. First, as is discussed below, public opinion has and continues to have little sympathy for teens having sex. Indeed, the themes of "family values" and of abstinence from premarital sex have been prominent since the early 1980s—yet more than half of the states have decriminalized teenage sex since that time. Thus, one may ask What might prompt a state to implement such a provision? Second, these age spans range from 0 years in those seven states choosing not to adopt such provisions to 6 years in others. What accounts for the variation across the states? Third, What do prosecutions look like after age-span provisions have been implemented? Are resources concentrated on relationships that fall just outside the span, on those which have very large age differences, or on (in some states) misdemeanor prosecutions of perpetrators close in age to the victim? These three questions are addressed in this chapter.

Background to Policy Adoption: The Pros and Cons of Age-Span Provisions in Statutory Rape Laws

Public Opinion—The Polls

It is somewhat surprising that any state implemented an age-span provision at all, given that the American public does not appear to be very accepting of adolescent nonmarital sexuality. Over the past 30 or so years, the National Opinion Research Center and General Social Survey (NORC-GSS) has repeated a number of its questions about attitudes toward sexual behavior. Their question on "premarital sex" is as follows: "There's been a lot of discussion about the way morals and sexual attitudes about sex are changing in this country. If a man and woman have sex relations before marriage, do you think it is always wrong, almost always wrong, wrong only sometimes, or not wrong at all?" Responses are charted in figure 2.1.

While the "sometimes" and "almost always wrong" stay relatively steady, there are increases in "not wrong at all" from 26% to 42%, and decreases in "always wrong" from 35% to 23%. The "blips" in the steady trends occur in the mid-1980s, a more conservative time than the 1970s and perhaps the 1990s. One might read these results as saying that the American public's attitudes on the subject of premarital sex have become somewhat more permissive over time.

But as with all public opinion surveys, there are potential problems in the wording of the question. First, it starts by noting "the way morals and attitudes about sex are changing in this country." Was the questioner implying that there is a perception that American attitudes about sex have become increasingly liberal? Is that what respondents thought he or she was implying?

FIGURE 2.1   Public Opinion on Premarital Sex, 1972–1998

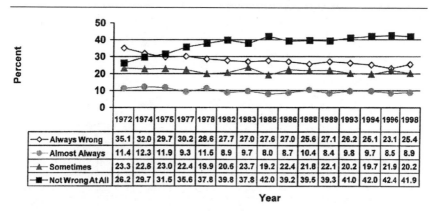

	1972	1974	1975	1977	1978	1982	1983	1985	1986	1988	1989	1993	1994	1996	1998
—◇— Always Wrong	35.1	32.0	29.7	30.2	28.6	27.7	27.0	27.6	27.0	25.6	27.1	26.2	25.1	23.1	25.4
—●— Almost Always	11.4	12.3	11.9	9.3	11.5	8.9	9.7	8.0	8.7	10.4	8.4	9.8	9.7	8.5	8.9
—▲— Sometimes	23.3	22.8	23.0	22.4	19.9	20.6	23.7	19.2	22.4	21.8	22.1	20.2	19.7	21.9	20.2
—■— Not Wrong At All	26.2	29.7	31.5	35.6	37.8	39.8	37.8	42.0	39.2	39.5	39.3	41.0	42.0	42.4	41.9

Year

Sources: For the years 1972 to 1989, data are drawn from Smith (1990: 415–435). For the years 1993 to 1998, data are drawn and percentages computed from http://www.icpsr.umich.edu/GSS/ rnd1988/merged/cdbk/premarsx.htm. Adapted by the author.

As such, did they make their responses more liberal? Second, the question asks about a "man" and a "woman," which clearly delineates heterosexuality and implies that the two parties are adults. Many Americans are willing to grant certain behavioral freedoms to heterosexual adults which they would not grant to heterosexual minors or to homosexuals of any age. Third, the phrase "if a man and woman have sex relations before marriage" could imply that the two are going to marry one another. Perhaps, then, the responses to this question really indicated an increase in permissiveness not of adolescent sexuality, but of two people who are engaged and have sex before they become married. Fourth, the question may point some respondents toward a negative response by allowing three gradations of "wrong-ness," beginning with the strongest negative. Most of the questions NORC-GSS uses about sexuality are framed in this way (i.e., "always wrong," "almost always wrong," and so on), so this problem in particular should be borne in mind throughout this assessment of responses.

NORC-GSS' follow-up question to the above, more specific about the age of the parties, would seem to point to the idea that people may have responded more liberally to the first "premarital" question because they were envisioning adults, possibly engaged adults. The second question was "What if they are in their early teens, say 14 to 16 years old? In that case, do you think sex relations before marriage are always wrong, almost always wrong, wrong only sometimes, or not wrong at all?" Responses are charted in figure 2.2. Not only are the "always wrong" numbers steady, but they also consistently include

FIGURE 2.2   Public Opinion on Adolescent Sex, 1986–1998

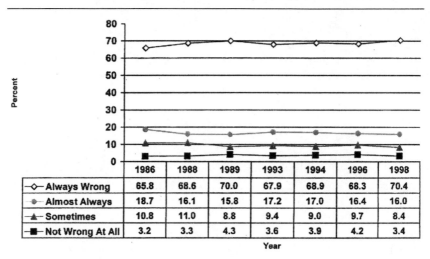

	1986	1988	1989	1993	1994	1996	1998
—◇— Always Wrong	65.8	68.6	70.0	67.9	68.9	68.3	70.4
—●— Almost Always	18.7	16.1	15.8	17.2	17.0	16.4	16.0
—▲— Sometimes	10.8	11.0	8.8	9.4	9.0	9.7	8.4
—■— Not Wrong At All	3.2	3.3	4.3	3.6	3.9	4.2	3.4

Year

Sources: For the years 1986 to 1989, data are drawn from Smith (1990: 415–435). For the years 1993 to 1998, data are drawn and percentages computed from http://www.icpsr.umich.edu/GSS/rnd1988/merged/cdbk/teensex.htm. Adapted by the author.

at least 65%–70% of the respondents. "Not wrong at all" responses hover between 3% and 4%.

The question wording is again a problem, as it implies that one's response to this question should be an exception to their response to the first question, by starting out with "What if?" Using the term "early teens," even if supplemented by "14 to 16,"[2] would probably set off red flags for many people, especially parents.

This is the only available measure of opinion on this subject, and even given its numerous flaws, the numbers are overwhelming enough that we can probably assume that the respondents believed that underage teenagers should not be having sex—period. Americans during this time period may have been particularly sensitive to the subject of the sexuality of young people, having witnessed numerous "moral panics"[3] having to do with young people and sexuality: "day-care" child abuse and satanic ritual abuse cases, crackdowns on child pornography, limits on young people's access to sexual content on the Internet, anxiety over pedophiles lurking in Internet chat rooms, an "epidemic" of "children having children," and sex offender registration laws.

Note also that figure 2.1 covers the period 1972–1998 and figure 2.2 covers 1986–1998. The responses in figure 2.1 for 1972–1985 vary by about 12 percentage points from those of 1986–1998. Even if the responses in figure 2.2 varied by 12 percentage points, they would still overwhelmingly condemn adolescent sex.

It appears that public opinion would not have been congruent with the adoption of an age-span provision of any size. Yet during the period charted above, the majority of the states did adopt them. Indeed, the age of consent in most of the states is 16, with an age span of three or four years. Why?

Laws criminalizing such activity operate at the state level, not the federal level. While one can look at the above polls and conclude that most "Americans" find adolescent sex to be a problem, one cannot necessarily draw the same conclusions about the residents of a particular region or state. What was happening at the state level?

The Feminists

Feminist lobbying to implement age-span provisions was part of a larger effort at overhauling forcible rape law (Bienen 1980a: 177–180; Searles and Berger 1987: 25–27).[4] But, as discussed in greater detail in chapter 1, the feminists were divided over statutory rape reform. Some advocated for age spans, while others argued actively against them.

Recall that feminist sex radicals argued that the laws denied the agency of young people, and that they presumed that all sexual activity involving a young person, particularly a female, was both heterosexual and coercive. Radical feminists, on the other hand, thought that young females required protection from males of any age, not just those a certain number of years older. They felt that adolescent females were simply the less powerful party in heterosexual relationships—particularly, sexual relationships.

Liberal feminists, many of whom were members of the National Organization for Women (NOW) and were involved in the lobbying effort, tried to split the difference: to empower young women while also protecting them. Specifically, reformers wanted to shift the focus from the double standard that assumed young women's incapacity to consent and sought to preserve their virginity, while having no similar assumptions about young men. They lobbied to decriminalize sex between similarly aged teens, while also providing increased protection for children.

More broadly, the reformers were seeking to change the traditional conception of the crime of statutory rape from one based on stereotypes of gender and the protection of "virtue" to one based on differences in sexual maturity and on age disparities between perpetrator and victim that would be reflective of potential inequality.[5] This was the point of the age-span provision:

[T]he implication [is] that if the parties are the same age then the offense is presumed not to be abusive. An age disparity, typically set at
three or four years, implies the element of coercion. In this respect,
the reform provision is not very different from the former statutory
rape: The purpose of the age limitation was and is to protect a
younger person from an older person. Statutory rape laws, however,
were structured around virginity. The age gap in the rape reform
statutes has a different resonance. The rape reform provisions are designed to protect against sexual exploitation and abuse. What constitutes the harm to be prevented is not the sexual activity itself, but
sexual activity in which one party is too young, or in which an older
person may be in a position to coerce a younger person, simply
because of the age differential. (Bienen 1998: 1570–1571)

Using age-span provisions in this way would also minimize the number
of consensual teenage relationships being prosecuted, at least at the felony
level.[6] Amid the infighting, feminist lobbyists pushed for age spans.

The Religious Conservatives

The idea of the young girl being taken advantage of by the wily older man is
the same image that drew in the support of conservative religious forces at the
turn of the twentieth century for the raising of the age of consent.[7] They supported statutory rape laws for this reason. Further, conservatives also supported
the laws as written (i.e., with no age span) because they appeared to serve as a
moral condemnation of premarital sexual activity. Thus, the exemption of
same-age sexual relationships from prosecution would send the wrong message
to young people.

It is important to note that here, as with some other issues having to do
with sexuality, there is some agreement on seemingly opposite sides of the political spectrum. This was true of statutory rape reform in the nineteenth century as well, when first-wave feminists joined with religious conservative groups
to raise the age of consent. Some feminists, generally considered liberal or even
radical, and some conservatives would both have problems with age spans. On
the left, the concern would be that a vulnerable teen might be left unprotected
simply because his or her sex partner was close in age. On the right, the concern would be that a decriminalization of unmarried teen sex might encourage
sexuality outside of marriage, thereby devaluing the institution and its construction as the sole proper arena for procreation.

Unlike the situation among feminists, there was no infighting among this
group during this period of statutory rape law reform: Those who might today

be described as the Christian Right or Religious Right were simply not at all in favor of age-span provisions for teenagers. What they had in common with the feminists early in the reform period was that they were not represented in large numbers in legislatures; they were on the outside trying to sway those on the inside, the legislators.

The Legislators

Feminists certainly could not implement such a reform alone, particularly with strong Christian-based opposition. At the beginning of the reform period in particular, although the same is true at present, women were extremely under-represented in legislatures at both the state and the national levels. I therefore use the terms *legislators* and *male legislators* interchangeably.

Most male legislators were generally unmoved by concerns about double standards of morality, or about a stereotype of young females as mentally incapacitated. Some on the left and most of those on the right were not inter-ested in decriminalizing consensual teenage relationships—there appeared to be nothing to gain from taking action. They did want to increase penalties for sexual activity with younger teens and with children, and were open to broad-ening the range of offenses beyond penile–vaginal penetration to other types of touching.

Other legislators worried that young males would be the victims of false reports (Bienen 1980a: 194). This latter concern was also cited by male legisla-tors during the campaign for statutory rape reform in the nineteenth century. Such a fear was a driving force behind the corroboration requirements of tradi-tional rape laws: Prosecution would not progress on the uncorroborated testi-mony of the female, or without proof that a female's utmost physical resistance was overcome by force. With statutory rape laws, male legislators were proba-bly even more concerned due to the stereotype that young women may be more prone to submit reports later found to be false (Bienen 1980a: 193–194). There is no clear evidence on this vis-à-vis young women or older women—that reports are found to be false does not necessarily mean that those reports were false. It could mean that evidence could not be obtained, that the female decided to drop the charges, that the prosecutor felt that the case was not strong enough, or that police officers did not believe the victim or believed that she had indeed shown consent.[8] Legislators were also concerned with the fact that statutory rape did not have the same kinds of evidence requirements about force as did rape laws. One only had to prove the female was underage and not the wife of the perpetrator.[9] In this line of thinking, a spurned young female or her outraged family might find it easy to charge a male with statutory rape for a variety of motives.

Second, these legislators did not want to see young males punished too harshly for exploring their "natural" sexual urges:

> Both reformers and conservatives seemed to agree upon criminaliz-ing sexual contact offenses involving children and adults, but when the question of defining consensual behavior among teenagers arises, debate usually reaches a stalemate, as each side retreats into a fortress built upon its own conception of appropriate female sex-ual behavior. Legislators often want . . . not to punish sexually ac-tive males who have not reached the statutory age of consent. (Bienen 1980a: 180)

Even though their goal was different from that of the feminists, the means were the same: exempt young males from felony-level statutory rape if he and the young female are close in age. But as noted, not all legislators agreed on this course of action.

In general, Democrats were more prone to support the liberal feminists' goals; Republicans were more prone to support religious conservatives' goals. These two sets of interests are part of the core constituencies of the two parties. Based on this, I would expect that a state with Democratic control of the legis-lature and the governorship to have adopted a large age span early on, and vice versa. This again brings up the question of what is liberal and what is conser-vative vis-à-vis statutory rape laws. One could argue, as I would, that a liberal age-span provision would be a large one that would catch potentially coercive relationships while decriminalizing same-age sexuality more likely to be con-sensual. One could also argue that this is a conservative, male-oriented measure because it could be read as securing access to young females by young males and as not protecting vulnerable young females. But, in general, I would label as conservative an absence of an age span, proscribing all unmarried teenage sexuality and thereby preserving the role of marriage as the only type of rela-tionship within which sexual activity should occur. This issue, of what types of statutory rape laws are liberal and what types are conservative, will recur throughout the case studies in this chapter as well as in chapters 3 and 4.

The Outcome

Forty-three states had age-span provisions in their statutory rape laws by 1999, ranging from two to six years. We know that some feminists lobbied for this change, although others were against it. We know that religious conservatives were opposed to age spans on moral grounds. And we know that some male legislators wanted to prevent young males from being falsely accused and from being punished too harshly, but that others had no interest in exempting same-age teens from prosecution.

What forces, then, account for the changes to the laws that decriminalized sex between teens close in age? Second, what accounts for their variation?

Adoption of Age-Span Provisions Across the States

Table 2.1 illustrates in what years 42 states adopted age-span provisions.[10] Hawaii, Kansas, Massachusetts, Michigan, New Hampshire, South Carolina, and Vermont had not adopted the provision by 1999.

In general, the expected pattern of policy adoption across the states and over time, regardless of the type of policy, is one of rising and falling like an S-curve: a few states adopt, followed by a point at which adoptions proceed rather quickly across the states, followed by a falling-off period during which the last few adopt.[11] This is attributed by some authors to a process of "social learning" across the states, in which a state that has not yet adopted watches the results in an adopt-state and then chooses whether and how it will adopt. While this social learning framework for examining policy diffusion can be useful in trying to determine which states tend to be leaders and which states laggards, and to analyze trends in the types of policy outputs across space and over time, it has a rather major problem in terms of getting at the root of the impetus for policymaking—it cannot tell us who is learning from whom.

The saw-toothed results in table 2.1 are somewhat different from the single, almost normal, bell-shaped curve one might expect if one assumed a smooth process of social learning over time. For one, there appears to be more than one "S," and so there is not one high point in the number of adoptions of a particular time period. Here there are at least two identifiable curves. One recent work has found a similar pattern, and hypothesized that with a morality policy, the pattern may be more saw-toothed because it reflects public opinion mobilization that truncates multiple S-curves (Mooney and Lee 2001). However, the pattern can be explained by interest group mobilization as well. The largest curve is in the late 1970s when NOW was pushing for rape reform. In the 1980s, NOW's priorities changed, particularly when they turned with concentrated resources toward abortion, domestic violence, and sexual harassment. No longer was there a concerted push for the provisions of statutory rape reform that had not gone through because most forcible rape provisions had.

One can readily see in table 2.1 that the states that adopted a span of two to three years (those in normal type) and those that adopted a span of four to six years (those in bold italic type) seem to be spread rather evenly across time. In other words, unlike some writers on morality policy would predict (Mooney and Lee 1995; Glick and Hays 1991), there does not appear to be a unidirectional

TABLE 2.1 Years of Adoption of Age-Span Provisions in Statutory Rape Laws

'71	'72	'73	'74	'75	'76	'77	'78	'79	'80	'81	'82	'83	'84	'85	'86	'87	'88	'89	'90	'91	'92	'93	'94	'95	'96	'97	'98
		MN																								MS	
		VA				AL																AZ					***WI***
		AR				LA																	GA				
			CO	***IA***	***NE***																	CA	IN	***NC***			
			ME	***MD***	***NV***												***DE***	SD									
	MT	TX									AK						***WA***	***TN***	***PA***								
OR	***OH***	***KY***	***NM***	***WV***	***ND***	***NJ***	RI		OK	***WY***	***UT***	***IL***									***ID***	CT	***MO***	***PA***	***FL***		

YEAR

Note: New York adopted the provision in 1950 and is not shown. States in normal type have an age span of two to three years; those in bold italic have a span of four to six years. Specifically: 2 Years—Alabama, Arizona, Connecticut, Louisiana, Minnesota. 3 Years—Alaska, California, Georgia, Indiana, Mississippi, Montana, Oklahoma, Oregon, Rhode Island, South Dakota, Texas, Virginia. 4 Years—Colorado, Delaware, Nebraska, New Jersey, New Mexico, North Carolina, Ohio, Pennsylvania, Tennessee, Utah, Washington, West Virginia, Wisconsin, Wyoming. 5 Years—Arkansas, Idaho, Illinois, Iowa, Maine, Missouri, New York, North Dakota. 6 Years—Florida, Kentucky, Maryland, Nevada.

Source: Adapted by the author from state statutes.

movement toward either a more liberal policy or a more conservative policy. Indeed, there appears to be no pattern, just as with the adoptions themselves.

Geographically, there is some pattern with contiguous states: Ohio, West Virginia, Pennsylvania, and New Jersey all have four-year age spans, as do Wyoming, Utah, Colorado, and New Mexico. Massachusetts, Vermont, and New Hampshire do not have age spans at all, but Illinois, Iowa, Missouri, and Arkansas all have five-year spans. Texas and Oklahoma, and Oregon and California, all have three-year spans. But these observations cannot tell us from whom the adoption of a particular policy is being spurred—is the learning from a group in one state to a group in another state, from policymaker to policymaker, from public opinion in one state bleeding into public opinion from another? At this point, I turn to case studies of three states: New Jersey, Georgia, and California.[12]

Case Studies: New Jersey, Georgia, and California

Case 1: New Jersey

SETTING THE STAGE   The New Jersey statutory rape amendments were passed in 1978, taking effect in 1979. Some additions were made between the date on which the main bill passed and the date before which it was to take effect. These are discussed in detail below. The previous statute, last amended in 1951, read "Any person . . . who, being the age of sixteen or over, unlawfully and carnally abuses a woman-child of 12 years or older, but under the age of 16 years, with or without her consent, is guilty of a high misdemeanor, and shall be punished by a fine of not more than $5,000, or imprisonment at hard labor of not more than 15 years, or both." This was basically the same as the 1905 statute, except then the fine was $2,000.[13]

In 1971, the New Jersey Criminal Law Revision Commission issued its final report on revising the penal code. It set the age of consent at 12, and recommended the mistake-of-age defense in which the defendant could claim he thought the female was over the age of consent. These provisions basically followed the American Law Institute's Model Penal Code. The institute's membership is that of lawyers, judges, and academics taking an interest in law revision. The 1962 version of article 213 of the code, "Sexual Offenses"— which was little changed in its latest 1995 edition—is ideologically mixed vis-à-vis rape law. Although some parts of it are more sensitive to rape victims, some feminists have criticized it for retaining notions of women as property of their husbands, and for setting the age of consent at 10. In New Jersey, the Law Revision Commission's recommended age of 12 was never adopted, although "[w]ithout the personal commitment [of the chairmen of the Senate and

Assembly Judiciary Committees], the two committees might well have adopted the 1971 Commission statute" (Bienen 1980a: 207 fn 206).

NOW, in conjunction with other feminist groups, began a nationwide campaign in the 1970s to reform rape laws and presented a standard package of reform legislation all around the country. In New Jersey, the feminists' rape reform bill was introduced as an amendment to what was basically the 1971 Law Revision Commission's draft. Committees held public hearings for two months in the spring of 1978, made numerous amendments to the 1971 draft, and included the NOW bill with their revised draft of the entire penal code. In short, according to one of the authors of the bill, the measure adopted in New Jersey "was drafted in the spring of 1978 by a coalition of feminist groups with the assistance of the NOW National Task Force on Rape. . . . The NOW bill, which was adopted by both houses of the legislature in 1978 without major definitional change, was modeled after the 1976 Center for Rape Concern Model Sex Offense Statute" (Bienen 1980a: 207). NOW influence appears to have been crucial to policy change.

Leigh Bienen, a research attorney at the Center for Rape Concern in Philadelphia, was responsible for drafting the Center's Model Statute. The Model Statute grew out of research done under a National Institutes of Mental Health grant to study the social and psychological effects of rape on victims, the victims' interactions with the criminal justice system, and the factors influencing case outcomes. A supplementary grant funded a compilation and evaluation of the rape laws in all 50 states. Reflecting their findings, "The model statute . . . was drafted with the explicit intent of incorporating a variety of reforms favorable to victims" (Bienen 1977: 90). Based in part on the groundbreaking 1974 Michigan code, the statute graded the crimes: "Sexual assault in the second degree" criminalized sexual penetration with a person 13 to 15, and required that the perpetrator be at least 21. It also banned the mistake-of-age defense. "Sexual assault in the third degree," a lesser grade of felony, criminalized sexual contact with a person 13 to 15, and required that the perpetrator be at least 21 (Bienen 1977: 92). Here was the age-span provision itself, with a large age span as would be expected if feminists were the main influence on policy adoption.

Bienen (1998) characterized the scene in New Jersey in 1978:

> In New Jersey, the effective decisionmaking body for rape reform legislation was the five-man Senate Judiciary Committee and the five-man Assembly Judiciary Committee. The most powerful legislator moving this package forward was a former law partner of the then Governor. The Chair of the Senate Judiciary Committee, State Senator Martin L. Greenberg, was himself a long standing member of the National Organization for Women. Both the Chair

of the Senate Judiciary Committee and the Chair of the Assembly Judiciary Committee were strong supporters of the feminist reform package in the Code of Criminal Justice, which included the redefinition of Incest. Without the support of these unlikely allies, rape reform legislation never would have passed in New Jersey. The reform statute would not have been formulated or brought forward without the women's movement, but it never would have passed in New Jersey without the specific politics surrounding the enactment of the Code of Criminal Justice in 1978 and 1979. (1512)

Her account tracks both the elements of group pressure and legislator partisanship as playing a major role in statutory rape reform adoption. Liberal feminists, with inside influence and support in a Democrat-controlled legislature, with a Democratic governor, were instrumental in drafting and lobbying for the reform.

LEGISLATIVE RESPONSE   Given the above, the 1978 amendment criminalized the act of "aggravated sexual assault": sexual penetration with a victim under 13 when the perpetrator was at least four years older. In other words, the age of consent in New Jersey was made 13, down from 16. Rather than a high misdemeanor, the crime was made a felony. The bill passed both Democrat-controlled houses and Democratic Governor Brendan Byrne signed it on August 10, 1978. The changes were to take effect September 1, 1979.

> The reclassifications of sex offenses were very difficult for several committee members to understand in 1977 and 1978. Sometimes the objections were religious and sometimes they were simply that the behaviors described were claimed to be outside the knowledge or experience of the legislators. Some of their hesitancies and objections seemed to this observer to be sincere matters of conscience, while others did not. Generally, the legislators favored policies that facilitated prosecutions. They were also highly suspicious of any change to the status quo or any change that might have an unintended effect. The intended effect was difficult enough. The legislators rightly anticipated that issues such as the decriminalization of consenting heterosexual conduct among teenagers would catch the attention of voters and be politically troublesome. (Bienen 1998: 1512–1513)

And troublesome it was. Between the signing date and the active date, the statutory rape law was amended again. Note that this participant mentions religious opposition to the reformed rape laws. Although the influence of religious conservatives was relatively weak in New Jersey, at least vis-à-vis the Republican Party, groups allied with their viewpoint would lobby against the bill before it took effect.

Certainly, the tone of the coverage of the bill that had been passed was inflammatory. One headline referred to a woman from New Jersey's State Coalition Against Rape, who worked with NOW on the code draft: "'I'm Trying to Help Teens,' Claims the Sex-at-13 Woman" (Norman 1979). Other articles appeared to imply that legislators must have been tricked into signing such a proposal: "No one—not even the legislators who voted to approve the entire penal code or the Governor who signed it—seemed to notice the sex abuse section until Lt. Joseph Delaney spotted it during a routine seminar on the code for law enforcement officers" (Norman and Wasserman 1979). When this policeman spoke out about the change, "parents [feared] that the state's criminal code would start a rash of sexual relationships" and a "petition drive [was] mounted in shopping centers and churches by angry parents, educators, and church groups" across the state. (Norman and Wasserman 1979). Along with church groups, antiabortion groups were also active in lobbying for amendments to the revised law in 1979 (Bienen 1980a: 209 fn 217). Some more conservative legislators, too, worried that the lower age (at 13 rather than 16) would "give the state's stamp of approval for young teenagers to engage in sex" (Waldron 1979b) and wanted it raised.

In response, NOW state coordinator Nancy Stultz noted that Planned Parenthood statistics showed a rising percentage of sexually active teenagers, and said that the organization was trying to avoid situations in which police would have to "throw a 15-year old boy in jail for having sex with his 15-year old girlfriend." Stultz also said, apparently in response to a reporter's question, that the new code "was in no way meant to legalize sex between a 13-year old and a 45-year old" (Norman 1979).

Six amendments were introduced. One, introduced by conservatives, criminalized all sexual penetration with a person under 16 and sexual contact between persons 13 to 16 and someone four years older (Bienen 1980a: 194). In other words, it restored the traditional statutory rape law, which criminalized any sexual penetration with a person under 16 and had no age-span provision. The predominantly Democratic legislature was uninterested and the measure failed.

The amendment that did pass also raised the age of consent back to 16, but required the perpetrator be at least four years older if the victim were under 16, and carried a 10-year maximum sentence. It also criminalized sexual contact (that is, nonpenetration) with a person between 13 and 16 and a person four years older, with a maximum of 18 months in jail as penalty. This was sponsored by Essex County Democrat Martin Greenberg, chair of the Judiciary Committee and as noted a NOW member of several years.

During the hiatus before the effective date, an enormous outcry over the reduction of the statutory age to 13, or the "repeal of the age of consent," as the protesters called it, produced sufficient political pressure to force the legislature to amend the age provisions in the 1979 amendments to the penal code. The 1979 amendments to the rape reform statute added an offense defined as sexual penetration with a victim under the age of 16. The term consent was not used, and after debate, the restriction of a four-year age gap between the victim and the act of sexual penetration with a person under 13 was removed. (Bienen 1980a: 208)

Bienen did not characterize the restoration of the age of consent at 16 as a loss for feminists. Indeed, they were consulted about the opposition's furor. The reformers felt, in the end, that they had accomplished what they set out to do vis-à-vis statutory rape: They had implemented an age-span provision. If the age of consent were 16 rather than 13 with a four-year age span, they reasoned that 14- or 15-year-olds in consensual relationships would probably not be reported to authorities anyway. In short, "If we could get the middle of the road to go along [with an age span], and they weren't trying to turn back the clock like the moral conservatives, why mess with it?"[14] It was not worth expending their resources on at that point. They let the matter drop.

The assembly voted 71–2 for the amendment. One reporter who covered the situation in Trenton throughout the debates in the spring of 1979 noted that the entire 80-member assembly was up for election that coming November (Waldron 1979c). "Many legislators who voted for the bill admit they were stampeded by public pressure to sign it" (Waldron 1979a). Interestingly though, another part of the penal code revision decriminalized sodomy. Attempts to recriminalize it failed. This was so even though the sodomy provisions were subject to as much or more publicity than the statutory rape provisions, such as protesters at the capitol carrying signs that "New Jersey is becoming Sodom and Gomorrah" (Bienen 1998: 1508 fn 14). However, the gay rights lobby did not back off, as NOW did. It appears that legislators were more concerned about facing the organized gay and liberal vote on the sodomy statute than the less-organized protesting public on the statutory rape statute.

One cannot know what would have happened had NOW and a coalition of feminist groups chosen to fight for 13 as the age of consent in New Jersey. While organized segments of the public in New Jersey, such as antiabortion groups, certainly brought the matter to attention and managed to garner news coverage, NOW still achieved its goal of an age span. On a final note, other scholars of morality policies have found that compromise is unlikely.[15] But here, the advocacy group did compromise; it was just done behind the scenes where quantitative analysis would not catch it. This underscores the importance of case study work.

Case 2: Georgia

SETTING THE STAGE   Until 1995, Georgia's statutory rape law read "A male commits the offense of statutory rape when he engages in sexual intercourse with a female under the age of 14 years and not his wife, provided that no conviction shall be had for this offense on the unsupported testimony of the female," with a penalty of 1 to 20 years.[16] In that year, a bill was introduced called the "Child Protection Act of 1995." It was actually two bills grafted together: Representative Matt Towery's (R-Vinings) bill to raise the penalties for cruelty to children and neglect of children[17] and Senator Steve Langford's (D-LaGrange) bill to overhaul the statutory rape law. Both these sponsors have acknowledged that Towery's bill would have flown through the process were the statutory rape portions not attached to it. By itself, Towery's bill passed the House unanimously in February 1995.

THE SENATE   At the same time the Towery bill was moving through the House, two statutory rape bills were in different committees in the Senate. The Senate Special Judiciary Committee bill set the age at 16 and had no age span. Langford's bill in the Senate Judiciary Committee raised the age of consent from 14 to 16, and included a three-year age span.[18] The difference between the two committees, according to Langford, was that Special Judiciary was chaired by a Republican, Judiciary by a Democrat. Special Judiciary was created by Lieutenant Governor Pierre Howard to catch the overflow from the regular Judiciary Committee. The Special Judiciary Committee bill was tabled, mostly owing to a lack of interest in raising the age of consent from 14 to 16. Judiciary Committee Chair Mary Margaret Oliver suggested tacking Langford's bill onto Towery's Child Cruelty Bill. Towery remembers, "She basically came to me and said we'll move [your] bill out, but we had to put Steve's bill on there as well. . . . I had no problem with it and they added it on in the Senate and it sailed out of the Senate."

By all accounts, neither the NOW Georgia chapters nor any other feminist-oriented group had anything to do with this policy adoption. Perhaps this is due to NOW and others having accomplished most of its concerns vis-à-vis forcible rape by the 1990s and having turned to other concerns such as abortion and sexual harassment, or due to their numbers in Georgia that were and continue to be quite low. Deputy Attorney General Mary Beth Westmoreland noted, "[NOW] was not a very strong presence and did not carry a lot of political weight."[19] In other words, Georgia's late adoption of a small age span may have stemmed in part from a lack of NOW strength and/or interest.

One cannot say much about public opinion on the matter in Georgia. The sponsors admit they conducted no polls and the measure passed with little outcry, unlike in New Jersey when organized groups responded to the new age span. District attorneys, responsible for implementing the law, were caught by surprise: "While we're all asleep one day, [the legislature] changes the age to 16. . . . No one asked our opinion. We were not even there at the Judiciary Committee hearings. We had no idea this was coming. Our lobbyist down there had no idea it was coming."[20]

Langford drafted the bill with his attorney and friend, Michael Key, who was a juvenile court judge increasingly frustrated with the statutory rape cases he was seeing—and not seeing—in his courtroom. A three-year age span would cut down the number of consensual teenage relationships he saw come through his court, and inclusion of victims aged 14 and 15 would allow more prosecutions of potentially coercive relationships. Langford noted, "There's not much room for making teenage sex against the law. It's societal, based on history. But our culture should have a say in it, and it's our responsibility to do so. [Like the law criminalizing sodomy, which (I) also made attempts to repeal], it can't be enforced and shouldn't be. Our children laugh at us and they don't respect the law." He admitted, though, "The age is an arbitrary thing. There's nothing magic about 16. If I had my druthers it would be 18. I won't say we did a lot of research, but we do have the benefits of what others have done. The three years was somewhat arbitrary as well."

THE HOUSE   There was plenty of opposition to the Langford portion of the bill in the House in March 1995. "When it got to the House, it became very clear to me that I had taken on something that was probably going to kill my bill," said Towery. All of those interviewed described those most opposed to the raising of the age of consent as older Democrats from rural districts, and those for the change as younger Republicans from urban districts. Many of these Republicans were transplants to Georgia, and Towery noted, "They came from states where [the age of consent] was higher anyway. . . . Many of the Democrats represent the more agrarian locations in the state, and as a result they were used to the old system and not inclined to change it. So you don't have your typical party line vote." Like the role of NOW, this element is different from New Jersey. Here, the Democrats were probably more conservative on sexual matters than were the Republicans.

What is interesting about this is the construction of what is liberal and what is conservative vis-à-vis statutory rape. Recall that in New Jersey the feminist bill in effect made the age of consent 13 so that same-age teenage relationships would not be prosecutable. Based on notions of privacy, and on the reality of teenage experimentation, one could classify this as a liberal provision. Other feminists, though, would take the stand that a higher age of consent, coupled with a large age span, would be the position further to the left—it would take into account that insecure females might be somewhat manipulated into sexual activity by a male not their own age. The Georgia Democrat position, which wanted to keep the age of consent at 14 and was, according to one of the bill's sponsors, a "Bubba" or "good-old-boy" notion of sexuality, is not completely incompatible with that of liberal feminists in New Jersey. While the feminist concern lay in part with restoring female agency within the law, the Georgia Democrat concern was with not punishing boys who had been enticed into sex. Indeed, Langford remembered, "One big argument I heard is these little girls dress up and lure these guys." This is the kind of gender stereotype that feminists were trying to get away from: that such a female could never be a victim because of her dress and demeanor; that she was either chaste or a temptress, and nothing in between. For disparate reasons, then, both groups sought to protect consensual relationships from prosecution.

As such, the Democrats' concerns were not assuaged by the age-span provision. Democratic Representative and Chairman of the House Judiciary Committee Tommy Chambless moved to amend the bill by removing the entire section pertaining to statutory rape, and amending the section on "enticing a child for indecent purposes"[21] to revert the age to 14 from 16. It was voted down 104–60. "Roy Barnes spoke against it . . . worried about 'our teenage sons' going to jail."[22] Towery characterized Barnes's argument and that of the House opponents:

> They're looking at their traditional, more rural based circumstance, in which . . . young people having relations and that sort of thing was not all that uncommon and many times resulted in early marriage. Their issue that they raised to me was what were we going to do . . . when our son had sex with a 15-year-old and they cart him off to jail because he's [18]. And it really didn't bother me that much because I felt that the true intent of this was adults and children. But they wanted to take it literally. . . . What they really wanted was not to have [the age span], period.

Also in opposition was the Christian Right. In 1995, both sponsors said, the more religious members were staunchly opposed to the age-span provisions. They preferred that same-age teens be prosecuted at the felony level as well in order to send a moral message about premarital sexuality. The final Child Protection Act, as a compromise to gain the votes of religious conservatives, read "If the victim is 14 or 15 years of age and the person so convicted is no more than three years older than the victim, such person may, in the discretion of the court, be punished as for a misdemeanor." In other words, same-age teens could still be punished at the felony level. Again, here is compromise on morality policy when those who treat it as a distinct subset of policies would predict that such a thing would not occur. Christian Right influence apparently affected the late adoption of a smaller age span—and one could argue, given the judge's discretion to prosecute as a felony or misdemeanor, that it is a much-weakened age-span provision.

Despite the objections, the act passed 113–58, and was signed. Towery credits its passage in some measure to pure electorally driven persuasion:

> [It was] very difficult for someone to cast a vote against something I had labeled the "Child Protection Act of 1995." Defeats are created in that. And when I went to the well to speak for it I did say I do think y'all will have a fine time explaining how you voted against the Child Protection Act of 1995. And it put everyone in a little bit of a box.

Again, though, the legislators had no idea how the public felt about the statutory rape reform; they had taken no polls on the subject.

Not long after the law went into effect, a case came up in which a 15-year-old was prosecuted at the felony level (a 1–20-year sentence) for sexual activity with his girlfriend. The case garnered attention because the male was from a low-income family while the female was a "society girl" from a somewhat prominent family. This spoke somewhat to a concern expressed by some members of the African American caucus during the debate over the bill in 1995: that minorities would be disproportionately prosecuted.[23]

With this case as a springboard, Langford in 1996 introduced the bill to remove the discretion of the judge and mandate that those who fell within the age span could only be prosecuted for a misdemeanor. He noted, "A Christian Coalition member of the Senate, who sat next to me and we fought all the time, was gone that year [1996]." Langford's bill was tacked on to another House bill requiring that if the defendant in a statutory rape case were at least 21, the punishment would automatically be 10–20 years.[24] This bundled act passed 108–55 by a Democratic legislature on March 13, 1996. Langford stressed that without that member of the Senate being absent, this revised age span would not have passed. Despite the party differences in the South, it was a Democratic legislature that liberalized the age-span provision by removing the "discretion" clause and implementing a new offense with an even larger age span of six years.

The Georgia situation appears at first to be an odd case on the ground, but it still conforms to the pattern one would expect: a three-year age-span provision (smaller than what feminists probably would have pushed for, were they interested and/or influential), that still allowed prosecutions without an age span and so in some sense was not an age-span provision at all (which feminists probably would have opposed, were they interested and/or influential) was in the end supported by Christian Right legislators who opposed a "true" age span. It may have been passed later rather than earlier because of the lack of organized feminist presence as well as the strength of the Religious Right. In effect, same-age teenage sex was still a felony in Georgia until 1996, when Langford's chief adversary from the Christian Coalition was not in the senate. Without that senator, the age span was passed.

Second, Democrats were responsible for voting for the policy change. But the Democratic Party in Georgia is more conservative than the Democratic Party in, for example, New Jersey, which may account somewhat for the measure not being passed earlier. And after the Christian Coalition member left the Senate, it was Democrats who voted for removing the judge's discretion in age-span cases and thus actually implementing the measure by exempting same-age sexuality from prosecution. Finally, neither the bill's sponsors nor the legislators as a whole took account of public opinion; indeed, they were entirely unaware of it.

Case 3: California

SETTING THE STAGE   Dating from 1859, California's statutory rape law until 1993 criminalized "sexual intercourse with a female not the wife of the perpetrator, where the female is under the age of eighteen years" at the felony level.[25] The 1993 amendment, which was also gender-neutral, made the following replacement that implemented age-span provisions while still allowing prosecution for those falling within the span:

> (a) Any person who engages in an act of unlawful sexual intercourse with a minor who is not more than three years older or three years younger than the perpetrator, is guilty of a misdemeanor [punishable by up to one year in county jail].[26]
>
> (b) Any person who engages in an act of unlawful sexual intercourse with a minor who is more than three years younger than the perpetrator is guilty of either a misdemeanor or a felony, and shall be punished by imprisonment in a county jail not exceeding one year, or by imprisonment in the state prison.
>
> (c) Any person over the age of 21 years who engages in an act of unlawful sexual intercourse with a minor who is under 16 years of age is guilty of either a misdemeanor or a felony, and shall be punished by imprisonment in a county jail not exceeding one year, or by imprisonment in the state prison for two, three, or four years.

The stage was set for this policy change in 1992, when 40-year-old Faye Abramowitz of Granada Hills was charged with having sex with eight males aged 14–16, among whom was Marcia Beckerman's stepson.[27] Because the law was still gender-specific at the time, Abramowitz could not be charged with statutory rape. Rather, she was charged with five counts of sex acts with a person under 18 and three counts of lewd acts upon a child, sentenced to five years probation, and ordered to undergo counseling (Moody 1993). She was also supposed to have no contact with anyone under 18 during the probation period unless their parents were present (Nikos 1993).

Marcia Beckerman founded a group in response, Mothers Against Sexual Abuse. "I was so upset about what happened in this case that I wrote letters to every senator, assemblyman—everyone I could find. . . . I thought it was just horrible that this woman could entice these boys into having sex, and not be charged with it" (Nikos 1993). This group, virtually on its own, conducted lobbying activity that followed the pattern of interest group politics: mobilize support and try to influence policymakers. But they were not completely successful alone.

NOW was not at all involved in this policy change, as they were not in Georgia. Although they have a large presence in California and its members were interviewed about the policy change, they took no position, did not testify at the hearings, and issued no letters or support or opposition. It is not necessarily surprising that they were not active players in this policy change in the 1990s, because as noted by that time NOW had focused more of their energies on other concerns. If not NOW, then who was responsible for the policy adoption and its nature?

LEGISLATIVE RESPONSE   Senate bill author Newton Russell (R-Glendale), the Minority Whip, was contacted by Marcia Beckerman and immediately introduced a gender-neutral bill, which at first had no age span. Comments on Russell's bill in various committees noted that "the author has introduced this bill in the wake of a Granada Hills case" (Judiciary, Comm Rep CA SB 22, 20 April 1993) and was more concerned (like Beckerman and Mothers Against Sexual Abuse) with prosecuting females than with not prosecuting teenagers. Legislators were concerned with the gender-neutral language in and of itself, as is described in detail in chapter 3. Their second concern had to do with the lack of an age span—without such a provision, how would a gender-neutral law decide who was guilty? The Senate Judiciary Committee asked, "If two seventeen year olds engage in consensual sexual intercourse, and one of them turns eighteen prior to the end of the relationship, should the 18-year-old be guilty of rape?" But, they acknowledged, "The author expressed concern, however, that [an age-span] provision may not impose severe enough penalties for defendants within the statutory age limits" (Judiciary, Comm. Rep. CA SB 22, 20 April 1993).

In the end, Russell relented due to pressure from prosecutors and other law enforcement personnel who had to deal with cases of consensual same-age sexual activity and found them to be a waste of resources. The problem, they said, was with predatory older adults (generally, male). A compromise was struck: A perpetrator falling within a three-year span would be prosecuted for a misdemeanor and sentenced to up to one year in jail. The Senate Judiciary Committee noted approvingly, "More often than not, consensual intercourse between two minors and intercourse between an older minor and young adult will go unprosecuted. Nonetheless, proponents of this bill argue, a statutory rape law is necessary in order to provide a means with which to punish those who prey on minors" (Judiciary, Comm. Rep. CA SB 22, 20 April 1993). This bill, then, was little different from the bill produced in Georgia—its tenor was due in large part to the concerns of those within the criminal justice system, and the absence of interested and organized feminists. Republican Senator Russell included an age span that he did not particularly want because it allowed the misdemeanor charge, as did the religious conservatives in Georgia.

Hearings in the spring of 1993 drew out supporters and those opposed. In support, the San Bernardino County sheriff noted that 16- and 17-year-old males were left unprotected by the current law, which included females under 18 and left males of that age to be covered by a "lewd and lascivious conduct" statute that criminalized activity with those under 16 when the perpetrator was at least 10 years older. Similarly, Los Angeles County District Attorney Gil Garcetti wrote Republican Governor Pete Wilson in support, approving of the fact that "in cases where the age difference is three years or less, the crime would be a misdemeanor" (letter, 21 September 1993). The California State Juvenile Officers Association endorsed it for the same reason (Tennen 1997).

At the forefront of the opposition were three Christian-based organizations: the Traditional Values Coalition of Contra Costa County, Shepherd's Gate (a shelter for homeless women and children), and the Committee on Moral Concerns. The last argued that the combination of gender-neutral language and an age span would result in parents never bringing charges against males because they would be too worried .that their daughter (in this "traditional" view of gender, always the victim) would wind up being prosecuted if she were the older party.[28] As in Georgia, there was some religious support for a small age span that was not really an age span at all because it still allowed teens within the span to be prosecuted.

The bill stalled, given the opposition and that no one was really pushing it forward. But at that point another case came to prominence. High school male A. T. Page had been coerced by his football coach, Randy Brown, to have sex with the coach's wife, by his estimate, about 1,000 times (Associated Press 1993; Kataoka 1993). Similarly to the Abramowitz case, the gender-specific statutory rape law allowed the Browns to be prosecuted only for oral copulation and conspiracy. They were given suspended 16-month prison sentences, placed on five years probation, and required to register as sex offenders.

Page and his friend Mark Searl, who had also been approached by Brown, went to local attorney Sherrill Nielsen to ask how to get the law changed because it was unable to protect them. Nielsen contacted Senator Russell's office and arranged to have the two go to Sacramento in July to lobby for the bill. Page testified before the assembly's Public Safety Committee: "I came here today to let you know just how much pain we've been through. If there was a law that was stronger and stood out a little more . . . it might have stopped coach Randy Brown from doing that to us." Searl pleaded, "I just want you guys to change the law so no one else has to go through this when they're eighteen or under." "The point, the teenagers say, is that boys can be coerced by dominant adults into having sex with a woman, leaving them emotionally traumatized. 'I was not forcibly raped, but I was emotionally raped,' Page said" (Gorman 1993).

At this point, the framing of the bill was completely changed in a way that would enable it to garner more interest among the legislators and the Republican governor. While in New Jersey and in Georgia the age-span provision was framed as decriminalizing consensual sexual activity between similarly situated teenagers, in California that thrust had failed. After the testimony of the young males, the Public Safety Committee sent it to the floor as a measure that would "broaden the crime of statutory rape" by including young males as victims and by adding another level of offense (and of penalty) for perpetrators of 21 or older who engaged in sexual intercourse with another person under 16. Indeed, while many other states completely exempt same-age couples from prosecution, California does not. Those within the three-year age span may still be prosecuted, with a penalty of up to one year in jail, even though the crime is classified as a misdemeanor. In this form as a law tough on crimes against young people, it was quickly passed and signed.

California appears at first to be an exceptional case: Even with high NOW membership, there was not a large age-span provision implemented early on. Indeed, the pattern looks more like a state in which NOW membership was low. The age span was implemented late, was three rather than four or five years, and is harsher than other age-span provisions that completely exempt same-age teenagers from prosecution. But, different from New Jersey in the 1970s in which NOW pushed for the policy change but the Christian Right was weak, in California in the 1990s NOW was uninterested in the thrust of the policy change and the religious influence was stronger. Indeed, it is important to note that in both Georgia and California the statutory rape reforms took place in the 1990s, during what might be called a "third wave" of statutory rape reform, more conservative in general than the wave of feminist reforms in the 1970s.[29] Second, the more prominent religious influence, albeit upon a

Democratic legislature, makes policy adoption in California look much more like that in Georgia in 1995, particularly in the passage of a law with an age span that still allowed prosecution within it. Third, the main sponsor of the bill was a Republican; so was the governor who signed it. Finally, the bill was framed much differently in California—rather than being spoken of as a measure that decriminalized teenage sex (a liberal construction), it was spoken of as a means to raise the penalties for statutory rape as a law-and-order measure to protect young people (a more conservative construction). The age span was a compromise, something that quantitative analysis could not have told us and that morality policy theorists would predict is not possible on such issues.

Conclusion

New Jersey showed the strong influences of NOW strength, Christian Right weakness, and Democratic partisanship on an early adoption (1978) of a large age span (four years). Even with inflammatory media coverage of the change, the general public did not really react; it was antiabortion and church groups who demonstrated against it. Georgia's late adoption (1995) of a smaller age span (three years) speaks to the lack of strength of NOW, the prominence of the Christian Right, and the more conservative nature of the Democratic Party in Georgia. In Georgia too, media coverage informed the public of the change; but legislators admitted they were not interested in gauging public mood. Sexual activity within the age span in effect remained a felony until a particularly prominent Christian Coalition state senator left office.

California, a state in which citizens are generally considered or measured as liberal, did not follow the path one might have assumed it would have, adopting in 1993 a small age span (three years) that still allowed jail time for perpetrators who fell within that span. While NOW influence was potentially high, the group did not press for reform. But the notion that policymakers respond to organized interests was still borne out in California: instead of NOW, it was Mothers Against Sexual Abuse, the Committee on Moral Concerns, Shepherd's Gate, and others; the last two Christian-based organizations. Even given extensive media coverage of the two catalyzing cases, there was no measurable reaction on the part of the mass public to the proposed changes or the policy adoption. Rather, the interplay of groups and the ideological leanings of legislators played the most prominent roles.

In short, Georgia and California, whose citizen ideological leanings tend toward the conservative and toward the liberal, respectively, had very similar policy adoptions. One might infer, then, that mass public opinion did not play a strong direct role in these policy changes. The comparable outcomes appear to be based on strength of Christian influence, lack of NOW activity, and partisan policymakers' compromises. Do these findings hold on a broader scale? I turn at this point to the event history analysis, to explore whether these microlevel observations are borne out at the macro level.

Modeling Policy Adoption

Many of the works in the state politics subfield test a host of political, economic, and social variables that correlate highly with policy outcomes. While I do not assert that I can "prove" what causes policy changes, I test political variables that speak to broad theoretical explanations of policy change in order to make causal links that would better explain the policymaking process. The pooled cross-sectional time series analyses in this chapter cover forty-nine states from 1971 through 1999.[30] This produces a set of 686 cases. Those seven states that did not adopt by 1999 are coded as 0 from 1971 through 1999.[31]

Table 2.2 shows the determinants of age-span adoption,[32] and table 2.3 shows the determinants of age-span reinvention, or how the states adopted different types of age spans.[33]

TABLE 2.2   States' Adoption of Age-Span Provisions

Independent Variables	Expected Direction	Coefficient	Standard Error	Coefficient/ Standard Error	Change in Probability
GROUP					
NOW	+	.010[+]	.007	1.465	.003
Christian Right Influence	−	−.174[+]	.139	−1.251	.043
ELITE					
Party of the Governor	−	−.437*	.189	−2.308	.108
Party Control of State Legislature	−	−.245	.233	−1.048	.061
Electoral Competition	+	.017	.021	.809	.004
PUBLIC OPINION					
Citizen Ideology	−	−.235	.275	−.858	.059
NEW ENGLAND	−	−2.869	1.164	−2.464	.446

Number of cases: 686
Number of y = 1: 42
Pearson Goodness-of-Fit Chi-Square: 648.317
Percent Correctly Predicted: 94%
[+]Significant at .10, one-tailed test; *Significant at .05, one-tailed test.
Note: The dependent variable is coded 1 if the state adopted in a given year, 0 if it did not.

TABLE 2.3   States' Reinvention of Age-Span Provisions

Independent Variables	Expected Direction	Coefficient	Standard Error	Coefficient/ Standard Error	Change in Probability
GROUP					
NOW	+	.011$^+$	.009	1.251	.003
Christian Right Influence	−	−.305*	.183	−1.663	.076
ELITE					
Party of the Governor	−	−.810**	.288	−2.811	.192
Party Control of State Legislature	−	−.087	.301	−.289	.022
Electoral Competition	+	.028	.027	1.034	.007
PUBLIC OPINION					
Citizen Ideology	−	−.106	.353	−.301	.027

Number of cases: 500
Number of y = 1: 24
Pearson Goodness-of-Fit Chi-Square: 478.098
Percent correctly predicted: 95%
$^+$Significant at .10, one-tailed test; *Significant at .05, one-tailed test; ** Significant at .01, one-tailed test.
Note: The dependent variable is coded 1 if that state adopted an age span of four to six years, 0 if it adopted a span of two to three years.

　　　The party of the governor appears to be the most significant variable, with the most impact on change in the dependent variable. This may be due to the fact that in the 1970s in particular, when states were revising their rape statutes as well as their overall penal codes, it was usually the governor who appointed a task force for those revisions—thus, those who were actually drafting the changes to the laws were probably of a similar ideological background as the governor. With this knowledge, outside groups may have sought to work more closely with these executive-appointed task forces rather than with sympathetic legislators. Given the relationship between NOW and the Democratic Party, NOW members probably assumed they would be more successful with Democratic governors. In the model, Democratic governors correlate positively with the adoption of an age span, particularly, a larger rather than a smaller one.

　　　Citizen ideology is insignificant in both models. Because I would argue that if public opinion has an effect on policy change it would be through the mediating influence of groups, I expected that when group variables were accounted for, the effects of public opinion would decrease. This weakness could be due to the measurement of the variable, a very general measure of citizen leanings on a variety of subjects. As noted, there are no state-level polls on statutory rape laws,[34] but recalling the national-level poll results on adolescent premarital sexuality, there is little reason to assume that public opinion was amenable to the adoption of an age-span provision. Electoral competition and party control of the legislature were insignificant as well, which was unexpected; both elements seemed integral to the case study work.

The group variables are significant, at a weak level.[35] While in table 2.2 the NOW variable is slightly higher in significance than that of the Christian Right, in table 2.3 the Christian Right variable is of a higher level of significance than that of the NOW variable. In both tests, though, the Christian Right variable has more of an impact than that of NOW in its influence on producing change in the dependent variable. There are two potential reasons for this. First, this could be an outcome of the way in which the variables are measured. The NOW variable measures membership and is a relatively suitable proxy, given the limitations of available data, for the influence of the NOW organization in that state.[36] The Christian Right variable is a direct measure of the influence of that group vis-à-vis that state's Republican Party.

Second, as Kingdon (1997) and others note, interest groups are sometimes more effective at blocking proposals than at pushing them through.[37] A high level of Christian Right influence on, for example, blocking a large age span from being introduced, could be more efficient than a group on the opposite side of the political spectrum trying to sway policymakers into acting on a particular issue. We saw this with the compromise on the age of consent in New Jersey, the felony-level prosecution retained for those perpetrators who fell within the age span in Georgia, and the stalled bill and inclusion of jail time for those within the age span in California.

While California and New Jersey are quite similar in their liberal citizen ideological leanings, they had completely different statutory rape policy adoptions. California and Georgia, dissimilar in citizen ideological leanings but similar in Christian Right strength, had very similar policy adoptions. If public opinion does have an effect on policy change, it is likely that its influence is conveyed through the organized and resource-rich groups upon whom policymakers must rely particularly for election and reelection in an era of low voter turnout. The models lend additional, albeit limited, support to the findings of the cases: Interest group activity vis-à-vis reelection-minded partisan policymakers appears to have a more direct influence on policy change than does mass public opinion.

Indeed, two recent works note that our electoral system may be in the second of two transitions: the first from party-centered to more candidate-centered campaigns; the second from candidate-centered to more interest-group-centered campaigns as "[g]roups that can effectively 'deliver their members' are sought after by parties and candidates trying to assemble electoral coalitions."[38]

This may be especially true of groups that are seen as an unwavering and integral component of a party's core constituency, such as feminist groups within the Democratic Party and Christian conservative groups within the Republican Party. Such a finding may have rather negative implications for those in the United States unrepresented by organized groups.

Beyond Policy Adoption: Enforcing the Laws

The adoption of age-span provisions is only the first part of the story of statutory rape reform. An exploration of prosecutions illuminates who is being arrested, charged, and sentenced; how cultural narratives of gender, sexuality, class, and race are implicated in the implementation of the laws; and whether the perpetrators are those whom feminist reformers intended to be targeted by an age span—that is, those in unequal and potentially coercive relationships, rather than in consensual ones in which the two parties are more similarly situated. To what extent were the feminists' goals achieved, or as in the nineteenth century is the enforcement of the laws a process more controlled by conservative forces and/or those within the legal system?

Common Prosecutions: Large Age Gap and/or
Abuse of Authority

"Prosecutors go after people in positions of trust or authority," says an Illinois prosecutor (Kiernan 1995). This is one of the benefits of an age span: Resources are more likely to be concentrated on egregious cases, as the intent of the span is to protect a younger person from sexual coercion or abuse by an older person.

Tara, a 23-year-old assistant teacher, had sexual intercourse with two of her 13-year-old male special education students; indeed, she was living with one of them and his parents. The parents "knew she was staying there, but they didn't have a clue" about the sex. The student asked her to move out after three weeks, feeling "strange" about the relationship, and requested that she not have sex with his friends. She moved back into her parents' house, and indeed began to have a sexual relationship with his best friend. Around this time, she also apparently performed sex acts on two other 12-year-old males at her parents' house. All of this was discovered by police after she confided in another student, who told a teacher's assistant, who told a principal, who told the authorities (Lefkowitz and Gardiner 2001).

A 37-year-old male with two prior convictions for sexual assaults on 8-year-olds was charged with the statutory rape of his stepdaughter, 14. She told the prosecutors that she did not want him punished, and sat with their infant daughter and her mother (the male's common-law wife) during his trial. Her mother asked the court for leniency as the defendant read into the court record, "I made a big mistake by falling in love with someone too young for me and not realizing what the consequences are" (Nowack 2000: 865).

Over 130 victims came forward against Catholic priest John Geoghan in the greater Boston area, most of whom were elementary-school-age males when the abuse occurred. About 50 such cases have been settled since 1997, and at least 80 were pending as of this writing. From the 1960s to the 1990s, Geoghan was transferred to six different parishes because of his behavior. He would befriend large Catholic families, some of whom he visited every day to take the kids out for ice cream, read them bedtime stories, and have oral and anal sex with them as he said their nighttime prayers. In one family, for instance, he abused seven boys aged 4 to 12. Said one victim to his mother, "We couldn't tell you because Father said it was a confessional." In admitting his behavior at one of the parishes, Geoghan sought to downplay his actions, saying it was "only two families" and that he did not feel it was a "serious or pastoral problem" (*Boston Globe* staff 2002).

These are the kinds of cases that one often sees in the newspaper or on television, and are not the types of cases that necessarily raise questions of privacy, consensuality, or agency among young people—a teacher and student, a stepfather and stepdaughter, a priest and an altar boy. Indeed, this is the type of case that many perhaps assume represents the universe of statutory rape, and builds support for enforcement of the laws.

Victims and Perpetrators within an Age Span

One could also argue that concentrating resources on cases in which one of the parties is in a supervisory relationship, or in which the parties are far apart in age leaves young people closer in age, or people whose ages fall within the span, unprotected.

Sixteen-year-old Sharon, mentioned in the introduction, recounts her encounter with Michael, 17:

> We were drinking at the railroad tracks and we walked over to this bush and he started kissing me and stuff, and I was kissing him back, too, at first. Then I was telling him to stop . . . he said ok, ok, but then he just kept doing it. . . . We was lying there and we were kissing each other . . . and we sat down on a bench and then he started kissing me again and were laying on the bench. And he told me to take my pants off. I said "No," and I was trying to get up and he hit me back down on the bench and then I just said to myself

"Forget it," and I let him do what he wanted to do and . . . He
slugged me in the face . . . on my chin . . . I had bruises . . . he hit
me about two or three times. (*Michael M. v. Superior Court of Sonoma
County*, 450 U.S. 464 [1981] fn*)

This is a case of forcible rape. But neither the California courts nor the Supreme
Court saw it that way, and this was exactly what some feminists feared. Even
though Sharon said no, and was punched, this case was immediately charged as
statutory rape. At the time, California's law had no age span; otherwise, the case
could not have been prosecuted at all. Here was a combination of events that
some feminists warned age-span provisions would not protect—a vulnerable female, coerced into sex in a way that cultural narratives of forcible rape (i.e., by
an armed male stranger, fought off physically with utmost resistance by the female) could not assimilate as being that crime. Justice Blackmun, author of *Roe
v. Wade* and widely considered a liberal stalwart on the court after his first few
years there, wrote a chilling concurrence in which he described exactly what he
thought of the case:

> I think, too, that it is only fair, with respect to this particular pe-
> titioner, to point out that his partner, Sharon, appears not to have
> been an unwilling participant in at least the initial stages of the
> intimacies that took place. . . . Petitioner's and Sharon's nonac-
> quaintance with each other before the incident; their drinking;
> their withdrawal from the others of the group; their foreplay, in
> which she willingly participated and seems to have encouraged,
> and the closeness of their ages (a difference of only one year and
> 18 days) are factors that should make this case an unattractive
> one to prosecute at all, and especially as a felony rather than as a
> misdemeanor. . . . But the state has chosen to prosecute in that
> manner, and the facts, I reluctantly conclude, may fit the crime.
> (*Michael M. v. Superior Court of Sonoma County*, 450 U.S. 464 [1981]
> at 483–487)

In other words, he had to "reluctantly" acknowledge that the statutory rape law
had been broken because Sharon was underage. But he clearly felt that Sharon's
behavior meant that she could not have been raped; she had encouraged
Michael's behavior by being willing to drink with him, walk off alone with him,
and kiss him just after they had met. The parts of her testimony recounting her
submission to Michael's violence were discounted. She was not seen as an underage innocent, deserving of the law's protection. There is no way of knowing
how many cases like this fall through the cracks in states with age spans, although one would like to hope that forcible rape prosecutions some 20 years

after the above events have become more inclusive of various scenarios of rape beyond the sterotypical.

Nushawn was told that he was HIV-positive in 1996, although he says he did not really believe it. In 1997, he had sex with at least 47 young women in a small town in western New York. Immediately after his arrest, 16 of these were confirmed HIV-positive, and 2 gave birth to infected infants. Many of the young females were runaways, homeless, and living occasionally in a shelter called Safe House (Gross 1997a). One, described as a high school dropout who lived on friends' couches and also in an abandoned building with Nushawn, re-called, "Me and [Nushawn], we had this bond. He told me everything, everything. Except this [his HIV status]. But I'll stand by him, because he said he loved me (Gross 1997b). Other females echoed this, talking about how charm-ing he was, how they liked to cook for him and braid his hair.

Of his sexual encounters, which he later said probably totaled over 300 partners, he said:

> I know, basically, my ways of talking to girls, associating with them, showing them the love that they want shown. When you're speaking with females, there's certain things they like to hear, cer-tain things they want to know. Me, I was always there to show them love, cook for them, invite them to my house when they got problems. When you're around females and you talk and you party and you listen to music that you want to listen to and you're smok-ing weed and chilling, nine times out of ten you're going to be in bed with that female. (Cooper 1999)

At the time of the offenses, he was 20, which meant that in New York he could only be prosecuted for statutory rape with someone who was under 14; to be prosecuted for statutory rape with someone over 14 but under 17, a per-petrator must be at least 21. While already serving a sentence for selling crack cocaine, he was sentenced to 4–12 years for one count of statutory rape with a 13-year-old, and one count of reckless endangerment; these were the only two young women willing to testify. A few of the females were 17 or over. Were they subject to coercion, manipulation? Or were their encounters consensual? Either way, the vast majority of his sex partners were not covered as potential victims by the statutory rape law of New York.

Uncommon Prosecutions: Fornication

Some states with age spans have recently begun to use another set of laws to charge those who fall within the age span when the perpetrator cannot be charged with felony-level statutory rape. Fornication statutes, criminalizing sex between any two unmarried people, have been retained by 17 states.[39]

In Idaho, fornication prosecutions have generally brought suspended jail sentences and enforced parenting classes for the convicted females, and fines and up to six months of jail for the males. Fifteen-year-old Amanda and her 16-year-old boyfriend Chris were charged. "[Amanda], like several of her friends in this town of 4,900, was charged with criminal fornication only after she applied for pregnancy-related state medical assistance." County Prosecutor Douglas Varie said Amanda was a "disgruntled, irresponsible teenager who [is bringing] something into the world that is going to cost taxpayers a lot of money" (Hardy 1996).

The article goes on to describe the town of Emmett in Gem County, where the prosecutions took place: "It is debatable how serious the teen-pregnancy problem is in Gem County. . . . But Emmett does wrestle with a lot of frustrations, including a plague of homemade amphetamines and chronic unemployment; many locals grumble about moral decay." As throughout the history of statutory rape laws, economic and moral problems are linked, with the assumption that targeting the moral will somehow ease economic and social ills. Amanda herself said she did not know the meaning of the word fornication: "My mom went down to the library and looked it up in the dictionary. Nobody ever told us it was illegal for two people of the same age to do that" (Whitmire 1997; Brooke 1996). Prosecutor Varie countered, "Children having children impose a heavy burden on society. It's a sad thing for a child to only know his or her natural father as someone who had a good time with his mother in the back seat of a car" (Brooke 1996).

In the end, Chris and Amanda were required to attend parenting classes together, complete high school, and stay off of drugs, alcohol, and cigarettes (Brooke 1996). With the punishment of both the male and female through fornication statutes, today's prosecutors have virtually re-created the situation that existed at the turn of the century when boys were punished lightly by the court and girls were funneled into rehabilitative reformatories which taught them domestic skills in hopes that they could be "uplifted" for later marriage.

Conclusions

Age spans assume that an age difference in the teen years is rife with the potential for manipulation or abuse. In marriages overall from 1940 to 1990, the average age gap between a husband and wife was about two and one-half years. Over that same time period, 12.9% to 17.4% of wives were more than five years younger than their husbands; 34.9% to 45.7% were two to five years younger; 30.2% to 40.9% were within one year; and the remaining 5% to 10% were older than their husbands (Kreider and Fields 2001: 10). So if any of these relationships involved teens, some would be prosecutable if sex occurred before marriage, but most of them would fall within the states' age spans. These figures are broken out no further to reflect the ages of the parties involved, but other available data tells us that in 1998, 115,000 females and 22,000 males aged 15–17 had been or were married, and 215,000 females and 102,000 males aged 18–19 had been or were married (U.S. Census Bureau 1998: 1). Clearly, many of these young women had married soneone older.

Age spans have accomplished the goals sought by some feminist reformers, but also live up to the fears expressed by others. Their implementation has concentrated resources on instances of sexual intercourse most likely to be coercive—that is, those in which the parties are far apart in age, or in which one is in a supervisory position over the other. However, they also leave a swath of vulnerable teens unprotected, open to coercion that is not recognized as meeting the legal definitions of forcible rape. Also, some sexuality within the span, however consensual, can still be punished in states that allow same-age teens to be prosecuted for misdemeanor statutory rape as in California, or for fornication as in Idaho. These types of examples show the ways in which statutory rape laws may be both protective and proscriptive, as well as the shortcomings of legal language in trying to encompass a continuum of forcible to coercive to manipulated to consensual sexual relationships.

Chapter 3

Prosecuting Mrs. Robinson
Gender-Neutral Statutory Rape Laws

Sex with a minor is a major crime.
  —*Billboard sponsored by the California Department of Health Services*

Introduction

Beginning in the 1970s, statutory rape was made a gender-neutral crime. Laws that formerly read, for example, "it shall be a felony for any male to have sexual intercourse with any female not his wife and under the age of 18" would be changed to "it shall be a felony for any person to have sexual intercourse with any other person not his or her spouse and under the age of 18." Such language had been imposed in every state by 2000. This revised definition of the crime allows both males and females to be charged as perpetrators of statutory rape, and acknowledges both males and females as victims.[1]

Unlike the other two sets of amendments to statutory rape laws discussed in chapters 2 and 4, age-span provisions and pregnancy-prevention programs, gender neutrality was an issue taken up by both state and federal courts at the same time the states were adopting the change. One might assume that states

Portions of this chapter were originally published in *Michigan Feminist Studies* 16 (summer 2002).

adopted gender-neutral language because the Supreme Court in the early 1970s had begun to strike down gender-specific language in some types of laws as being unconstitutional. State legislators may have thought that the change would be forced on them anyway. However, numerous state courts upheld gender-specific statutory rape laws into the late 1970s, providing legal cover for legislative inaction. And in 1981, the Supreme Court declared that gender-specific statutory rape laws were constitutional. The rest of the states, after that decision, still implemented gender-neutral language.

Why, when they no longer felt the threat of unconstitutionality, would risk-averse policymakers change the statutory rape laws in their states to be gender-neutral? Following from this, what forces other than court-mandated requirements would have brought about such action? And what are the implications of such laws in action—how have prosecutions changed in light of gender-neutral language?

Background to Policy Adoption: The Pros and Cons of Gender-Neutral Language in Statutory Rape Laws

The Courts

In the latter half of the twentieth century, in the wake of the passage of Title VII of the Civil Rights Act prohibiting discrimination based on sex and as part of the women's rights movement, liberal feminist movements sought to make numerous types of laws gender-neutral.[2] Given their lobbying, and under pressure from the implications of Title VII, courts began to strike down gender-specific language in certain areas of the law when that language was challenged. As one Supreme Court opinion noted, "Legislative classifications which distribute benefits and burdens on the basis of gender carry the inherent risk of reinforcing the stereotypes about the 'proper place' of women and their need for special protection" (*Orr v. Orr*, 440 US 268 at 283 [1979]).

The Supreme Court was at the forefront of declaring gender-specific language unconstitutional in a number of areas; for example, executing wills (*Reed v. Reed* [1971]), insurance coverage from a spouse in the military (*Frontiero v. Richardson* [1973]), Social Security benefits (*Weinberger v. Weisenfeld* [1975]), the age at which one could drink alcohol legally (*Craig v. Boren* [1976]), and alimony proceedings (*Orr v. Orr* [1979]). In *Craig v. Boren*, the court recommended that the states take action to avoid such suits, saying they should "choose either to realign their substantive laws in a gender-neutral fashion, or to adopt procedures for identifying those instances where the sex-centered generalization actually comported to fact" (429 US 190 at

199). Some states had already begun to gender-neutralize virtually all of their laws, including both their statutory rape and forcible rape laws. Others had not, and identified rape laws as "those instances" about which the court wrote. But in short, in the 1970s, the courts seemed more than willing to strike gender-specific language in laws and require that they be rewritten as gender neutral.

The Feminists

Feminist lobbying to implement this gender-neutral language at the level of individual states was led by NOW's Task Force on Rape.[3] But the feminists were and are divided over the issue of gender-neutral language vis-à-vis statutory rape.[4]

Those who lobbied for gender-neutral laws, generally liberal feminists who were members of NOW and were concerned with formalizing equality between men and women through the language of the law, argued that the gender-specific laws undermined female agency and equal rights, and did not recognize that young males could be victims as well. Implementing gender-neutral laws was thus viewed as a win–win situation: Females would still be protected, males would be protected as well, and females and males would be viewed as equals in the eyes of the law. The language, covering activity in which a younger person might be manipulated into sexual intercourse, would protect a person based on his or her age rather than his or her gender. Over time, in theory, the wording of the law would have an influence: People would begin to think of statutory rape in terms of vulnerable teens, rather than in terms of a victimized female.

Radical feminists and sex radicals agreed with the inclusion of males as victims. But at a more theoretical level, the radical feminists argued that the formal equality in the language of the law would do nothing to serve the cause of substantive equality. Female teens did need distinct legal protection from that required for male teens; most sexual assaults were and are committed on females by males. Gender-neutral language would neither empower nor protect young females in any way; rather, the language would make it seem as if they were similarly situated with young males when they simply were not. This is not to say that radical feminists necessarily preferred gender-specific laws, but that gender-neutral laws in and of themselves could not change and would not reflect female subordination.

Feminist sex radicals, in a third point of view, charged that gender-neutral statutory rape laws would just extend the laws' invasion of privacy and denial of agency from females to males. Some of these feminists also feared that a gender-neutral law might be used disproportionately against gay men and lesbians.[5]

In short, here as on age-span provisions, feminists were divided. The liberal feminists again navigated a path between the two poles of the radical feminists and sex radicals, and again were well represented in groups such as NOW. Lobbying for the language change went forward.

The Legislators

Male legislators at first saw little point to having gender-neutral language in statutory rape laws. Perhaps swayed by stereotypes of gender in which females were viewed as physically unable to coerce or manipulate sex from a male if the latter were not a willing participant, they were unconcerned about relationships in which a female was older than the male. Those agitating for such a change presented lawmakers with three scenarios, the first two of which one feminist lobbyist summed up as "boy scouts and prisons."[6] In other words, when lawmakers realized that males could be charged for conduct with underage males that occurred within an uneven playing field, they were much more prone to support the change of language. The third selling point was that while legislators were unwilling to hold female perpetrators responsible for initiating sexual activity as such, they were willing to hold a female responsible for "aiding and abetting" if she were assisting a male in initiating activity that could be charged as statutory rape.

In the end, most legislators supported the idea of making the change as a way by which to cover more potentially coercive conduct than traditional statutory rape laws. As with age-span provisions, they had no real sympathy for at least one of the feminist lobbyists' goals—here, to remove stereotypes of females as victims and males as aggressors in the sexual arena.

The Religious Conservatives

The "females-as-victims" perspective was echoed by the more conservative religious forces both within and outside of the legislatures, who felt that gender-specific laws with a marriage exemption adequately covered nonmarital heterosexual activity in which a young female was manipulated into that activity. A gender-neutral law would dilute the purpose of the laws: to protect young unmarried females from aggressive males. Further, it would equate homosexual activity with heterosexual activity rather than continuing to cover sodomy as a separate crime that had nothing to do with the age of the parties, but only with the moral wrong of the activity. Gender-neutral laws, which would cover homosexual activity criminal only because of age-based distinctions, would be akin to a tacit acknowledgment that homosexual activity could be permissible if those age-based distinctions were not met. This in some ways parallels the arguments against legalizing same-sex marriage. In short, gender-neutral language was distasteful to the religious conservatives.

The Outcome

The cause of gender neutrality prevailed in all states by 2000. But is this story about NOW and other liberal feminists agitating for change, or is it merely about the courts? Given that the Supreme Court in the 1970s was striking down gender-specific language in virtually all of the cases that came its way, state legislators may have simply been responding to the potential for their laws to be declared unconstitutional. As noted, the Supreme Court in one opinion told the states in no uncertain terms to rewrite their laws (*Craig v. Boren*, 429 US 190 at 199). Indeed, in other areas of the law, states did act in anticipation of court activity, particularly if a relevant case was "in the pipeline" on its way to being decided.[7] States do have to amend their laws if court decisions demand it, and numerous state courts heard statutory rape cases that were appealed for the express purpose of having the court rule on the gender-specific language. The next section assesses the influence of the courts on the adoption of gender-neutral language.

Court Reviews of Gender-Specific Language

While other aspects of statutory rape laws, such as age-span provisions, have not been subjected to court scrutiny, gender-specific versus gender-neutral language in those laws has commanded judicial attention. Nearly half of the states have heard cases specifically about the language in these laws. This factor must be taken into account to determine whether and how courts have affected the adoption of this policy in the states.

CIRCUIT AND STATE COURTS   In 1977, the First Circuit Court in *Meloon v. Helgemoe*[8] declared unconstitutional New Hampshire's gender-specific statutory rape law by holding that it violated the equal protection guarantees of the Fourteenth Amendment. Although by 1977 the state had already implemented gender-neutral language, Meloon's case was still justiciable because the sexual act occurred before the law was changed. The state argued that the gender-specific language of the statute, punishing only males and considering only females as victims, was warranted because:

1. males were physiologically incapable of being victims of the offense,
2. adult males were more likely to commit the offense than adult women because males can suffer from the psychological disorder known as pedophilia,
3. only females could get pregnant and it was in the state's interest to try to prevent teenage pregnancy,
4. females were more likely to suffer physical damage from sexual activity, and thus
5. a gender-specific law concentrated resources on the class [males] most likely to break the law. (564 F2d 602 at 605)

The court rejected all of these arguments. Although the opinion was not binding outside of the court's jurisdiction and the court took pains to specify that only New Hampshire's law was the issue at hand, its reasoning was adopted by those in other states seeking to challenge the law. There was one success: an Eighth Circuit Court case from Iowa (*Navedo v. Preisser*, 630 F2d 636).[9] But like New Hampshire, Iowa had already adopted gender-neutral language by the time the case was decided.

Table 3.1 displays state court cases in which gender-specific statutory rape laws were upheld. Note that a case may be handed down even after the law was changed to be gender-neutral, if the act in question was committed while the gender-specific law was still in force. Also note that most of these cases are clustered in the years 1978–1980, between the First Circuit Court's decision in *Meloon* in 1977 and the Supreme Court's decision (discussed below) in 1981. The cases decided in 1982 had most likely been in the pipeline since 1980 or 1981.

Forty state court decisions in 22 states upheld gender-specific language. Most of those courts had little trouble distinguishing their cases from *Meloon* by quoting that opinion's caution that the court's reasoning applied only to the New Hampshire statute and was passing no judgment on statutory rape laws in general. Those decided after 1981 could easily cite the Supreme Court as commanding precedent.

But almost all of these states adopted gender-neutral language after such a case was decided; a few did so while the case was moving up. The other 28 states had no court decisions on the matter. And the two circuit court cases that declared gender-specific language unconstitutional did so after the two pertinent states had already changed to gender-neutral language. There is no discernible pattern between the states in which there was a court case and the states in which there was none; most adopted in the mid- to late 1970s regardless. Perhaps most important, not one state court struck down gender-specific language, which would have forced legislators to amend the law to make it gender-neutral. There is little reason, then, to construe state court decisions as

TABLE 3.1 Years of State Court Rulings Upholding Gender-Specific Statutory Rape Laws

```
                                 UT
                                 TX
                           NY NC
                           NJ NY
                           ME NJ                        TX
                  WV       IA NV                        SC
                  OR       DE LA RI                     NV
                  NH       CA GA NY                     ID
            MO                                          AL
            CO IA CA WV       AL AZ DE           CA              GA
           '69 '70 '71 '72 '73 '74 '75 '76 '77 '78 '79 '80 '81 '82 '83 '84 '85 '86 '87 '88 '89 '90 '91 '92 '93 '94 '95
                                            YEAR
```

Note: The dotted lines represent the Supreme Court's 1981 decision upholding gender-specificity.

Source. Adapted by the author from Trenkner (1998).

having a strong influence on the propensity to adopt.[10] But what about the influence of the Supreme Court?

THE SUPREME COURT OF THE UNITED STATES: MICHAEL M. V. SUPERIOR COURT OF SONOMA COUNTY   In 1981, the one Supreme Court case concerning statutory rape was decided. In short, it found gender-specific language in statutory rape laws to be constitutionally sound, as had every state court that decided on the issue before it. Ten states implemented gender-neutral language between the Court's decision and 1999: California, Delaware, Georgia, Idaho, Louisiana, Mississippi, New York, Oklahoma, Virginia, and Texas. Four of them—Idaho, Mississippi, Oklahoma, and Virginia—had no state court decisions before 1981 that might have been a factor in their "waiting" on the Supreme Court to force them to implement a gender-neutral provision. The other six did have state court decisions upholding gender-specific language, and thus one could surmise that they felt no compulsion to change the law. Yet all of those states did adopt gender-neutral language.

The case that went to the Supreme Court had come from California, which at the time criminalized sexual intercourse with an unmarried female under 18, and concerned a 17-year-old male (Michael) and a 16-year-old female (Sharon). For a gender-specific statute to be upheld, the state must show that the gender classification is substantially related to the achievement of an important governmental objective.[11] This would include the state having to prove that the gender-specific law would meet that objective better than would a gender-neutral law. In the aforementioned *Meloon* case, the First Circuit Court found that New Hampshire did not prove that point and that therefore its law was unconstitutional.[12]

The Supreme Court upheld the gender specificity of California's statutory rape law—that only males could commit the crime, and only females could be its victims—in a much-cited, much-criticized opinion. Rejecting the plaintiff's argument that the gender specificity of the statute had as its purpose the anachronistic protection of female chastity, the Supreme Court found that the statute served as a legitimate means to deter teenage pregnancy. Chief Justice William Rehnquist wrote the majority opinion, which briefly summarized and also agreed with the findings of the California Supreme Court:

> Canvassing "the tragic human costs of illegitimate teenage pregnancies," including the large number of teenage abortions, the increased medical risk associated with teenage pregnancies, and the social consequences of teen childbearing, the court concluded that the State has a compelling interest in preventing such pregnancies. Because males alone can "physiologically cause the result which the law properly seeks to avoid," the court further held that

the gender classification was readily justified as a means of identifying offender and victim. . . . [W]e affirm. (450 US 464 at 467)

The majority argued that while only the female party could get pregnant
from a (heterosexual) sexual encounter, "[n]o similar natural sanctions deter
males" (450 US 464 at 473). Thus a law punishing only the male would "'equal-
ize' the deterrents on the sexes" (450 US 464 at 473) when they decide to engage in sexual activity. If the female were under threat of punishment, she
might then be deterred from reporting the statutory rape violation.

Pregnancy prevention was certainly not the historical purpose of California's statutory rape law. As Justice William Brennan noted in his dissent,
from People v. Verdegreen in 1895 (106 Cal 211) through People v. Hernandez in
1964 (61 Cal 2d 529), the purpose of the law was stated to be the protection
of "the virtue of young and unsophisticated girls" (450 US 464 at 495 fn 10).
The pregnancy-prevention notion was not advanced until 1978 in People v.
McKellar (81 Cal App 3d 367). Further, the two cases mentioned previously
that declared gender-specific statutory rape laws unconstitutional on equal
protection grounds (Meloon v. Helgemoe in the First Circuit Court in 1977 and
Navedo v. Preisser in the Eighth Circuit Court in 1980) considered and dismissed
the pregnancy-prevention argument. The former noted it to be "an available
hindsight catchall rationalization for laws that were promulgated with totally
different purposes in mind" and further said that there was not "an iota of testimony . . . that the prevention of pregnancy was a purpose of the statutory
rape law" (564 F2d at 602 at 607).[13]

Michael's lawyer, perhaps sensing the Supreme Court's disagreement with
Meloon and Navedo and agreement with the California Supreme Court, tried to
argue that the statute was overinclusive because it also applied to (heterosexual)
sexual activity with prepubescent females who could not get pregnant, to sexual activity in which one or both parties was using contraceptives, or to sexual
activity in which for some other physical reason the female party could not become pregnant. But Justice Potter Stewart's concurrence with the majority
opinion dismissed these arguments as fostering unwieldy defenses that would
be "difficult if not impossible" to prove (450 US 464 at 480, fn10).[14]

Justice Harry Blackmun's concurrence contains two interesting threads.
First, he briefly discussed the seeming incongruity that while minor females
have significant privacy rights after they are pregnant (i.e., to choose abortion
or not), they do not have these same rights to engage in sexual activity in the
first place. This concern may have stemmed from his authorship of the majority ruling in Roe v. Wade (410 US 113) in 1973, which found that the constitutional right to privacy encompassed the right to choose to have an abortion.
The logic of treating the two situations differently appears to have been that
while one's pregnancy takes on an "inevitability," one could refrain from sexual

activity (450 US 464 at 483). Although challenged as illogical hairsplitting in later state-level cases, lower courts picked up on the Supreme Court's reasoning to uphold the constitutionality of statutory rape laws while granting that minors have other substantial privacy rights having to do with contraception, abortion, health care, and marriage.[15]

Ultimately it was Blackmun's characterization of the activity between Sharon and Michael that convinced, or reconvinced, many feminists of the need for statutory rape laws. As noted in chapter 2, Sharon testified that Michael punched her in the face two or three times, causing bruises. "I said, 'No,' and I was trying to get up and he hit me back down on the bench and then I just said to myself, 'Forget it,' and I let him do what he wanted to do" (450 US 464 at 484–486, fn*). Yet Blackmun wrote:

> Sharon appears not to have been an unwilling participant in at least the initial stages of the intimacies that took place the night of June 3, 1978. Petitioner's and Sharon's nonacquaintance with each other before the incident; their drinking; their withdrawal from the others of the group; their foreplay, in which she willingly participated and seems to have encouraged; and the closeness of their ages (a difference of only one year and 18 days) are factors that should make this case an unattractive one to prosecute at all. (450 US 464 at 483–485)

In other words, it seemed that unless a rape was committed by a stranger with a weapon—as opposed to an acquaintance with a fist—it was not recognized as coerced. But when the female is a minor, one has recourse to prosecute for statutory rape and neither "force" nor "nonconsent" have to be proven. In statutory rape cases, one need only prove that the act occurred with an underage person to whom the perpetrator is not married. Michael could be prosecuted because California had no age span at the time; an age span assumes that sex between teens close in age is more likely to be consensual.

Many feminists also picked up on the fact that Blackmun used the word *foreplay*, which tends to connote activity that is intended as a precursor to intercourse rather than an end in itself. It appeared that Blackmun was unsympathetic to Sharon because she seemed to be leading Michael toward intercourse with her behavior.

Neither Justice Brennan's dissent nor Justice John Paul Stevens's separate dissent directly addressed the various facets of feminist concerns about statutory rape laws: (1) that they perpetuated stereotypes of females as innocent victims and males as aggressive perpetrators and thus should be gender-neutral, (2) that males and females are not similarly situated on the sexual playing field; thus, females may need further protection, or (3) that they conflate children with female adolescents, violate privacy rights, and may be unconstitutional.

Brennan did say in a footnote that the door may be open to a challenge on privacy grounds (450 US 464 at 491 fn 5), but the thrust of his short opinion was that California did not meet the "burden of proving that there are fewer teenage pregnancies under its gender-based statutory rape law than there would be if the law were gender-neutral" (450 US 464 at 491). Stevens expressed his support for the protective nature of statutory rape laws in general, although he found both parties "equally guilty" (450 US 464 at 502) and he characterized the majority's idea about prosecuting males to be the same effective deterrent as a females' fearing pregnancy as "fanciful" (450 US 464 at 498). Like Brennan, he confined his analysis to California's lack of proof.

In sum, the majority seemed content with California's pregnancy-prevention defense, while the dissenters were more concerned with punishing teens equally rather than with the perpetuation of stigma, with the potential inequity in sexual relations, or with the privacy rights and agency of minors that were the concerns of liberal feminists, radical feminists, and feminist sex radicals, respectively. The decision's message was clear: Gender-specific statutory rape laws, unlike other types of gender-specific laws, were perfectly constitutional as written. Despite the string of Supreme Court cases in the 1970s that had struck down other types of gender-specific laws, states were basically free to keep the language of their statutory rape laws as they chose. Yet 49 states implemented gender-neutral language by 1999; the last in 2000.

Conclusion

We are then left with two interrelated puzzles. First, why would a state implement gender-neutral language after its own court declared gender-specific laws constitutional? And second, why would a state implement gender-neutral language after the Supreme Court declared them constitutional?

Adoption of Gender-Neutral Language Across the States

Table 3.2 graphs the years in which 49 states adopted gender-neutral provisions.[16] The dotted line between 1980 and 1981 represents the Supreme Court decision in *Michael M. v. Superior Court of Sonoma County*, declaring gender-specific statutory rape laws to be constitutional. Note that most of the 10 states that adopted gender-neutral language after the *Michael M.* decision in 1981 were in the South (New York and California, as generally liberal "leader" states, do not seem to fit in with the others): Texas, Oklahoma, Louisiana, Mississippi, Georgia, and even Virginia. Alabama, contiguous with these states, was the only state to retain gender-specific language by 1999; it adopted in 2000. All of

TABLE 3.2 Years of Adoption of Gender-Neutral Statutory Rape Laws

'69	'70	'71	'72	'73	'74	'75	'76	'77	'78	'79	'80	'81	'82	'83	'84	'85	'86	'87	'88	'89	'90	'91	'92	'93	'94	'95
				WA			WY																			
				SD			WI																			
				NM			VT																			
				NH			UT																			
				NE			TN																			
				MT			SC																			
				MN			OR																			
			MI	ME			NV			RI																
				MA	CT	WV	MO		NC																	
			PA	KY	CO	MD	IN	NJ		IL																
											VA															
KS		OH	ND	FL	AR	IA	AZ	AK	HI			OK														
														TX		MS	DE	NY				ID	CA		LA	GA

YEAR

Note: As of 1999, Alabama still had a gender-specific law and is not shown. The dotted lines represent the Supreme Court's 1981 decision upholding gender specificity.

Source: Adapted by the author from state statutes.

these states except Georgia still criminalized consensual sodomy by 1999, and Georgia's oft-challenged law was struck down by its high court only in 1998.[17] Idaho, while not in the South, is also generally viewed as a conservative state in sexual matters vis-à-vis the law.

The pattern here is much closer to that of an S-curve than table 2.1 in chapter 2 representing the adoption of age-span provisions.[18] Looking at the the mid-1970s, one could surmise that time itself was a significant factor in the adoption of this policy; that states felt some kind of pressure to adopt at that time, probably because feminist reformers were pushing strongly for gender-neutral language. But, as noted, this type of chart is a rather fuzzy measure, unable to tell us about who is pressuring whom in a given state or about what caused policy change in a particular place at a particular time. At this point, I turn to case studies of three states.[19]

Case Studies: New Jersey, Georgia, and California

Case 1: New Jersey

SETTING THE STAGE   The New Jersey rape statute was made gender-neutral in 1978, taking effect in 1979. The previous statute, last amended in 1951, was clearly gender-specific and read "Any person . . . who, being the age of sixteen or over, unlawfully and carnally abuses a woman-child of 12 years or older, but under the age of 16 years, with or without her consent, is guilty of a high misdemeanor."[20]

The revision adopted in 1978 "was drafted in the spring of 1978 by a coalition of feminist groups with the assistance of the NOW National Task force on Rape. . . . The NOW bill, which was adopted by both houses of the legislature in 1978 without major definitional change, was modeled after the 1976 Center for Rape Concern Model Sex Offense Statute," which among other things was gender-neutral in language (Bienen 1980a: 207).[21]

Chapter 2 discussed the age-span provisions enacted in New Jersey. The law was drafted and pushed forward by liberal feminists from NOW, with inside influence and support in a Democrat-controlled legislature and from a Democratic governor. But what was the process like vis-à-vis gender-neutral language? Feminist groups wanted to remove stereotypes of female victimhood. One of the drafters of the gender-neutral law, Leigh Bienen, spelled out the goals of changing the language:

> Reform statutes typically adopted sex neutral terms for the persons involved. This language change had several ramifications: Legislators and judges were moved away from terms such as prosecutrix

and complainant that reformers regarded as sexist, biased by negative and derogatory connotations. The reformers wanted to cut any
connection with the line of cases incorporating that language and
the attitudes they symbolized. The adoption of sex neutral language for offenders and victims was part of a strategy to reformu-
late sex crimes in more objective, serious, and clinical terms.
(Bienen 1998: 1567)

At the same time, the reformers wanted both homosexual and heterosexual acts with young people to be included, and the new definitions of *sexual assault* and *sexual contact* in the law written to make clear that both were equally
criminal. Part of the impetus here was ensure that incestuous acts were covered,
particularly those by parents or stepparents on young children. Pressing for
sexual assault to be gender-neutral, and for the decriminalization of adult consensual sodomy, the feminists joined with the gay rights movement (Bienen
1998: 1574). This alliance was successful on both issues.

LEGISLATIVE RESPONSE   The gender-neutral language was not troubling to the
New Jersey legislators, who were predominantly members of the Democratic
Party. The chairman of the Judiciary Committee, in fact, was a NOW member
himself. As one participant characterized the amendment, "It went down without a squawk."[22] But the legislators' reasons for wanting to adopt that language
differed from that of the feminists:

The sex neutral aspect of the offense was appealing to legislators
because it protected boys from homosexual assaults by adults. That
was a policy change that male legislators understood and endorsed,
especially when presented with examples of abusive scout masters
or camp counselors. These examples were highly persuasive in
other jurisdictions as well. . . . Indeed, those lobbying for rape reform legislation, when faced with a suspicious all male judiciary
committee, had only to talk in terms of the sexual abuse of young
boys to find a sympathetic audience. (Bienen 1998: 1513, 1578)

The lobbyists made the issue hit home for the legislators in two other
ways. One was by raising the specter of the prison, and the notion of the
forcible rape of juvenile males. This situation had apparently received some
publicity in the local papers at the time of the rape reform. Second, the feminists spoke of women being able to be prosecuted as aiders and abettors. For instance, if a female assisted a male in the rape or statutory rape of a young female
or young male, she could be charged as an accessory to the crime. Legislators
readily accepted the idea of holding females responsible in this way.[23]

It is interesting that the male legislators almost automatically conceived of the gender-neutral language as protecting young males from homosexual activity. They apparently did not imagine females to be the principal perpetrators of statutory rape; they did not seem concerned about sexual relationships between older females and younger males. They did conceive of it as a way in which to prosecute homosexual males, even though the same bill package decriminalized sodomy between two adults. The notion of a male perpetrator, heterosexual or homosexual, was a better fit with the legislators' notions about gender and sexuality. Either way, gender-neutral language was an easy sell, and probably aided the feminists in moving through other elements of their reform package.

In short, the legislators' concern was not with removing the gendered stereotypes from the law as many liberal feminists would have hoped; rather, it began and ended with protecting young males. By shifting the focus to the latter, NOW enlisted the support of "'law and order' groups, and nonfeminist legal reformers, and many were linked to conservative concerns about rising crime rates and lenient criminal justice practices. Feminist proposals . . . which failed to resonate with these latter concerns met with more resistance" (Searles and Berger 1987: 27; Bienen 1980a: 171).

This provision was passed almost unanimously by a Democrat-controlled legislature, despite the fact that during the debate over the statutory rape reform bills two court cases in New Jersey upheld gender-specific language.[24] It was pushed through by NOW and its allies because of the way in which they played to legislators' construction of whom a gender-neutral statutory rape law should prosecute.

Case 2: Georgia

SETTING THE STAGE   Georgia's statutory rape law was made gender-neutral in 1995, one year after a Georgia state court reaffirmed the constitutionality of gender-specific statutory rape laws.[25] Until that time, the law read "A male commits the offense of statutory rape when he engages in sexual intercourse with a female under the age of 14 years and not his wife."

THE LEGISLATURE   One part of the bill to amend the statutory rape law raised the penalties for cruelty to children and neglect of children; the second consisted of an age-span provision for the statutory rape law and made the offense gender-neutral. Representative Matt Towery (R-Vinings) and Senator Steve Langford (D-LaGrange), respectively, sponsored the two parts of the bill separately before they were cobbled together in the Judiciary Committee. In its final form, it was called the "Child Protection Act of 1995."

As was the situation in Georgia with age-span provisions, neither NOW nor any other feminist-oriented group lobbied for this policy adoption. Nor were any district- or state-level polls taken on the issue, asserted the sponsors. Nor was there a push toward inaction because of the court decision the year before; neither sponsor felt the case had an impact on reform. In Georgia, it appears, policy adoption was the work of a Democratic senate sponsor, voted for by a predominantly Democratic legislature, and signed by a Democratic governor.

From the beginning, said Langford, his intent was to create a gender-neutral statutory rape law: "Arguably, the number of male–female is greater, but it does happen the other way." House sponsor Matt Towery acknowledged the same, while also noting, "At that point [1995] you had issues of teachers having sex with male students and that sort of thing."[26]

Other legislators were generally unconcerned with the gender-neutral language in the law, in large part because they still viewed the offense as one of female victims and male perpetrators. Towery commented, "The issue they really raised to me was . . . what were we gonna do when our son . . . had sex with a 15 year old and they cart him off to jail?" Likewise, Langford said, "[Opponents of the bill] were worried about 'our teenage sons' going to jail." Those affiliated with the Christian Right were unconcerned as well.

Both sponsors characterized these arguments as coming from some of the older Democrats from the more rural districts. But aside from the problems of their perceptions of the typical statutory rape case, it is apparent that they cared little about the gender-neutral language. And as Towery told many opponents, "Y'all will have a fine time explaining how you voted against the Child Protection Act of 1995." The act passed, 113–58, apparently based in large part on electoral concerns.

Case 3: California

SETTING THE STAGE   Until 1993, California's statutory rape law had been left untouched since 1859, punishing "sexual intercourse with a female not the wife of the perpetrator, where the female is under the age of eighteen years." Part of the puzzle of California's inaction is that by the end of the 1970s, most states had made their rape statutes (both statutory rape and forcible rape) gender-neutral. Indeed, California had made its forcible rape statute gender-neutral in 1979 but left its statutory rape law alone.[27]

In *People v. Mackey* in 1975 (46 Cal App 3d 755) and *People v. McKellar* in 1978 (81 Cal App 3d 367), the state court had upheld the constitutionality of the still-gender-specific statutory rape law. But as we saw in New Jersey and in Georgia, the legislatures adopted gender-neutral language almost immediately after court cases upheld the constitutionality of gender-specific language in statutory rape laws. California did not.

It was in *People v. McKellar* that the notion of the law's gender specificity as deterring illegitimate teenage pregnancies was first advanced.[28] When *Michael M.* was heard at the state level in 1979,[29] the California Supreme Court majority opinion cited *McKellar* and its rationale and dismissed the petitioner's arguments about privacy and equal protection being violated by a law that would punish the male partner in what was often consensual sex. The state court dissent does take on at least one feminist concern more directly by noting that the gender-specific law perpetuated gender stereotypes and codified a double standard of morality.[30] But the majority opinions of the state court and the Supreme Court, where the case was heard in 1981, are little different: Both found the "pregnancy as deterrent for the female/jail as deterrent for the male" argument a valid one; both dismissed the petitioner's argument that the conduct of those using contraception or of those otherwise unable to conceive was unfairly criminalized because pregnancy was not an issue. In short, California's much-scrutinized gender-specific statutory rape law was not unconstitutional.

FAILURE IN 1990: THE CATALYZING EVENT AND LEGISLATIVE RESPONSE   California, then, had little reason to expend resources to gender-neutralize its statutory rape law after *Michael M.*[31] But in 1990, Assemblywoman Gwen Moore (D-Los Angeles) introduced a bill to make California's statutory rape law gender-neutral. The initiative came from Larryann Willis, a law student who wrote a paper on the laws. Further, an aide to Moore noted, cases such as that of 14-year-old actor Chris Barnes demonstrated the need for change. Barnes had moved in with a 31-year-old female karate instructor. While the two denied that they had had a sexual relationship, his mother tried to prosecute the instructor. But the mother waited until Barnes was 15. Had she prosecuted while he was still 14, the instructor could have been charged with child molestation. At 15, no state law covered him because the statutory rape law, with the age of consent set at 18, included only females as victims and males as perpetrators.

The bill passed the Democrat-controlled assembly 59–1. But the measure "generated little discussion in the assembly. Nor has it attracted strong support from women's organizations." A legislative advocate for NOW was quoted as saying, "We support the principle that rape should be gender-neutral. In truth, though, the problem of women raping men is not the major problem. The real problem is men raping women" (Hull 1990). This is the response one might expect after the push for formal equality in rape reform in the 1970s: Priorities had shifted, and the reality that males tend to perpetrate the crime of rape on females did not provoke feminist groups into expending organizational resources and political capital on fighting for further gender-neutral reform. Thus despite high NOW membership in California, there was no positive action from the group on this matter because their was no interest in expending group resources on it. Republican Governor George Deukmejian vetoed, saying that he was "concerned that the bill didn't receive the proper attention it deserved in the legislative process" (Hull 1990).

SUCCESS IN 1993: CATALYZING EVENT 1   As noted in chapter 2, 40-year-old Faye Abramowitz was arrested for having sex with several teenage males in California in 1992. She was charged with five counts of sex acts with a person under 18, and three counts of lewd acts upon a child. Like Chris Barnes's karate instructor, she could not be charged with statutory rape because of the gender-specific language of the law. She received only a probated sentence. The stepmother of one of the teenage boys, Marcia Beckerman, founded a group called "Mothers Against Sexual Abuse," which engaged in various lobbying activities and succeeded in putting the issue into the public eye (Nikos 1993).

However, the numerous comments that were made publicly about the situation were mostly tongue-in-cheek and along the lines of those made by Deputy District Attorney Craig Richman who prosecuted the Abramowitz case: "A lot of males have the attitude, 'Where were women like this when I was growing up'?" (Moody 1993). Likewise, the Sacramento deputy district attorney who prosecuted a similar case "found that attitude, just in conversation, oftentimes a gut reaction, or initial reaction [from people]: 'Oh, well, he's a boy and it's probably the greatest thing that happened to him. . . . If it's a young girl, it's clear to people that it's a molest" (Moody 1993). Unnamed policemen were quoted as saying that "some of the boys, ages 14 to 16, consider the experience a badge of honor," and one detective even pressed, "I really think the parents are more upset about it than the kids are" (Wharton 1992). Jeff Beckerman, the father, said that "he was not as disturbed as his wife about the incident." Marcia Beckerman herself noted, "All the kids thought she [Faye Abramowitz] was cool" (Moody 1993). Such comments reflect the assumption that males are sexual agents and would therefore welcome any sexual attention.

Finally, others came forward to squash the snickering and noted the double standard of almost praising boys who have sex with older females, while the reverse sparks horror. Law professor and feminist theorist Susan Estrich summed up, "It has to do with old notions. Society had traditionally put a prize on female virginity and on male experience" (Wharton 1992). Mark Stevens, a psychologist who runs a support group for men molested as children, commented, "There's some kind of status that society believes men have if they have sex early . . . [but with an older woman] it's an abuse of power. . . . On the one hand, it feels very good physically, yet there is a feeling something is wrong, some guilt about it" (Moody 1993). And Deputy District Attorney Richman gave the bottom line, "If you're a 30-year old man and a 6-year old girl takes off all her clothes, lies spread-eagle on your bed and says 'take me,' she is a victim. . . . This case is no different. Even if these boys wanted it, it doesn't matter" (Wharton 1992).

LEGISLATIVE RESPONSE 1   Beckerman's representative, Paula Boland (R-Granada Hills), and State Senator Newton R. Russell (R-Glendale, and Minority Whip) introduced slightly different bills in response, at the end of 1992 and beginning of 1993. Comments on Russell's bill in various committees note that "the author has introduced this bill in the wake of a Granada Hills case where a 40-year-old woman had sex with 10 boys, ages 14 to 16. Under the current gender-specific law, the woman could not be prosecuted for having sexual intercourse with any of the 16 year old boys" (Judiciary, Comm. Rep. CA SB 22, 20 April 1993). The lewd and lascivious conduct statute under which she was charged criminalized that conduct with anyone under 14, or with a 14- or 15-year-old if the perpe-trator were 10 years older—16-year-olds were excluded.

Boland's bill called for gender-neutral language. Russell's bill criminalized adult females having sex with underage males. But to retain the idea of females needing protection, he would still have had the male charged if two teenagers were involved and the older one were female. One of his legislative assistants elaborated, "Senator Russell feels real strongly right now in discouraging teenage pregnancy" (Moody 1993). This retaining of gender specificity speaks to a more conservative orientation toward statutory rape based on stereotypes of female and male adolescent sexuality; its emphasis on teen pregnancy, un-dercutting the gender-neutral language, also foreshadows the next set of amendments to California's statutory rape law discussed in detail in chapter 4.

The bills would not go far. In May 1993, the Senate Rules Committee noted that the conservative Christian Committee on Moral Concerns was in opposition to the bills:

> If the law were to become gender neutral as proposed, and two mi-nors, say a boy 17 and a girl 15, have sexual intercourse, no parent would ever bring charges against the boy regardless of how ad-versely the girl may be affected. Charging the male would mean that charges would also have to be filed against the girl, since both would be considered guilty. A gender neutral law would offer no protection for females whatsoever. The practical effect of this bill would be like repealing the existing statutory rape law. (Rules, Comm. Rep. CA SB 22, 26 May 1992)

Similarly, Alice Ann Cantelow from the Shepherd's Gate Christian Emergency Shelter for Homeless Women and Children was concerned that "by broadly defining rape to be a gender-neutral activity [the bill] places both males and fe-males in danger of charges of being the perpetrators rather than the victim" (Tennen 1997: fn 18, quoting letter). The Traditional Values Coalition of Con-tra Costa County wrote letters in opposition to senate and assembly members as well.

On the other side of the political spectrum, Jeanne Dreisbach, director of Women's Advocate, wrote that her organization opposed the passage of the bill because it would "eliminate the right of a young, minor woman to be protected as the presumed victim in such a rape" (Tennen 1997: fn 17, quoting letter). This is similar to the radical feminist point of view that males and females are in need of different types of protection because it is males who usually perpetrate the crime of rape, not females. Recall that it was the liberal feminists who pushed forward the two sets of reforms, but here there were no liberal feminist proponents of the law to counter this influence; indeed, recall that the NOW legislative advocate asserted that the problem was one of men raping women, not women raping men (Hull 1990). But the strange bedfellows of the nineteenth century on statutory rape reform here come together again: religious conservative and radical feminist ideas from different perspectives but with similar goals.

As noted in chapter 2, a second concern with the bill had to do with the lack of an age-span provision. Without an age span, argued its proponents, a gender-neutral statutory rape law could not tell prosecutors which of the two parties was the perpetrator. Given the conservative opposition and lack of interest and support from the other side of the political spectrum, progress on the bill stalled.

CATALYZING EVENT 2   In the summer of 1993, the second case came to light, involving a person in a supervisory position pressuring a minor into sexual activity. This particular crime is included as its own offense in some states' statutory rape laws, although in California it is not. The importance of this case stems from its victims traveling to Sacramento to express their support for Russell's bill. As noted in chapter 2, A. T. Page and Mark Searl were 17-year-old high school students when their football coach, Randy Brown, asked them to have sex with his wife, Kelly. Searl refused; Page did not (Associated Press 1993; Kataoka 1993).

As in the Abramowitz case, the gender specificity of the law did not cover these young males as victims. The Browns were prosecuted only for oral copulation and conspiracy and given suspended prison sentences, placed on five years probation and required to register as sex offenders. Page and Searl contacted a local attorney to change the wording of the law so that future male victims could seek redress. The attorney in turn contacted Senator Russell's office and arranged to have the two boys go to Sacramento to testify. They did so with great emotion, which appeared to affect the progress of the bill. The two also filed suit against the school district for not protecting them further, but the district rejected the claim outright (Smith 1993).

This is not the best example of a "typical" statutory rape case because not only does it involve a person in a position of authority over the victims, but also that person solicited the victims for a third party. Thus it does not fit into the narrative of the older woman enticing or seducing a perhaps willing participant. But this may have made the situation easier to understand for lawmakers. Recall that in New Jersey the strongest arguments for gender-neutral language were to punish males for homosexual sex, and to punish females by charging them as accessories. This allowed feminists to push the bill through while skirting the age-old cultural presumption that a young male would be more than willing to engage in sexual activity with an older female. Here, with a male accessory who was doing the overt coercing, the acts were more easily assimilated into existing cultural frames of reference—namely, that females cannot really coerce males into having sex.[32]

LEGISLATIVE RESPONSE 2   By this time, Russell's accompanying letter with the bill shows that he was more willing to endorse the idea of prosecuting young females: "According to current law, if a 17-year old girl seduced a 14-year old boy, the boy would be guilty. . . . In the past, we believed that only females needed the protection of this law. Now, however, with the increasing evidence of the existence of female perpetrators and the devastating effects they inflict on male minors, I think that equal protection is needed" (Tennen 1997: 3, quoting letter). The bill passed the committee and cleared the full assembly with little trouble, given the above events and the revisions to the bill. Republican Governor Pete Wilson signed the bill in late September 1993, just after Page and Searl filed civil suits against the Browns for assault, battery, conspiracy, and infliction of emotional distress (Kataoka 1993).

Note that the misdemeanor portion of the final bill read "Any person who engages in an act of unlawful sexual intercourse with a minor who is not more than three years older or three years younger than the perpetrator, is guilty of a misdemeanor [punishable by up to one year in county jail]." Although this provision is gender-neutral, it does not name the perpetrator as necessarily the older party; one might assume this was intended to allow the prosecution of males who were younger than their female partners, thus conforming to gendered stereotypes of sexual behavior.

At first, the California situation here seemed just as puzzling as the way in which the state adopted age-span provisions. Opposition by religiously affiliated groups stopped the initial policy adoption process, but in the end, a Democrat-led legislature amended the law. But in a state with high NOW strength, gender-neutral language was implemented quite late in the period under study and was not at all part of a feminist agenda—they had succeeded in implementing gender-neutral language in the forcible rape statute and turned to other concerns. They took no action on this matter. The amendment was introduced not by Democrats concerned with gender stereotypes but by Republicans concerned with law and order.

Conclusion

California again appears to be an outlier, which at first one might ascribe to its state court having upheld gender-specific language in the 1970s—but so did New Jersey's and Georgia's state courts. That the one Supreme Court case on statutory rape came from California may have been influential in the lack of adoption of gender-neutral language in the 1980s, but no policymaker mentioned it as a deterrent. On partisanship, California differs as well: Although the legislature was controlled by Democrats, the bill sponsors and the governor here were Republicans.

That policymakers responded to organized interests was evident in all three states. In California in particular, while NOW was not concerned with the policy change and did not fight for it, indeed almost scoffed at it, the opposition of religious conservative groups such as the Committee on Moral Concerns and Shepherd's Gate appeared at least to stall the policy adoption. This configuration of influences makes this policy adoption in California again look much more like policy adoption in Georgia, even though their citizens are thought to be ideologically on opposite sides of the political spectrum. The similarity in their policy adoption processes allows us to say with some confidence that the leanings of the public had little to do with policy adoption. Whether these results are generalizable is taken up in the next section.

Modeling Policy Adoption

Covering all 50 states from 1969 through 1999, this model includes a set of 511 cases of "state-years." Alabama did not adopt by 1999 and is coded as 0 from 1969 through 1999.[33]

Tables 3.3 and 3.4 show the determinants of the adoption of gender-neutral statutory rape laws. The first model includes all cases; the second excludes New York and California. I constructed the second model out of the concern that New York and California's rather puzzling "late" adoptions were skewing the effects of the variables. Both adopted gender-neutral forcible rape laws early on, but specifically excluded the statutory rape laws from that change. Both have very large NOW membership bases, and for much of the measured period, generally liberal electorates and innovative legislatures. The other late adopters, as noted, are completely different in profile. In excluding them, the fit of the second model is slightly better than that of the first, and the effects of the NOW variable are more clearly displayed while that of the Christian Right weakens.

In both models, the variables measuring elites are the most significant, each in the expected direction. Adoption was more likely when the governor was a member of the Democratic Party, when the legislature was controlled by

TABLE 3.3 States' Adoption of Gender-Neutral Language

Independent Variables	Expected Direction	Coefficient	Standard Error	Coefficient/ Standard Error	Change in Probability
GROUP					
NOW	+	.000	.000	.193	.000
Christian Right Influence	−	−.185[+]	.139	−1.333	.046
ELITE					
Party of the Governor	−	−.335*	.178	−1.881	.083
Party Control of State Legislature	−	−.478*	.231	−2.064	.117
Electoral Competition	+	.038*	.182	2.054	.009
PUBLIC OPINION					
Citizen Ideology	−	−.253	.251	−1.008	.063

Number of cases: 511
Number of y = 1: 49
Pearson Goodness-of-Fit Chi-Square: 532.094
[+]Significant at .10, one-tailed test; *Significant at .05, one-tailed test.
Note: The dependent variable is coded 1 if the state adopted in a given year, 0 if it did not.

the Democratic Party, and when there was a high level of electoral competition. The measure of electoral competition is in some sense a control for the South. The Democratic parties in southern states were generally more conservative than those elsewhere in the country for the period under study. It was these same states that tended to be "laggards," adopting in the 1980s and 1990s while most other states had adopted in the 1970s (see table 3.2). But these states were also characterized by low levels of competition.

The party of the governor and of the legislature also have the highest scores under "change in probability," and thus had the most independent influence on the dependent variable. Again, there were and continue to be strong links between feminist forces and the Democratic Party; women who describe themselves as "liberal" tend to vote for the Democratic Party, and organizations working on behalf of women tend to be more welcome in the Democratic Party. Finally, electoral competition, while significant, does not have the same influence as the partisanship variables.

Citizen ideology, although in the expected direction, is insignificant in both models as expected. This is not to say that public opinion is insignificant to policy change; it is merely to say that it probably does not have a direct

TABLE 3.4   States' Adoption of Gender-Neutral Language, Excluding New York and California

Independent Variables	Expected Direction	Coefficient	Standard Error	Coefficient/ Standard Error	Change in Probability
GROUP					
NOW	+	.000$^+$	.000	1.505	.000
Christian Right Influence	−	−.095	.147	−.642	.024
ELITE					
Party of the Governor	−	−.421*	.190	−2.213	.104
Party Control of State Legislature	−	−.438*	.126	−1.899	.108
Electoral Competition	+	.033*	.018	1.867	.008
PUBLIC OPINION					
Citizen Ideology	−	−.080	.262	−.303	.020

Number of cases: 477
Number of y = 1: 47
Pearson Goodness-of-Fit Chi-Square: 497.227$^#$
Percent Correctly Predicted: 90%
$^#$Significant at .10, two-tailed test; $^+$Significant at .10, one-tailed test; *Significant at .05, one-tailed test.
Note: The dependent variable is coded 1 if the state adopted in a given year, 0 if it did not.

relationship to it even when congruent with it. When group variables are accounted for, we can expect the effects of public opinion to decrease. Note that in the second model, in which more variation is captured in the NOW variable because the potentially skewing effects of New York and California are omitted, ideology is even less significant.

The group variables do not perform exactly as expected; each is only modestly significant in one but not both of the models. In the first model, which includes the exceptional cases of New York and California, Christian Right influence is barely significant at the .10 level, and NOW influence is insignificant.[34] These two states have the highest NOW memberships among the states. In other areas of rape reform, they were leaders, reflecting NOW's influence. Yet they were among the last few states to adopt gender-neutral language, by which time the organization's priorities had shifted to other policy areas, particularly abortion, domestic violence, and sexual harassment.

The combination of an insignificant NOW variable and a significant Christian Right variable was not as surprising as it might seem. Indeed, "[t]he actual creation of policy agenda items by interest groups may be a less frequent activity than blocking agenda items or proposing amendments to or substitutions for proposals already on the agenda" (Kingdon 1997: 51; Wiggins, Hamm, and Bell 1992: 90). Recent empirical studies of policy adoption have found that opposition group strength may be an even more important factor in the type of policy adopted than that of the group pushing the particular policy.[35] This follows from the conventional wisdom that a group whose values are threatened would be more likely to mobilize.

The second model, with the skewing effects of New York and California omitted, reflects the strength of NOW more clearly. The NOW variable is significant at close to .05, and in the expected direction; the Christian Right variable is insignificant. I was expecting the influence of NOW to increase, but was not expecting the decrease in the significance of the Christian Right variable. Note, though, that while the NOW variable is significant, it does not have proportionate influence on a change in the dependent variable; the Christian Right variable is stronger in this regard, as in the tests on age-span provisions.

Overall, the effects for partisanship are much stronger than those for group influence. Note the connection between the parties and the groups: liberal feminist women and men usually vote Democrat, and Christian conservatives usually vote Republican. With this in mind, and with slight results for the NOW variable, we can say that the pooled cross-sectional time series shows some limited support for the findings of the case studies: that interest group activity (here, NOW activity) on partisan legislators concerned about reelection is a strong direct influence on policy change, and that public opinion's more indirect influence will show weaker effects when groups are taken into account.

Beyond Policy Adoption: Enforcing the Laws

Has gender-neutral language changed the face of statutory rape prosecutions? Have feminists succeeded in contributing to changing cultural assumptions about gender and sexuality?

Two types of prosecutions in the 1990s have further buttressed the gendered undercurrents of statutory rape laws. Spurred on by bonus monies offered through the welfare reform act of 1996, several states have begun using stepped-up statutory rape prosecutions as a means of decreasing teen pregnancy. This type of prosecution is discussed in detail in chapter 4.[36] Focusing on this one particular type of relationship not only excludes cases in which abuse but no pregnancy has occurred, but also subverts the gender neutrality of the law by purposely prosecuting only males who have impregnated young females.

A second type of case making its way through the court system in various states encompasses females convicted of statutory rape for relationships with young males, but who have then become pregnant, given birth, and sued the male for child support. Thus far, in a number of different states,[37] those young males have been forced to pay—even though they are minors as well as victims of sex crimes, and their partners are, in some cases, felony-level sex offenders. "The State's interest in requiring minor parents to support their children overrides the State's competing interest in protecting juveniles from improvident acts, even when such acts may include criminal activity on the part of the other parent" (*State ex. Rel Hermesmann v. Seyer*, Kansas 1993, 847 P.2d 1273, quoted in Tennen 1997). The issue of consent to sex under criminal law is apparently irrelevant in a civil action to establish paternity and receive child support. That the young male may have been emotionally or physically harmed is virtually dismissed, outweighed by the cultural assumption that he should be a provider.

Much of the discourses surrounding "nontraditional" statutory rape cases in which the victim is male tend to categorize the "older woman" perpetrator as a manipulative or mentally ill seductress, and to categorize the "older man" perpetrator as an abusive predator, doubly outside the bounds of society by being homosexual as well. Such language maintains the boundaries of traditional gender roles: The older woman is constructed as an almost sympathetic aberration of her gender who tries to obtain love by seducing a young male, while the older man is seen simply as a sexual aggressor and is therefore more universally excoriated for his behavior. Three examples follow.[38]

Mary Kay LeTourneau

Mary Kay LeTourneau's first arrest on statutory rape charges ended in a suspended 89-month prison term, completion of a three-year sex offender treatment program, and avoiding all contact with minors (including Vili Fualaau, the victim). For a repeat statutory rape offender to serve no jail time is extremely unusual. Her second arrest, after she violated these terms by seeing Fualaau and indeed becoming pregnant with their second child, resulted in the 89-month sentence being imposed.

In television interviews, Fualaau objected to being called a victim although he was 13 at the time of the initial offense (LeTourneau was then 35); told of his pursuit of LeTourneau, which she at first resisted; and professed his love for her and his willingness to wait to be able to be with her. He wrote a book in 1998 entitled *Only One Crime, Love* that was published in France. His own mother pleaded with the judge not to sentence LeTourneau to prison. In the spring of 2001, Fualaau noted that he was about to turn 18, and was hopeful that prison officials would allow him to marry LeTourneau (Giles 2001).

It appears that, somewhat like the discourse on infanticide, female offenders are more subject to solely medicalized language than their male counterparts, who tend to be described with a mixture of medical and criminal terms. Her lawyer's main argument, repeated frequently, was that "Mary still does need treatment . . . locking her up is not going to cure her and, in fact, could cause her delusional beliefs and the boy's to continue to grow. . . . A developmentally disabled person cannot be held responsible for some of their actions . . . she needs some help, she needs some extra supervision" ("Excerpts" 1998). A number of therapists echoed this view: Roger Wolf, a Washington state sex offender treatment specialist, said, "What we're dealing with here is obviously not 'love' as most people define it. . . . We treat this as just another cognitive disorder" (Egan 1998). Robert Kolodny, a sexologist at the Behavioral Medicine Institute, commented, "To behave in such a dangerous way, one would think this woman is indeed psychologically unstable. We are talking about someone who needs professional care" (Peterson 1998).

When LeTourneau pled guilty the first time she was arrested, she used this same language—apparently in order to receive a more lenient sentence. After her second arrest and during her interview on *Oprah*, she said that she preferred being in jail and being "true" to herself, rather than pretending in the sex offender program that she felt remorseful and wanted treatment.

In general, the word *abuse* occurs less frequently in press accounts of this older woman perpetrator than in the example that follows in which the older party was male. She is portrayed more as influential and exploitative seducer than coercive or violent abuser. This appears to reach back to a construction of a woman as a temptress, who while invested with sexuality still required a male to act. Such a narrative withstands the language used for men who commit the same crime—that of pedophilia.

Stephen Simmons

Beginning in 1996, 15-year-old Samuel Manzie had frequent phone and E-mail contact with and was "sexually abused . . . by [Stephen Simmons, 43] who lured him from an on-line chat room [for gay men]." His parents found out, forced him to end the relationship, and sent him to counseling. The police enlisted the teen's help to entrap Simmons; Manzie went along briefly with the plan and then smashed the recording equipment, refusing to cooperate further. His parents first forced him to stay in a shelter for teen runaways and then tried to have him committed to long-term psychiatric care—the hospital refused. A few days later he sexually assaulted and killed 11-year-old Edward Werner (McFadden 1997a,b,c; Hanley 1997a,b).

Simmons was charged under New Jersey's gender-neutral statutory rape law, among others. The potential penalty for his nine offenses totaled 46 years. Manzie, on the other hand, had committed murder, which had a potential sentence of 30 years. One typical front-page article noted that the teen was not forced to have sex, yet referred to Simmons as "the pedophile" four times, roughly the same number of times he was referred to by his last name (McFadden 1997a). While using the subject's last name is journalistic convention, using the term *pedophile* reinforces the repeatedly constructed link between homosexuality and pedophilia that is unshaken by evidence to the contrary.[39] At Simmons's sentencing hearing, Manzie told the judge as he refused to testify against Simmons, "I would like to shed some light on my relationship with Simmons. It was a good one. . . . Please keep in mind that he never forced me to do more than I wanted to, and please keep in mind that I never regretted the relationship" (Mansnerus 1999a).[40] While the prosecutor did note how "clever" Manzie was in setting up meetings with Simmons, the assistant prosecutor dismissed this agency, saying "Mr. Simmons committed a criminal act which we believe not only victimized Sam Manzie but was also an assault on our society" (Masnerus 1999b).

In both the Simmons and the LeTourneau cases, the victims asserted that they were active and willing participants in the sexual activity. But in striking difference from the LeTourneau case is the use of the terms *sexual assault* and *sexual abuse* in every article on the Simmons case. A typical article on LeTourneau is entitled "Lovesick" or "Statutory Rape: A Love Story"; a typical article on Simmons is entitled "Pedophile Admits He Abused Young Killer" (Fielder 1998; Egan 1998; Hanley 1999b). Simmons was not portrayed as having some sort of medical disorder; he was merely a violent offender, assumed to have indirectly caused a murder, facing jail time.[41] He was not given the possibility of outpatient treatment as was LeTourneau. No feature articles were written about whether he was a sympathetic figure in love with Manzie (or vice versa). By the same token, LeTourneau was never referred to as a pedophile although Fualaau was actually younger than Manzie. It appears as if the homosexual nature of the sexual encounters feminized Manzie; during Simmons's prosecution it was assumed that Manzie was not a sexual agent, while in LeTourneau's case Fualaau was assumed to be one.

But these cases do not appear readily able to tell us much about statutory rape cases involving a female perpetrator with a female victim. Given that the laws prohibit sexual intercourse, that is, penetration of a vagina by a penis, are there such cases? If so, would a "lesbian" perpetrator be treated by the media more like LeTourneau or more like Simmons?

Sean O'Neill [Sharon Clark]

While it is not difficult to find statutory rape cases in which males have been charged for statutory rape of young females, and there are a small but increasing number of cases involving females charged for statutory rape of young males, there is but one accessible case over the last decade that involves two females[42]—and the perpetrator, Sean O'Neill, would undoubtedly say that this characterization of him would not be accurate. Because the laws as written criminalize sexual intercourse, a female perpetrator would not technically fit into the legal definition of the crime. She could be charged with statutory sodomy (or oral copulation depending on the phrasing used by that state), or perhaps under a sexual contact law that includes digital or object penetration.[43] The lack of such cases in itself serves to remind us of the limits of legal language, of the heterosexual assumptions of the laws, and of the strict gender stereotypes enshrined by rape and statutory rape laws in particular.

In Colorado in 1994, 19-year-old Sean O'Neill was prosecuted for having sexual relationships with four young females, two of whom were underage. "The parents [of the females] made no objection to the relationship, until it emerged that Sean had a vagina and the relationship was 'lesbian'" (Wilchins et al. 1996). Apparently, he had "posed as a 17-year-old boy to woo young girls into sexual encounters" (Foster 1994). Born Sharon Clark, O'Neill was charged in the end with 12 counts of sexual assault, sexual assault on a child, and criminal impersonation (having represented himself as a male rather than a female), crimes that together could have brought him almost 50 years in prison ("Plea" 1995). Recall that Simmons's potential penalty for nine counts could have brought him 46 years in jail; LeTourneau's potential penalty was, at first, a probated seven and one-half years, imposed only when she violated the terms of the probation.

Each of the females, who apparently did not want to prosecute, stated that they never suspected that Sean "was a woman." One recalled at trial, "She had her shirt off, had her jeans on, and had a condom and was putting it on herself" (Minkowitz 1995: 140). Another testified that "during the fifty or so sexual encounters, the defendant never removed his shirt completely and that she never saw a penis, but felt it" (*National Law Journal* Staff 1995); she later said that she had performed oral sex on him (Minkowitz 1995). Most of the news coverage identified O'Neill as "Clark" or "Ms. Clark," and when using pronouns such as "he," tended to put them in quotation marks. A typical headline read "Woman Accused of Playing Boyfriend to Girls" (Foster 1994).

"I don't call myself gay or straight. I consider myself in the masculine form," said O'Neill (Minkowitz 1995: 101). Because he identified as male, but did not identify as lesbian or transgendered, it is difficult to make generalizations from this case about how a perpetrator who claimed such an identity might be treated. It seems, though, that the use of an object for penetration,[44] coupled with a fluid sense of gender identity, both masculinized and queered O'Neill for the purposes of statutory rape prosecution, "During cross examination and closing arguments the DA repeatedly cast Sean as a dangerous predator, a pedophile of the worst sort, driven to sexual relations with 'children.'" Noted only once as he was characterized this way was O'Neill's physical appearance: he was less than five feet tall, and weighed under 100 pounds (www.brentpayton.com/trans/transgendered).

His lawyer remarked, "The disparate treatment between transsexuals and 'normal' sex offenders makes it that much easier for the prosecution to stack and maximize the charges. . . . The simple fact of a defendant's being transgendered dramatically shrinks the 'presumption of innocence' impossibly complicating any chance of mounting a fair and effective defense" (Wilchins et al. 1996).[45] As in the Simmons and the LeTourneau cases, the victims did not want to prosecute, but the language surrounding this case is much more similar to that of Simmons's crime than that of LeTourneau's. O'Neill was not assumed to be a "sick" heterosexual female like LeTourneau, with her mental illness explaining how she could stand outside gendered boundaries as a female sexual agent. Rather, he was assumed to be a lesbian, with his sexuality itself placing him outside the boundaries of femaleness and enabling his sexual agency.

O'Neill's sexuality and his gender were collapsed so that he was constructed not as a transperson, but rather as homosexual and as male, both suspect categories in statutory rape prosecutions. Indeed, the legal director of the Lambda Legal Defense and Education Fund commented that statutory rape cases in which the parties are close in age are more likely to be prosecuted when the parties are of the same sex (Minkowitz 1995: 145).

Conclusions

In the preceeding examples, the presumption of innocence, or of consensuality, begins to fade when the perpetrator is male, and in particular, when the perpetrator is a homosexual male.[46] At the same time, victims of statutory rape, particularly by older males, are constructed as unwilling, or at best, passive and manipulated participants in sexual conduct. Yet children are also perceived to be "invested with sexual capacity" (Kincaid 1992: 174). Cases involving young males with older females are most readily perceived as falling into this category, as if one's male gender surpasses one's age as enabling or encouraging sexual behavior.

Liberal feminists' goals for gender-neutral statutory rape laws—that they would enshrine gender equality into law and thus dismantle stereotypes of female sexuality as passive and male sexuality as aggressive—may have been unfortunately too ambitious, particularly in a climate in which homosexuality is still often constructed as suspect. Rather, the criticism by feminist sex radicals that such laws might essentialize young people as victims, punish consensual sex, and single out homosexual relationships may prove to be more accurate.

Chapter 4

From "Welfare Queen" to "Exploited Teen"

Targeting the Partners of Pregnant Females

Es un delito con una menor de 18 años [It's a crime with a (female) minor under 18 years].
> —Billboard sponsored by the California Department of Health Services
> (*emphasis added*)

Think twice about sex with an older guy.
> —Billboard sponsored by the Connecticut Department of Social Services
> (*emphasis added*)

Introduction

Since 1996, 10 states have revised their statutory rape laws to target sexual activity resulting in teen pregnancy.[1] The intent of the policy, say public officials, prosecutors, pressure groups, and parents who support the targeting, is

Portions of this chapter were originally published in the *National Women's Studies Association Journal* 14, no. 2 (summer 2002).

to protect young and vulnerable girls from further abuse, and to deter predatory men from having sex with teens. In turn, fewer unmarried teens will get
pregnant, the welfare rolls will be greatly reduced, and the government will
spend less money on public assistance.

But the connection between statutory rape prosecutions and a reduction in the number of people who need public assistance seems rather tenuous. First, while about 70% of U.S. teens report having had sexual
intercourse in high school (Alan Guttmacher Institute 1999a),[2] only a small
fraction of mothers receiving public assistance are under the age of consent
in any given state. Second, it is also unlikely that all statutory rape cases resulting in pregnancy, particularly those between similarly aged teens, are the
result of exploitation. Third, the lawmakers who have urged the commitment of resources to statutory rape prosecutions to protect young unwed
mothers are the same politicians who have actively sought cuts in an-
tipoverty programs that assist those mothers financially. Yet despite these
precarious assumptions and contradictions, numerous states have allotted
millions of dollars to these prosecutions.

The above debate occurred in the context of the overhaul of the welfare
system in 1996, through the Personal Responsibility and Work Opportunity
Reconciliation Act (PRWORA). The PRWORA gave states financial incentives
to decrease out-of-wedlock births to teens without increasing abortions. But
detailed or surefire policy solutions were not suggested, let alone required. One
might assume that policymakers would ignore the federal call on illegitimacy,
and concentrate on the collection of child support and on the work requirements of the PRWORA. Most have. Then why have 10 states adopted measures
intended to target the partners of impoverished pregnant teens? Why these
states and why this policy?

Background to Policy Adoption: Linking Statutory Rape Prosecutions to Rates of Teen Pregnancy

In times of economic, political, social, and moral uncertainties, changing justifications for statutory rape laws have been constructed. These historically
specific justifications have linked adolescent sexuality to the broader socioeconomic dislocations, and have proposed the social control of that sexuality
as a means by which to alleviate the larger problems. In the 1880s and 1890s,
for instance, unmarried sex was linked to the problems wrought by urbanization, industrialization, and immigration. In the 1980s and 1990s, unmarried
sex was linked to teen pregnancy, which has come to signify family breakdown, moral decay, and welfare dependency.

Setting the Stage for the Language of Welfare to Strengthen Statutory Rape Laws

The late 1960s and 1970s saw social upheaval in the United States, exemplified by the civil rights, antiwar, gay, and women's movements. These movements, under the umbrella label of *counterculture*, appeared to many to foster a general social and sexual permissiveness. Specifically, this encompassed access to birth control and abortion, sex education in schools, more women in the workplace, a decriminalization of sodomy in some states, busing and affirmative action, and so forth. Certainly, prosecutions for statutory rape decreased. As Jeffrey Weeks (1989) notes, "These long-term changes in the social structure tended to undermine the orthodox moral framework—and generate a sense of moral collapse" (260). Organization against these changes began to solidify in the 1980s. As a researcher from the conservative Heritage Foundation put it, "Why are issues such as when human life begins, and the authority of the state to protect it, religious freedom, the sexual activity of minors, and pornography political issues in the first place? These issues became political because liberal ideologues insisted on using the mechanisms of the state to impose their own values and policy goals on American society" (Diamond 1995: 232).

As such, Ronald Reagan's "talk of 'getting the government off people's backs' was thus assumed by the Christian Right to mean legislation to reinstate traditional morality" (Diamond 1995: 232). One of President Reagan's more popular appeals, which persists through today, was in his attacks on "children having children" and on "welfare queens."[3] Such language tied in the backlash against permissiveness and changing sexual mores to the simultaneous backlash against the perceived overexpansion of the welfare state:

> Economic conservatives wishing to dismantle the New Deal safety net and moral conservatives offended by government subsidies of nonmarital sex transformed the issue into a referendum on teenage pregnancy, single motherhood, and "welfare queens," all the while implying that the problem was one of immorality and irresponsibility among people of color. . . . Whether based in fear, anger, or envy, the charge of sexual impropriety shaped a policy debate in a way that statistical evidence could not. (D'Emilio and Freedman 1997: 375–376)

The issue was one that could unite different factions on the right. As Kristin Luker notes, "What's toxic about teen-age pregnancy is that it combines a threat to the public purse with a threat to morality" (quoted in Goodman 1996b).

Family planning advocates, who can be conceived of as being on the left of the political spectrum, encouraged the links between teen pregnancy and welfare. Framing their concern as economic, not moral, they fought to increase teens' access to contraception and abortion based on the rationale that teen pregnancy was a symptom of poverty which then produced more poverty. They medicalized the debate by arguing that such access in and of itself would stem the tide of teen pregnancy and its costs; but by doing so they implicitly acknowledged that teen pregnancy itself was a problem (Nathanson 1991).

Debate across the political spectrum seemed to converge on the figure of the poor teen mother. It was at about this point that the Supreme Court heard *Michael M. v. Superior Court of Sonoma County* (450 US 464 [1981]). As detailed in chapter 3, the majority opinion said that gender-specific statutory rape laws were constitutional because the laws served to deter the "epidemic" of teen pregnancy. Young females should be deterred from sex by the threat of pregnancy, and young males should be deterred by threat of prosecution. In doing this, the court linked together teen pregnancy and statutory rape. This judicial support dovetailed with the more conservative movements described above vis-à-vis sexuality, pregnancy, and the economy.

The Alan Guttmacher Institute Study

Since 1995, when the Alan Guttmacher Institute (AGI) released a study on teen pregnancy entitled *Sex and America's Teenagers*, both the discourse about and the activities around statutory rape have increasingly centered on teen mothers. It was this study that provided the numbers for those who asserted increases in statutory rape were leading to increases in teen pregnancy and welfare dependency.

The following AGI statistic would come to be cited by virtually every article on the topic across the political spectrum as well as by public officials: 65% of teen mothers had children by men who were 20 or older, and, often, the younger the mother, the larger the age gap between her and the baby's father. Feminists, liberals, and conservatives were similarly alarmed.

But a closer look at the numbers, undertaken by the Urban Institute reveals more.[4] For one, the AGI study included as teen mothers women of 19 and their partners of 20 or older. The distribution of births of 15–19-year-olds reveals that 62% in the year of the study were 18 or 19, 28% were 15–17 but had a same-age partner, and 2% were 15–17 and married. Thus, only 8% of teen mothers in the United States had male partners who could be prosecuted at the felony level for statutory rape. Twenty-three percent of the 15–19-year-olds were married at the time of delivery, and 49% were living with their partner at the time of the interviews, which were up to 30 months after delivery. The

Urban Institute also found that having an older sex partner had no strong association to the girl's race or household income.

At the same time, given the percentages of teens who claim to be sexually
active—that is, those who, depending on their state of residence, may be engaged in criminalized sexual activity—a rather small percentage becomes pregnant *and* gives birth *and* is considered poor enough to require public assistance.
Approximately 24% of females and 27% of males age 15, 39% of females and
45% of males age 16, 52% of females and 59% of males age 17, 63% of females
and 68% of males age 18, and 77% of females and 85% of males age 19 report
having had sexual intercourse (AGI 1999a).[5]

However, higher-income teens who make up 62% of females aged 15–19
only account for 17% of teen births because over 70% of those who become
pregnant choose to have abortions. By contrast, impoverished pregnant adolescents represent 83% of females aged 15–19 who give birth because only
about 39% of them choose to have abortions. This is indeed alarming, for various reasons. But it does not mean that every female in the latter group requires
public assistance. Only about 5% of mothers receiving public assistance are
teens, and only about 1% are under 18 (AGI 1998, 1999a,b,c).

Regardless of the delicate nature of the links in the chain, teen sex, particularly between an older male and a younger female, became conceived of as
leading inexorably to single motherhood, and to welfare dependency.[6] The
"two-thirds of teen mothers are impregnated by older men" catchphrase per-
sisted. Support for renewed efforts at rooting out sexual abuse through statutory rape laws seemed to range across the political spectrum.

Just one year after the AGI statistics appeared, the federal government
was deep into negotiations on reforming public assistance. Given the link between statutory rape and the number of young women on the welfare rolls that
the statistics were construed as establishing, public officials were eager to "get
tough" on the predatory men responsible for impregnating young women who
would then require public assistance. The next section details debates surrounding those parts of the new welfare plan related to statutory rape laws and
then reviews the viewpoints of three sets of actors on the statutory rape playing field: legislators, feminists, and religious conservatives.

The Legislators: Punishing Predators and Preventing
Pregnancy through the PRWORA

The PRWORA established Temporary Assistance to Needy Families (TANF),
the block grant to states that replaced the federal guarantee of cash assistance
formerly provided by Aid to Families with Dependent Children.[7] The new plan
stressed replacing welfare with work, collecting child support, and reducing

dependency. Specifically, it imposed time limits on the receipt of benefits, required work in exchange for full benefits, restricted food stamps, reduced monies for nutrition programs, instituted a separate application process for Medicaid, and provided money for child care (to be determined by the state) for adult parents but not teen parents.

But the PRWORA had social objectives as well, most of which emphasize the need to change the sexual and reproductive behavior of the poor and unmarried. The language might not have been so strong but for the Republican takeover of Congress in 1994. Indeed, President Bill Clinton vetoed two previous versions of welfare reform, seeking more compromise between the Republicans' ideas and his own 1992 pledge to "end welfare as we know it." He would sign this bill during his reelection campaign of 1996.

About 350 pages long, the PRWORA begins with Congressional "Findings," or the rationale for this major overhaul of the U.S. welfare system. Virtually all of the findings have to do with children born out of wedlock and born particularly to unmarried teen females.

The Congress makes the following findings:
1) Marriage is the foundation of a successful society.
2) Marriage is an essential institution of a successful society which promotes the interest of children. . . .
3) Promotion of responsible fatherhood and motherhood is integral to successful child rearing and the well-being of children. . . .

The increase in the number of children receiving public assistance is closely related to the increase in births to unmarried women. . . .

It is estimated that the rate of nonmarital teen pregnancy rose 23 percent from 54 pregnancies per 1,000 unmarried teenagers in 1976 to 66.7 pregnancies in 1991. . . . In contrast, the overall pregnancy rate for married couples decreased. . . .

If the current trend continues, 50 percent of all births by the year 2015 will be out-of-wedlock. . . .

An effective strategy to combat teenage pregnancy must address the issue of male responsibility, including statutory rape culpability and prevention. The increase of teenage pregnancies among the youngest girls is particularly severe and is linked to predatory sexual practices by men who are significantly older. . . . Available data suggests that almost 70% of births to teenage girls are fathered by men over age 20. . . .

Therefore, in light of this demonstration of the crisis in our Nation, it is the sense of the Congress that prevention of out-of-wedlock pregnancy and reduction of out-of-wedlock birth are very important government interests. (PL 104-193, sec. 101, 1996)

Note that the Congress cites the AGI statistic on the percentage of teen births fathered by adult men, without the caveats of the Urban Institute, that is, that most teen mothers are 18 or 19 with partners of 20 or 21, and many either live with or are married to their partner.

Also note that Congress has cited the rate of "nonmarital teen pregnancy." This figure, for any age group, is always higher than the corresponding birthrate because it includes pregnancies ending in miscarriages and abortions. If out-of-wedlock birth is the concern, Congress should be citing the birthrate—the lower, and not as dramatic, number. For example, the findings cite the nonmarital teen pregnancy rates of 54.0 (per 1,000) in 1976 and 66.7 (per 1,000) in 1991. A closer look reveals the following: the *overall* teen birthrate in 1976 was 52.8. The *unmarried* teen birthrate, though, was 23.7, which is half of the number they cite. The *married* teen birthrate was 313.1, skewing the overall teen birthrate higher. The overall teen birthrate in 1991 was 62.1—among unmarried teens it was 44.8, and among married teens it was 410.4 (Ventura, Matthews, and Hamilton 2001: 10). It is interesting that the Congress chose to cite this figure from 1991, because that particular year has otherwise been widely noted by health officials to be part of a short uptick in the otherwise steady decline of the teen birthrate from the 1950s to 2000.

Indeed, the overall teen birthrate peaked at 96.3 in 1957. It ranged between 89.1 and 65.5 in the 1960s, and 68.3 to 51.5 in the 1970s. In the 1980s when the United States was cited as being in the midst of an "epidemic" of teen pregnancy, the rate ranged from 57.3 to 50.6; in the 1990s, it ranged from 62.1 to 49.6. By 2000, it was 48.7 as efforts to combat teen pregnancy were reinvigorated. In other words, the teen birthrate in 2000 was almost exactly half that in 1957 (Ventura, Matthews, and Hamilton 2001: 10). But in 1957, the year of the highest teen birthrate in the last 100 years, 87.1% of teen births were to married women; in 2000 with the lowest teen birthrate in the last 100 years, 78.7% of teen births were to *un*married women (Ventura, Matthews, and Hamilton 2001: 10). As the teen birthrate has steadily declined, the percentage of births to unmarried teens has steadily risen. The first year in which the percentage of unmarried teen mothers exceeded the percentage of married teen mothers was 1984 (Ventura, Matthews, and Hamilton 2001: 10). So, while far fewer teens are having children, far more of those teens are unmarried and apparently are assumed by the PRWORA to be impoverished. Although Congress finds that if the "current trend continues, 50 percent of all births by the year 2015 will be out-of-wedlock," they did not mention that most unmarried mothers are women in their twenties who do not require public assistance.[8]

The Findings go on to cite several ills that have been associated with both teen mothers and their children such as low birth weight, low educational attainment, persistent poverty, juvenile crime, and long-term welfare dependence. While these problems have been statistically correlated with teen births, one cannot assert that they are caused by teen births. Indeed, recent in-depth studies of teen pregnancy tend to refute the notion that giving birth as a teen is the source of these problems and suggest that delaying childbearing would have little effect on them (Geronimus 1997; Lawson and Rhode 1993; Luker 1996). Rather, these studies have found, such problems may have much more to do with poverty itself and other related disadvantages suffered by teenage females before they became pregnant.

The concern here, as with the various debates over and amendments to statutory rape laws in the past,[9] appears to be with marriage rather than with protecting young people. The moral, the social, and the economic are completely conflated as marriage is here constructed as the key to the American nation; if people were married they would apparently be a morally upstanding unit, a stable social unit, and a self-sufficient economic unit. There is no mention of any potential structural causes of poverty such as a low minimum wage, lack of health care and child care, unequal pay for equal work, or a national ideology of self-sufficiency that stigmatizes the economically unsuccessful.

Rather, here as a guiding principle of the new welfare plan is the notion that there exists a direct connection not only between unmarried teen pregnancy and welfare dependency, but between adolescent sexuality and welfare dependency. One attempt at curbing adolescent sexuality is reflected in "Section 912 Abstinence Education," which funds any state program that:

> Teaches abstinence from sexual activity outside marriage as the expected standard for all school-age children.
> Teaches that a mutually faithful monogamous relationship in the context of marriage is the expected standard of human sexual activity.
> Teaches that sexual activity outside of the context of marriage is likely to have harmful psychological and physical effects. . . .
> Teaches that bearing children out-of-wedlock is likely to have harmful consequences for the child, the child's parents, and society. . . .
> Teaches the importance of attaining self-sufficiency before engaging in sexual activity.

This passage is quite clear in linking the moral and economic concerns about people receiving public assistance: not only do they engage in an offensive lifestyle that is outside of the "expected standard of human sexual activity," but also that behavior and its "harmful consequences" directly affects society as both a religious affront and an expensive fiscal outlay. It is not so clear on the definition of sexual activity, or on what kind of structure a state would need to implement and evaluate abstinence education.

The second prong of the attempt to stem teen pregnancy, linked to the previous section on abstinence, was contained in amendments introduced by Senator Joseph Lieberman (D-CT).[10] Speaking on behalf of the amendments, Lieberman said, "The Senate is sending sexual predators an unequivocally stern message—that we choose abstinence for children, and that we will not tolerate those who take advantage of a child's inability to form and articulate a decision about her body."[11] The pertinent sections, 401–403, begin with the Congress charging the states to:

> [provide assistance to the needy,] end the dependence of needy parents on government benefits by promoting job preparation, work, and marriage, prevent and reduce the incidence of out-of wedlock pregnancies, with special emphasis on teen pregnancies, and establish numerical goals for reducing the incidence of these pregnancies, and encourage the formation and maintenance of two-parent families.[12]

Arguing on behalf of these amendments, Lieberman took to the floor to urge "district attorneys to be very aggressive in working with welfare authorities to once again take statutory rape as a serious crime and to prosecute it, understanding that this is done to deter adult men from committing a sexual act that will result in a child born to poverty" (quoted in Levin-Epstein 1997: 5). His colleagues apparently agreed. One congresswoman debating the bill cited teen pregnancy as being at the heart of the well-being of the United States: "Devoting more resources to preventing teenage pregnancy will not only save us money in the long run, but it will strengthen the social fabric by improving the health, education, economic opportunities, and well-being of our Nation's youth."[13] A senator, speaking of illegitimacy in general was more colorful: "I suggest it may be the great social ill that can be the cancer within to destroy this civilization."[14]

With the amendments in place, states were required to submit a "TANF plan" to the Department of Health and Human Services (DHHS). Among the six requirements are these two: states must submit plans on how they will reduce the "illegitimacy ratio of the State . . . [and] conduct a program designed to reach state and local law enforcement officials, the education system, and relevant counseling services, that provides education and training on the problem of statutory rape so that teenage pregnancy prevention programs may be expanded in scope to include men" (PL 104-193, sec. 402[a][1], [v], [vi], 1996). The Justice Department, too, was granted $6 million to research the "linkage between statutory rape and teenage pregnancy, particularly by predatory older men committing repeat offenses," to educate state law enforcement on the same, and to ensure with DHHS that at least 25% of communities put teenage pregnancy-prevention programs in place. Up to five states each year can receive a "Bonus to Reward Decrease in Illegitimacy" of up to $25 million each if they have the highest rates of decrease in both illegitimate births *and* abortions (PL 104-193, sec. 403[E] [Z]), 1996; emphasis added). However, the federal government provided no money in advance, no definition of the teenage pregnancy-prevention program, and no mention of access to or education about birth control.

In linking welfare dependency, teen pregnancy, and statutory rape, rhetoric on the teen mother shifts from demonization ("the welfare queen") to victimization ("the exploited teen"). While her sexual behavior is an object of reform, the welfare queen is somewhat redeemed. No longer seeking to have children to collect state monies, she is now the child victim, an innocent on whom a crime of violence is committed by a man much older than she. "At times regarded as irresponsible, promiscuous, or as users of the welfare system, this teenage population is now being viewed by many as prey and even victims of child abuse" (Navarro 1996). And as the director of the Center on Children and the Law of the American Bar Association put it, "It's important we look at these teen mothers not as welfare queens but as victims of sexual exploitation" (quoted in Navarro 1996).

This revised image of the teen mother at first seemed to serve a broad audience—the Left could claim it was protecting the young and vulnerable who are unable to help themselves, while also nodding to the supposed distaste of people for the liberals' "soft" stance on both curtailing an immoral lifestyle and decreasing public assistance monies; and the Right could further condemn nonmarital sex and out-of-wedlock births while also attacking the perceived failures of the welfare system in a new manner. As Lieberman characterized the agreement, "Democrats and Republicans alike wish to use our Nation's welfare programs to combat social ills—particularly the growth in out-of-wedlock pregnancies among teenagers."[15] Three days later, he was more specific, "By focusing on the problems of teenage pregnancy and statutory rape, we are economizing our future welfare expenditures and improving the lives of poor children."[16] In other words, both sides of the aisle would gain because this initiative meant both less government spending and raising up the poor. As few legislators would have stood up to defend the sin of teen pregnancy; as the target populations were disempowered by virtue of their age, class, race, and/or ethnicity; and as the framing of the problem was one that pulled in support across the political spectrum, the targeting of the poor pregnant teen and her equally poor and amoral impregnator was bound to succeed. But what about groups on the outside?

The Feminists

Where were the feminists during this debate? NOW, always concerned with nonconsensual sex and with violence against women, protested outside the White House the day that President Clinton signed the PRWORA into law. But not over the statutory rape/teen pregnancy provisions. The organization had two concerns: that the emphasis on reducing the "illegitimacy ratio" would prompt states to restrict access to abortion, and that the mandatory naming of a child's father by a pregnant woman or mother was not taking into account the number of impoverished women who were victims of domestic violence (from a 1996 Feminist Majority newsletter). Tracking down the father based on the mother's report, in order to force him to contribute financially, might leave her vulnerable to additional abuse. Nowhere in their extensive literature on the PRWORA does the organization even mention the connection between statutory rape, teen pregnancy, and welfare reform.[17]

A few female voices criticized the plan even as they reiterated that relationships in which one person was much older than the other were still cause for concern. Michelle Oberman, feminist law professor and author of one of the most cited law review articles on statutory rape (1994), commented, "Drawing a connection between enforcing these laws and lowering adolescent pregnancy rates flies in the face of everything we know about why girls get pregnant. . . . The problem is much more complicated than simply older men preying on younger women" (quoted in Donovan 1997). The feminist *Ms.* magazine wrote that health care providers in particular were concerned that a young woman might not seek prenatal care if she thought her partner would be arrested as a result, and that the arrest and jailing of the male would worsen the female's impoverishment by cutting off whatever support he might have been willing to give (Shin 1998). Former Surgeon General M. Joycelyn Elders also emphasized that young women might delay seeking medical care or social services, and expressed further concern that girls who named their partners and exposed them to statutory rape charges might be risking physical abuse from the male depending on the type of relationship the two had (Elders and Albert 1998).

But these criticisms were not organized into any kind of united front in support of protecting young women but in opposition to the method. The support of some feminists for renewed statutory rape prosecutions just after the publication of the AGI statistics fell away during the debate on the new welfare plan. Silence prevailed from the feminist corner on the national level. As one observer characterized the situation, "Feminists seemed to back off when they

saw the strange bedfellows who became their allies: family policy groups, welfare reform advocates, and Republican governors" (Maynard 1999: 3).

The Religious Conservatives

At the same time, the bill elicited great support from some religious conservatives. "The teen pregnancy problem is inextricably linked to statutory rape" stated
an article in *World* magazine, described alternately as *"Time* or *Newsweek* from a
Christian perspective" or "an evangelical Christian weekly" (Maynard 1999: 6).
The magazine is edited by Marvin Olasky, a poverty theorist who advocates the
privatization of the administration of public assistance and who was also an informal adviser to former President George H. W. Bush's campaigns. Matt Daniels,
whose Massachusetts Family Institute urged the state to be more stringent about
enforcing the law, laid out why the Religious Right should support prosecuting
pregnancy: "This is more about statistics and bringing down the teen pregnancy
numbers. It's about protecting our children." Young females have to be protected
from themselves as well, and the author of the article wrote that "the overwrought
emotions of teenage girls lends credence to [Daniels's] view." More to the point
of political maneuvering, Daniels noted, "We are losing badly in the social debate, so we have to find ways to reframe that debate. The statutory rape issue allows us to do so. It puts us on the side of women, on the side of children. It puts
the other side on the defensive" (quoted in Maynard 1999: 7).

The Family Research Council (FRC), a noted conservative group, em-
bodies the views held by many religious conservatives on the subjects of
teenage nonmarital sexuality and pregnancy, views that are perhaps shared by
a "silent majority" who feel threatened by the economic, political, social, and
cultural changes of the past few decades. In her 1996 "Statutory Rape," Gracie
Hsu wrote:

> In many respects, the rise in statutory rape is the tragic and pre-
> dictable consequence of the larger moral free-for-all that began
> during the sexual revolution of the 1960s and 1970s. As sex was
> severed from the context of marriage and perceived barriers to per-
> sonal "freedom" were torn down, the door was opened to a "libera-
> tion" in which predators were given easier access to the most
> vulnerable in our society. (2)[18]

She cited four main factors as contributing to the rise in teen pregnancy: fatherless households, lack of parental supervision as measured through whether the
mother was employed, erosion of "cultural protections" such as the media and the
schools, and erosion of legal protections. Lack of a father figure results in statu-

tory rape: "With more girls lacking the love and attention only a father can give, more of them are . . . seeking intimacy with predatory older men" (Hsu 1996: 3).

One solution: Prosecute statutory rape more effectively. In particular, Title X of the Public Health Service Act, which guarantees patient confidentiality so that health practitioners are not bound to report teens who come in for gynecological care to their parents, is a problem. Rather, health practitioners should be allowed to report the crime of statutory rape when they see it (Hsu 1996: 7).[19] The law "can and should encourage behaviors which strengthen the family through the use of incentives and disincentives" (Hsu 1996: 9). The FRC's solution was as follows: "What children need now is what they have always needed—for adults to protect their innocence. They need fathers and mothers who will love them and supervise them, laws that punish statutory rapists, and a culture which values and upholds the sacredness of marital sex, the permanency of marriage, and the authority of parents" (Hsu 1996: 9). In short, unlike the other two sets of changes to statutory rape laws, then, here the feminists were opposed and the Christian Right was in favor. This illustrates the ways in which there is no continuum of statutory rape reform from the 1890s to the present; rather, the issue of statutory rape has been used for different purposes at different times by different groups.

The Outcome

With the potential of TANF resources to back them, a few states began to dust off their statutory rape laws to target men for the impregnation of young impoverished females. A *New York Times* article that noted the shift in the construction of the teen mother continued, "While Congress has focused on proposals like denying teen-age mothers cash payments as part of an overhaul of the welfare system, state officials have begun looking at these older fathers as the unaddressed half of the teen-age pregnancy problem and its cost to taxpayers" (Navarro 1996). Statutory rape laws, often ignored through prosecutorial discretion, were not only revitalized but also in some states supplemented with amendments mandating longer sentences for male perpetrators of a certain age, or in cases in which pregnancy resulted. The latter has occurred in ten states.

Delaware, for instance, passed the "Sexual Predator Act" in 1996 to lengthen the sentences of the sexual partners of pregnant teens. The preamble to the amendment reads:

> Whereas illicit sexual activity between adult males and teenage girls is contributing to the high teenage pregnancy rates in Delaware and the nation. . . .
> Whereas, many of these adult males are repeat offenders. . . .

Whereas, $69 million was spent on the consequences of teen pregnancy in Delaware in 1993. . . .

Whereas society can no longer ignore or disregard statutory rape and the consequent increase in teen pregnancies. . . .

Whereas our state agencies and schools must recognize these cases as child abuse cases and make appropriate referrals to law enforcement (Ch. 600, SB No. 346).

In other words, statutory rape leads directly to teen pregnancy, it is caused by predatory sex criminals, and it costs a lot of money. Because the act pulls together statutory rape and child abuse, teachers and others are required to report suspected cases. The same is true in Florida, which passed a 1996 amendment called "MAMA—Make Adult Males Accountable" (L. 1996, c. 96–409) to include in mandatory reporting the "impregnation of a child under 16 by a person 21 years of age or older" (McCullough 1997).

Another method of finding the partners of young, unwed, impoverished, pregnant females is to mandate those who apply for Medicaid to identify their partners in order to receive assistance. Senator Lieberman implied this method when he urged law enforcement to work closely with welfare authorities on the subject. A third method is operative in several states as well: require health care providers to report to state authorities any suspicions of statutory rape. Tennessee uses both of the above methods since its 1996 amendment: "The purpose of this part is to curtail the crime of statutory rape" (Acts 1996, Ch. 842, §1). It includes the section, "Notice of Statutory Rape from Public Assistance Providers to Law Enforcement Agencies." Health care providers are required to report when examining females under 18 who are pregnant through the "Report of Pregnancy and Identity of Alleged Father to Judge or Law Enforcement Official" section.[20]

Several states have moved ahead with such prosecutions. California, for instance, has been prosecuting about 10 times the number of statutory rape cases as it was a few years ago. In addition to the states mentioned above, Connecticut, Idaho, Pennsylvania, Texas, Virginia, and Wisconsin have also begun targeting the partners of pregnant teens with additional resources, enhanced penalties, and special prosecutors. But can we say for certain what forces in those states account for the changes to their laws? Were their actions merely responses to the federal welfare reform act?

Adoption of Pregnancy-Prevention Provisions
Across the States

This set of changes made to statutory rape laws differs from those discussed in chapters 2 and 3, age-span provisions and gender-neutral language, respectively. Those changes were made beginning in the early 1970s, diffusing across almost all 50 states over a period of 30 years. The integral role of feminists, in particular, was quite clear vis-à-vis these policy adoptions; indeed, NOW virtually drafted the changes to the laws in the early part of the period under study. With this policy adoption, regarding pregnancy, the situation is not similar. The 10^{21} (rather than 43 or 50, as with the other two types of policies) policy adoptions occurred in the mid-1990s and were pushed by conservative groups; the two sets of reforms that occurred in the 1970s were part of a feminist program of rape law reform. One cannot necessarily assume that this amendment will diffuse throughout the states over a particular period; nor can one determine who in one state has learned from whom in another state— organized groups from organized groups, public officials from public officials, the public from the public, or some combination of these—and then agitated for policy change.

Case Studies: California and Georgia

Unlike the previous two chapters in which I also covered New Jersey in the case study section, I do not do so here. This is because after intensive research in this area, I find no evidence that this measure was ever even pushed forward or considered, let alone debated or fought over. None of the pertinent groups or legislative officials had any comments on the matter; there was no news coverage of such a concern over the time period under study. Thus I exclude New Jersey from the case studies.

Case 1: California

INTRODUCTION

> One of the most disturbing things about [the] exploding [rate of] teen pregnancy is that so many of the fathers are . . . men, 26 and 28 years old, having sex with 14-year-old girls. We've got to enforce statutory rape laws.
>
> —Governor Pete Wilson

California is perhaps the national leader in devoting great time and resources to statutory rape cases, allotting millions of dollars to the effort since 1995 through its four-pronged Partnership for Responsible Parenting: community challenge grants, stepped-up statutory rape prosecutions, a mentor initiative, and a public awareness campaign.[22] Its "Teenage Pregnancy Prevention Act of 1995" strengthened statutory rape laws and provided for civil penalties as well.[23] In 1997, it mandated reporting of sexual relationships in which one person was under 16 and the other at least 21 (AB 327, Reg. Sess., chap. 83). In 1998, it denied public assistance to pregnant women and single mothers who refused to name the fathers of their children (Lopez 1998). And in 1998 the California Court of Appeals declared that minors do not have a constitutional right to privacy to engage in consensual sex (*In Re T. A. J.*, 62 Cal. App. 4th 1350).

BACKGROUND TO POLICY CHANGE   "Every threat to the fabric of this country—from poverty to crime to homelessness—is connected to out-of-wedlock teen pregnancy" (Alter 1994: 41). So stated a December 1994 article clipped by the office of Assemblyman Louis Caldera (D-Los Angeles) and member of the centrist Democratic Leadership Council.[24] A second clipping asks, "What are post-school adult men, six to seven years older, doing fathering children with junior high school girls?" (Abcarian 1995).[25] And a third asks, "Does at least some of the blame for soaring teen birthrates and the enormous societal costs that follow rest on the shoulders of a society that looks the other way while adult men seduce minor girls? I'd say yes" (Erwin 1994). There is a large arrow drawn toward these statistics: "Statewide, adult men, most between the ages of 20 and 24, are responsible for two-thirds of births to teen mothers" (Erwin 1994). Note this is the same proportion as the AGI statistics, which had just been published and were about to gain national attention.

At the same time, Governor Pete Wilson proposed that $32 million of the budget go to preventing teen pregnancy. He declared in his 1995 State of the State Address on January 2:

> The costs are simply too high for society to continue tolerating the promiscuity and irresponsibility that have produced generations of unwed teen mothers. It is monstrously unfair to the children; to their sad, ill-equipped teen mothers; and certainly to working taxpayers, who must support them at a cost to their own children. . . . Too often the fatherless child of a teen mother becomes a teen predator, and the trigger man for his gang.

Although there is no evidence of direct correspondence between Caldera and Governor Wilson on this matter in January 1995,[26] it was only one month later that Caldera introduced the "Teenage Pregnancy Prevention Act of 1995" (AB 1490) into the Democrat-controlled California legislature. By all accounts, he was approached by no individual or group in order to pass this legislation—he drafted this bill himself with the support of two aides. Each bill introduced in the California legislature requires the attachment of a cover sheet listing the support for and opposition to the bill. It also asks "Which group or individual requested introduction of this bill?" While other bill files do name those groups or individuals, this one merely names the author as Caldera. This was somewhat unexpected. He was a moderate Democrat in the mold of President Clinton, whom Caldera noted in correspondence and interviews to be in favor of punishing statutory rape and decreasing teen pregnancy. As noted, many moderates and liberals would tend to support prosecuting coercive relationships; particularly those involving disadvantaged young people. The legislation initially introduced, however, was made more conservative in subsequent drafts.

The bill itself, as well as virtually every one of the hundreds of pieces of correspondence about it, contains the AGI teen pregnancy statistics and claims that California has the highest teen pregnancy rate and teen birthrate in the nation. It also points to statutory rape as the direct cause of teen pregnancy.

But note the statistics cited here. First, the teen pregnancy rate and teen birthrate are not the same. As noted, the teen birthrate is much lower than the teen pregnancy rate due to the high percentage of middle- to upper-income teenage females who have abortions, as well as miscarriages and other such incidents among all teens. The teen pregnancy rate in California was 149 per 1,000 but the teen birthrate was 62.6 per 1,000 (39.2 among 15–17-year-olds). Recall also that the teen birthrate was highest in the 1950s–1960s, almost double these rates. Note also that the literature cites the teen birthrate per 1,000 rather than births to teen mothers as a percentage of all births. The teen birthrate itself does not mean much, because in terms of demographics it could just be part of a larger overall birthrate to mothers of all ages. Births to teen mothers as a percentage of all births is the more pertinent statistic, but was not cited in the act or any of its supplementary material. California does have the highest teen birthrate, but also has a higher overall birthrate. It does not have nearly the highest percentage of births to teen mothers. In California, births to teen mothers as a percentage of all births was 12.0%. Compare Massachusetts' teen births as a percentage of all births at 7.3%, Georgia's at 15.9%, and Mississippi's at 21.3% (Statistical Abstract 1998, table 103; DHHS News "Teen Birth Rates Down in All States," 30 April 1998).

LEGISLATIVE RESPONSE: ATTEMPT 1   The first draft of Caldera's Teenage Pregnancy Prevention Act began:

> The Legislature finds and declares all of the following:
>   1) Statutory rape of teenagers in this state is resulting in the nation's highest teenage pregnancy and birth rate. . . . Sixty-six percent of the fathers of those children were adult males.
>   2) Society can no longer ignore this epidemic. . . . Adult males must be held accountable for their conduct.[27]

These findings were changed after the Committee on Public Safety reviewed the bill in March and sent it back to Caldera to be strengthened—for the link between statutory rape and teen pregnancy and the prosecutorial solution to be made more clear.[28]

Caldera amended the bill and it was read again (additions are in italics):

This act shall be known and may be cited as the Teenage Pregnancy Prevention Act of 1995. . . .

The Legislature finds and declares all of the following:

1) *Illicit sexual activity between adult males and teenage or younger girls* in this state is resulting in the nation's highest teenage pregnancy and birth rate in the nation. . . . *Many of these adult males are repeat offenders who have fathered more than one child by different teenage mothers, yet accept little or no responsibility for their actions or for the support of their children.*

2) Society can no longer ignore *the disregard of statutory rape laws and the consequent increase in teenage pregnancies.* . . . Adult males *who impregnate minor girls* must be held accountable for their conduct.[29]

The amended bill thus created a new crime, and would fund "Underage Sex Offense Units" to prosecute it: statutory rape by a male resulting in the pregnancy of a female under 18.

As of 1993, statutory rape in California has been defined as an adult (18 or older) of either sex having intercourse with a minor (under 18) of either sex.[30] Within a three-year age span, the crime was a misdemeanor although still punishable by jail time. Caldera's April 1995 amendment to this part read "An adult who impregnates a minor in violation of this subdivision shall be punished by imprisonment in a county jail for not less than six months or by imprisonment in the state prison for not more than two years." Outside the three-year span was a "wobbler," either a misdemeanor or a felony. The amendment for that subdivision extended the punishment, in cases in which the female were pregnant, to county jail for six months to one year, or state prison for no more than five years. The third part of the law concerns a teen under 16 and an adult of at least 21; this was also a wobbler. If the female were pregnant, read the amendment, the state prison term for the offense was to be extended to three, four, or five years. Further, the amendment added a provision for "repeat offenders": A second conviction for impregnating a minor would result in an automatic 10-year term in state prison.

Finally, the April 1995 amendment added civil penalties of varying amounts:

a) An adult who impregnates a minor less than 2 years younger than the adult is liable for a civil penalty not to exceed one thousand dollars ($1,000).
b) An adult who impregnates a minor at least 2 years younger than the adult is liable for a civil penalty not to exceed two thousand dollars ($2,000).
c) An adult who impregnates a minor at least 3 years younger than the adult is liable for a civil penalty not to exceed ten thousand dollars ($10,000).
d) An adult over the age of 21 years who impregnates a minor under 16 years of age is liable for a civil penalty not to exceed twenty-five thousand dollars ($25,000).

This money, after subtracting costs of prosecution for which the offender would also be liable if the district attorney chose to pursue it, was to be de posited in a new "Underage Pregnancy Prevention Fund" in the State Treasury. The money would be appropriated by the legislature to prevent pregnancy in some unspecfied way.

The Democrat-controlled Committee on Public Safety held hearings on the revised bill two weeks later. They had three basic criticisms: "This measure seems to only attack one part of the problem. Should teen mothers also face a civil penalty?" This would be an interesting question, if the intent of the law were about age and not about gender. But it missed the bill sponsor's point. Those arguing for further enforcement of statutory rape laws targeting predatory men were not looking to punish those whom they saw as exploited and manipulated young females. The second criticism was to question if the penalty should only be imposed after the live birth, because "it would seem that proof problems may arise unless a blood test was performed." As a corollary, they were unsure whether Caldera intended pregnancies ending in abortions to be prosecutable. Third, the committee noted, teens might not report the father of the child for fear of reprisal. Here then is the recognition of the potentially exploitative relationship, but with skepticism on whether cases would really be prosecuted. The committee thus far was unconvinced by the merits of the bill, and heard testimony from organized groups.

OUTSIDE SUPPORT AND OPPOSITION   The conservative religious Committee on Moral Concerns expressed support for the bill. Recall that this group had opposed both age-span provisions and gender-neutral language. In this case, they did not mince words about teen pregnancy:

The most serious problems facing society today are the result of unmarried teenage sexual activity. Teen parenthood, single parent households, high school dropout rates, sexually transmitted diseases including HIV, welfare dependency, poverty, youth gangs, and abortion are all caused primarily by minors having unlawful sexual intercourse. (letter, 10 April 1995)

The links here were explicit. The director of the committee characterized renewed enforcement of statutory rape laws as being the "single greatest deterrent government can offer" to stopping the "roughly two-thirds of the males who father a child out of wedlock with teenage girls [who] are over 20 years old." This is the AGI statistic, and is virtually the language that Caldera incorporated into the amendment. Other support came from the Junior Leagues of California, from Attorney General Dan Lungren who wrote to the Committee on behalf of the bill, and from editorial pages in California newspapers. An example, 'These adults take advantage of impressionable young girls and leave taxpayers to pick up the ever-increasing tab for child support. . . . Putting the heat on these young offenders [through Caldera's bill] should make many of them think twice before they prey on young girls" ("Put the Heat on Predators" 1995).

The American Civil Liberties Union (ACLU) and the California Attorneys for Criminal Justice were opposed. The ACLU was concerned mostly with privacy: that the poor in particular would be subject to invasive questioning and potential punishment over the very personal matters of sexuality and reproduction. "Creating sex patrols to investigate and prosecute 18 and 19 year old young men for having consensual sex with their 17 year old girl friends is not on our support list. [This bill] raises the specter, if not the reality, of the sex police snooping into the private lives of young people" (letter, 10 April 1995). The California Attorneys for Criminal Justice, a relatively liberal grouping of legal practitioners, found the link between statutory rape prosecutions and teen pregnancy rates spurious and were concerned that the bill would backfire: "Criminal prosecution of men who father children by teenage mothers may be counterproductive, giving these men every incentive to deny paternity, and if they are convicted and jailed or imprisoned, making it nearly impossible for them to contribute to support their children" (letter, 10 April 1995). This criticism cut to the heart of the intent of the bill: making men psychologically and financially responsible for the pregnancy.

The clear ideological split between the groups supporting and those opposing evidently had an effect on the committee. The groups on the Right, with more of a working relationship with the Republican Party, were for the bill; those on the Left, with more of a working relationship with the Democratic Party, were against the bill. The measure failed the motion to pass out of Public Safety and be referred to the Committee on Appropriations. In the committee of eight, the vote was 4 to 1, with three people absent or abstaining (Public Safety Committee, 18 April 1995). The split was even between the parties, with Republicans in favor. In short, the Democrats on the Committee did not support the bill and killed it.

LEGISLATIVE RESPONSE: ATTEMPT 2   The bill made a comeback in the beginning of 1996, for two reasons. First, elections brought more Republicans into the legislature. Second, as one source noted, "[Governor] Wilson was able to act independently of the Caldera legislation" (Jacobs 1996). The governor continued to campaign against teen pregnancy throughout the summer, fall, and winter of 1995.

In June 1995, Governor Wilson hosted a "Focus on Fathers Summit" that he had called for in his State of the State Address "as a way to examine the growing number of fatherless families. Studies indicate that children without fathers are more inclined toward violence, suicide, school failure, teenage pregnancy, divorce, and other problems" (Wilkie 1995). Enforcing statutory rape was one of the topics taken up at the meeting. Summit panelists noted, "A driving force behind the rise in juvenile crime . . . is father absence and adult men fathering children of teenage girls."[31] In response, the governor proposed funding to enforce statutory rape laws, particularly in those counties with the highest rates of teen pregnancy.[32]

In August, Wilson announced his new budget, which included $12 million to reduce teen pregnancies through more aggressive enforcement of statutory rape laws and a media campaign. It also cut Aid to Families with Dependent Children payments from between 4.9% to 9.8% depending on one's location in the state (Mendel 1995). This was part of Wilson's urging the enforcement of statutory rape laws and limiting payments to teen mothers as a dual-pronged approach to combat teen pregnancy (Lesher 1996).

In the fall, he announced the "Statutory Rape Vertical Prosecution Program," part of California's TANF plan as submitted to the federal government under the PRWORA. It allotted $2.4 million of the $12 million (and an additional $6 million for the following year) for extra lawyers who would work exclusively on statutory rape cases and remain on the same case from beginning to end. This, in theory, would result in more convictions as prosecutors would get to know the people involved in the case. The rest of the money was to go to the media campaign, and be spent on various types of advertising, including billboards such as the ones shown in figure 4.1. This campaign was in some sense a co-opting move by Wilson, incorporating Caldera's ideas as well as those of the Senate leader, Democrat Bill Lockyer, who had introduced a bill on allotting money to public service announcements and billboards that would send a message about teen pregnancy. Figure 4.1 displays two such billboards: one gender-neutral and one not.

The money for the prosecutions was released in December 1995; at the same time, Wilson announced he would end his administration's three-year-old

FIGURE 4.1   Billboards in English and Spanish from California's
Partnership for Responsible Parenting Initiative

Source: Photographs taken by the author, San Francisco, CA, November 1997. Note that the billboards are sponsored by the California Department of Health Services, Partnership for Responsible Parenting—the Governor's Initiative.

"Education Now and Babies Later" counseling and education program because it had failed to stem the rates of teen pregnancy (Perry 1996). The thrust of these three initiatives here, as it would be on the federal level, seems both contradictory and punitive. While policymakers cited concern for female victims of statutory rape as the reason for the stepped-up prosecutions, they curtailed financial and psychological assistance for that same group of young women.

Finally, Wilson's January 1996 State of the State Address called for a "re-alignment of the state's focus, turning from an economy that is gaining steam to teen pregnancy—"a social problem considered so dangerous that it threatens every facet of life in California, from schools and police departments to the resources available for environmental and transportation departments . . . [creating] a perceptible degradation in the state's quality of life" (Lesher 1996). Bill Lockyer agreed, "This is the most basic, fundamental social problem of our day. We have got to change that behavior." This bipartisan agreement seemed to herald a renewed effort to legislate measures that might stem the tide of teen pregnancy. Indeed, a news release from Caldera's office stated, "Both President Clinton, and more recently Governor Wilson in his State of the State Address . . . have focused on teen pregnancy and the need to strengthen statutory rape laws."[33]

Taking up the language of Caldera's last amendment, Wilson predicted in his address that the Statutory Rape Vertical Prosecution Program would "send a loud message that there will be serious consequences for adult men who impregnate minors, thereby creating a significant deterrent effect." Clearly, the governor played an enormous role in the push for this policy. Caldera had been unable to get it passed by himself, and had virtually no support from his own Democratic Party. Recall, though, that Republicans on the Committee on Public Safety had voted in favor of his bill.

COMMITTEE HEARINGS   The same week as the State of the State Address, the Caldera bill was reconsidered in the Committee on Public Safety in which it had died the year before. But elections had produced a much different assembly: "In an indication of how the Assembly has changed since Republicans seized control this month, the bill sailed through the committee" (Jordan 1996). While the ACLU and then Planned Parenthood of California forcefully opposed the bill, the makeup of the committee had changed. The same four Republicans who had voted yes the first time voted yes once again, but they were joined by a fifth new member (Jan Goldsmith), which made the vote 5 to 3. The bill passed 15 to 3 in the Committee on Appropriations on January 24, passed 62 to 11 on the assembly floor the following week (6 of the 11 were the same who voted against in Public Safety and in Appropriations; all 11 were Democrats), and was moved on to the senate.

The Senate Committee on Criminal Procedure was assigned the bill and held hearings in May 1996. The Democrat-led committee recommended some amendments before it would vote. First, the committee felt that the fines were disproportionately high given the conduct, and that they would discriminate based on the income of the perpetrator. Caldera reduced them.[34] Second, the senators were concerned with the mandated dual penalty of both prison time and a fine. They therefore required some discretion: that the penalty be either jail time or a fine or both jail and a fine. Third, they required that civil penalties in the amounts of the April 1995 amendment be imposed in lieu of criminal prosecution. In other words, the amendments forced by Criminal Procedure allowed perpetrators to be fined rather than serve any jail time at all, and to be fined rather than be prosecuted at all.

OUTSIDE OPPOSITION   Again, the ACLU opposed the bill. They put forth the following concern:

> Young women may feel that they must have illegal abortions in order to protect their partners from misdemeanor or felony prosecutions . . . [and] if minor women know that their partners will be imprisoned if they become pregnant, they may be reluctant or afraid to get the health care they need to ensure that they and their babies are healthy. (letter, 8 May 1996)

Working with the American College of Obstetricians and Gynecologists (ACOG) and with Planned Parenthood, representatives from the ACLU met with one of Caldera's aides on May 1, 1996, to try to incorporate their concerns. They wanted to add language guaranteeing the confidentiality of information disclosed to health care providers. As ACOG put it, "This makes us very nervous as patient physician confidentiality is both crucial to and the center of the medical relationship . . . the linking of incarceration to prenatal care is literally the death of that care" (letter, 6 May 1996). The language was not added, and all three groups remained opposed for the reasons previously stated. Also opposed were California Attorneys for Criminal Justice (as they were the first time around); Children Now, an advocacy group for issues concerning minors; and the National Center for Youth Law. The last noted that females in nonconsensual relationships not only might be deterred from prenatal care, but also may be hesitant to seek a child support order for fear of reprisal from the father or for fear of losing whatever informal financial support she may have from him (letter, 13 May 1996). All six of the groups in opposition, in short, argued that the female in each case would be more burdened than the male, with various deleterious consequences for her and her child, and that prosecutions would disproportionately target the poor.

Despite the arguments of those opposed, the bill passed out of the committee 4 to 1 with two abstentions after the amendments mandated by the committee itself were made. But once the bill reached the floor, the Senate Democrats would attempt to change its intent.

THE SENATE FLOOR   In the Democrat-controlled senate in August, numerous revisions were mandated for passage. The penalty for repeat offenses was removed entirely, partly over concern about whether conviction for statutory rape would count as a "Three Strikes and You're Out" offense, sending a person found guilty of three such offenses to jail for life. The author was also asked to change the fines again, and raised them back to or beyond the original levels he had sought. Due to the outside objections about the varying income levels of the perpetrators, the fines were no longer mandatory, nor were they to be given in lieu of prosecution. Instead, they "may be imposed" as an additional penalty.[35] As noted in reviewing the case studies vis-à-vis the other two sets of amendments to statutory rape laws, here is compromise on a morality policy while others in the field would predict there would be none.

Perhaps most important, senate Democrats changed the wording of the bill entirely: "Strike out 'impregnates'" (AB 1490 as amended in Senate, 28 May 1996). One more round of testimonies in opposition focused on the fact that the bill seemed to be making sexual intercourse resulting in pregnancy a more serious crime than perhaps coercive sexual intercourse itself. While minor females do not have a constitutional right to engage in sexual intercourse if they are unmarried, they do in theory have a constitutional right to become pregnant, and such a bill would infringe on that right. The California Regional Family Planning Council, for instance, had sent out to all parties affiliated with them an "Action Alert," with the goal of pushing people into faxing letters of opposition to Caldera and senators telling them to "raise the current penalties for statutory rape instead of creating the crime of impregnation of a minor" (letter, 2 August 1996). Planned Parenthood, the ACLU, the National Council of Jewish Women, and the Los Angeles Free Clinic echoed this.[36]

The former language of the bill is in strikethrough, and the revised language in italics, "An adult who ~~impregnates~~ *engages in an act of unlawful sexual intercourse with* a minor."[37] The intent of the original bill to create a crime of impregnation of a minor, and the much more severe form in which it was passed by the Republican-controlled assembly, was deleted. Democrats clearly took into consideration the opposition of more liberal groups that objected to this construction of the crime.

After that amendment was made, Planned Parenthood contacted Caldera to say that they would revise their position from "opposed" to "neutral."[38] Again, here is compromise because of the input of those uncomfortable with the language of impregnation and how it would be prosecuted. Yet the bill was still titled, and passed as, the Teenage Pregnancy Prevention Act; its findings still linked statutory rape and teen pregnancy.

The amended bill passed unanimously in the senate and was concurred upon by the assembly on the last night of session by a vote of 45 to 8, with 25 people—including Louis Caldera—either absent or abstaining. He later wrote to the assemblyman who had pushed it through, "Thank you very much for jockeying AB 1490 for me. I understand it took quite a bit of work for you to get it to clear the floor. I knew I left it in the right hands; it meant a lot to me that you did this for me. I owe you one!"[39] The governor signed the bill on September 22, 1996.

THE OUTCOME   Since that time, California has been prosecuting many more statutory rape cases than before. The majority of such cases stem from mandatory reporting. Note, though, that the funding for these prosecutions is allotted by the governor's Statutory Rape Vertical Prosecution Program, not by the legislature's Teenage Pregnancy Prevention Act. Without the gubernatorial mandate and its attendant funding, it is possible that prosecutions in California would have gone on as before and not concentrated on pregnancy at all.

Partisanship clearly mattered to the debate over and passage of this bill in California. In general, the partisan arguments mirrored those of outside groups on respective sides of the political spectrum. Democrats forced the removal of language offensive to, for instance, Planned Parenthood and the ACLU; Republicans incorporated language favored by the Committee on Moral Concerns and the Junior Leagues of California. The role of the governor was crucial. Governor Wilson took the lead in promoting the link between statutory rape and teen pregnancy, and acted independently from the legislation being debated while also forcing the issue in the legislature. His executive program retains the language of targeting statutory rape prosecutions at males who impregnate females; the final Teenage Pregnancy Prevention Act passed by the legislature did not although it did allow for potential civil penalties. In all, the measure was one basically debated by organized groups and insider elites over the course of more than 18 months, and the signed bill represented some compromise between groups while generally being more supported by Republicans than by Democrats.

Case 2: Georgia

BACKGROUND   January 1996 in Georgia, as in California, was when the governor attempted to kick off a statewide campaign against teen pregnancy, that linked statutory rape and a high teen pregnancy rate. Indeed, elites in both states asserted in interviews, press releases, and preambles to legislation that they had the highest teen pregnancy rate in the nation, which is not quite accurate in either case. Again, one should note that the teen pregnancy rate and teen birthrate are not the same; the latter is much lower than the former due to the high percentage of middle- to upper-income teen females who elect to have abortions, as well as miscarriages and other such incidents among all teens. For instance, the teenage pregnancy rate in California cited in the Teenage Pregnancy Prevention Act is 149 per 1,000 but the teenage birthrate was 62.6 per 1,000 (39.2 among 15–17-year-olds). Births to teen mothers as a percentage of all births was 12.0%.

In Georgia, the "teen" pregnancy rate in 1996 was about 100, an undercount because it included 10–19-year-olds rather than 15–19-year-olds. Its teen birthrate was 68.2 per 1,000 (45.4 among 15–17-year-olds), and births to teen mothers as a percentage of all births was 15.9%. Recall as points of comparison, Massachusetts' teen births as a percentage of all births was 7.3%, Mississippi's teen births as a percentage of all births was 21.3% (Statistical Abstract 1998, Table 103; DHHS News "Teen Birth Rates Down in All States," 30 April 1998). So although both Georgia and California asserted that they had the highest teen pregnancy rates in the nation, there are a number of ways in which to examine births to teens. But for the purposes of this analysis, it is enough to assume that the parties involved believed, or wanted the public to believe, that the teen pregnancy rate was very high, and a costly phenomenon out of control.[40]

In Georgia, Democratic Governor Zell Miller's office drafted a bill in January 1996 that would require a mandatory 10–20 years in prison for adults of at least 21 who had sexual intercourse with those under 16; it also mandated the same sentence if the teen was under 14, regardless of the perpetrator's age. The following week began the Georgia Campaign for Adolescent Pregnancy, funded by Ted Turner's Turner Foundation. The foundation conducted a statewide poll the week before the opening of the campaign, and found that an overwhelming 89% of Georgians considered teen pregnancy a "very important" problem, and an additional 7% considered it "somewhat important" (McKenna 1996).

In conjunction with the campaign, the *Atlanta Journal-Constitution* began a weeklong in-depth series on teen pregnancy, covering about two full pages each day. The editors introduced the series:

> Georgia is leading the nation in the number of teens having babies. . . .
>
> Many of [the males] aren't boys, they're young adults who've committed statutory rape. We need to enforce the laws and start making examples of these young men. Others need to get a job and be forced to support their children.
>
> Years ago broad-shouldered daddies stood watch on front porches to protect young daughters from adolescent boys. Today, many fathers are absent, and society has put in place its own mechanisms to discourage boys.
>
> Society certainly has a strong incentive. Taxpayers pay the huge medical bills of low birth weight babies born disproportionately to teens; we pay $25 billion a year in AFDC and related assistance to teen mothers and their babies, and we lose thousands of potentially productive citizens to a life of near-certain poverty. Teen sex is everybody's problem. We've got to deal with it. (16 January 1996)

   Miller made the keynote address at the opening meeting on January 19 as
a springboard to highlight the issue of statutory rape. His floor leader, Thurbert
Baker (D-Decatur) introduced the bill on January 25, 1996.[41]

   One of the *Atlanta Journal-Constitution* editorials praised Miller's bill to
strengthen statutory rape laws because "Georgia must be aggressive in enforcing statutory rape laws. At least half of the fathers of babies born to teenage
girls are adults aged 20 or older" (14 January 1996). This is the same type of figure used in California, again without noting that the majority of teen mothers
are 18 or 19. Indeed, while the California bill went though a dozen amendments, the findings section regarding adult males and teen females remained.
But in the Georgia bill, the authors in Miller's office attached no findings section and no title to the bill—the link between statutory rape and teen pregnancy remained verbal and was not inscribed into the law. The legislators did
not consider the thrust of the bill to be about teen pregnancy.[42]

LEGISLATIVE RESPONSE   A number of Georgia Democrats, led by Special Judiciary
Committee Chair Billy Randall (D-Macon) were concerned about the possibility of two young teens engaged in sexual activity, and having to punish the male
with 10 years in jail: "I have no problem whatsoever with sticking it to a grown
man who takes advantage of a child. But taking a 14-year-old boy who has sex
with a 14-year-old girl and sending him to prison is wrong" (*Atlanta Journal-
Constitution*, 25 January 1996). The *Atlanta Journal-Constitution*, also concerned with
such an outcome, noted that more than one in four Georgia teens has engaged
in sexual activity by the age of 13 and that the "Bible Belt" location of the state
was causing parents to react in disbelief and not talk to their children about sex
(14 and 25 January 1996). Under pressure from Randall in particular, who had
lined up close to a majority of Democrats against the bill, the provision regarding those under 14 was omitted by the authors in the first week of February
1996. The bill then passed the assembly with 160 ayes and 10 nays; the final bill
was not passed by both houses until April, at which point it was bundled with
the removal of the marital exemption in rape and sodomy laws to ensure passage
of the latter.

   Recall that the 1995 amendments to Georgia's statutory rape law (see
chapters 2 and 3) had implemented a three-year age span that allowed for those
within the span to be prosecuted for a misdemeanor at the discretion of the
court. This was done mostly as a compromise with the state's religious conservatives who did not want an age-span provision and wanted to retain the ability to prosecute male teens. With one particularly powerful Christian Coalition
member absent from the state senate in 1996, the word *discretion* was removed
and activity within the three-year age span became a misdemeanor.[43] From con-
cept to passage, the act moved quickly through the Democrat-controlled legislature. It is important to note the absence of this representative during the final

passage of this bill. When asked by whom the linkage between statutory rape and teen pregnancy was being made, one Georgian was succinct: "The Religious Right."[44] With that presence missing from the proceedings, there was no pressure to make the link explicit as it had been in California.

Thus, the Georgia bill was passed and signed in the spring, while the California bill was not passed and signed until early fall. This is significant because it was over the summer of 1996 that the PRWORA overhauling welfare became law. It was the PRWORA that urged connections between teen pregnancy and statutory rape, required states to submit plans on how they would prosecute statutory rape, and offered financial incentives for reducing the rates of teen pregnancy and abortion.

A second difference between the two states lies in the way in which the bills were conceptualized and on what terms they were considered. Even in its final incarnation, the California bill in its findings explicitly linked statutory rape prosecutions to the rate of teen pregnancy in California. The Georgia bill was passed with no findings section and no title, unlike the previous bill that had overhauled the statutory rape law, the Child Protection Act of 1995. Nowhere in the bill was pregnancy mentioned, even in its first draft. And while initially considered in isolation, in April it was lumped in with the removal of the marital exemption in forcible rape and sodomy cases. True, the passage of the bill was contemporaneous with Georgia's campaign against teen pregnancy and linked by the governor and media coverage as a potential tool with which to punish adult males who were responsible for much teen pregnancy. But the links were not inscribed in the law or in the executive branch or among prosecutors as they were in California. In Georgia, then, the bill was more about punishing one class of perpetrators in particular—those at least six years older than the victims, which is what one might expect from a Democrat-led legislature.

The following January, Miller announced that teen pregnancy would be the centerpiece of welfare reform in Georgia, and called for at least $5 million for measures targeting prevention such as abstinence programs, changes in sex education, and family planning clinics (McKenna 1996). But although this was the point at which a number of states drew up "TANF plans" for the federal government as to how they would combat teen pregnancy, the link was not made explicit between statutory rape prosecutions, teen pregnancy, and welfare dollars. While prosecutors in California were interviewed repeatedly and expressed support for what was seen as the governor's program, and while the number of statutory rape prosecutions increased tenfold due to reports from welfare authorities and from medical professionals, the opposite was true in Georgia. An Atlanta district attorney, who had worked on sex crimes for eight years prior to his election noted, "Some people were saying that if we were prosecuting [statutory rape cases] a lot more aggressively there would be fewer teenage pregnancies. [But] no one advised us to go out and carry that banner. There's no formal program in place."[45] That 96% of Georgians considered teen pregnancy an "important problem" apparently made little difference to policy adoption in the state. Public opinion had little effect on pushing policy adoption.

Conclusion

The adoption of pregnancy-prevention provisions appears much different at first from the amendments to statutory rape law previously investigated: age spans and gender-neutral language. For one, California adopted while Georgia did not. New Jersey did not even consider the measure. In the other two sets of changes to the laws, the two states had similar adoption patterns that seemed to point to the importance of the two commonalities in those states: Democratic legislatures and Christian Right influence. The two differ in that California residents were measured as much more liberal than those living in Georgia, that California had a Republican governor and Georgia a Democratic governor, and that feminist lobbyists were much more numerous in California than in Georgia although they were silent in both states.

For this policy adoption unlike the other two, California's assembly was Republican-led while Georgia's was Democrat-led. As noted, California's Teenage Pregnancy Prevention Act may not have made it out of committee were it not for Republican control. Conservative support for the prevention of teen pregnancy was evident in both states. The crucial difference is that in Georgia the most influential self-described Christian Right state senator left office just before the new statutory rape bill was debated; in California, outside Christian groups were strongly supportive and were consulted and thanked by the bill's author.

Note though, that once the bill in California reached the Democrat-controlled senate, it was changed completely. The bill's original intent was basically gutted, as the language of impregnation was removed for passage. What the Democratic senate agreed to pass was a bill that noted the link between statutory rape and teen pregnancy. Its thrust was to allow prosecutors to impose civil penalties if they so decided. This is similar to the policy adoption in Georgia: It was a bill that imposed strong penalties for relationships in which there was a large age span, but prosecutors were given discretion as to whether the sentence is to be served or entirely probated. Partisanship in both states was key to the policy initiatives actually passed by the legislatures, regardless of the shouting. Whether partisanship was key to whether the other 48 states did or did not adopt this type of statutory rape law is taken up in the next section.

Modeling Policy Adoption

In this chapter, the tests are performed on a set of 167 cases of state-years. This includes all states from 1996 through 1999. Those states that did not adopt by 1999 are coded 0 on the dependent variable from 1996 through 1999.[46]

Table 4.1 shows the determinants of the adoption of pregnancy-prevention provisions in statutory rape laws. The results are clearly statistically insignificant. The party of the governor is the only variable that even approaches statistical significance at the .10 level. Is the problem that there are only 10 adopt-states and the period is only four years? In theory, that should make little difference to whether a clear pattern emerges unless some or all of these 10 states are exceptional cases. It is difficult to say what the results might have been for the tests in the other two chapters if I had conducted analyses of only the first four years and/or the first 10 adopt-states. Second, there are far fewer cases of state-years than in the other two chapters, which could also be skewing potential effects. Comparing adopt-states' measures of central tendency with those of nonadopters shows that they are quite similar with two exceptions: Adopt-states were more likely to have had Republican governors, and slightly more likely to have divided legislatures.

TABLE 4.1   States' Adoption of Pregnancy-Prevention Provisions

Independent Variables	Expected Direction	Coefficient	Standard Error	Coefficient/ Standard Error	Change in Probability
GROUP					
NOW	−	.00590	.02043	.28862	.00148
Christian Right Influence	+	.05004	.29045	.17230	.01251
ELITE					
Party of the Governor	+	.48744	.42980	1.13410	.11950
Party Control of State Legislature	−	−.06072	.43288	−.14028	.01518
Electoral Competition	+	−.01169	.03543	−.32994	.00292
PUBLIC OPINION					
Citizen Ideology	−	.27950	.58807	.47529	.06942

Number of cases: 167
Number of y = 1: 10
Person Goodness-of-Fit Chi-Square: 160.531
Note: The dependent variable is coded 1 if the state adopted in a given year, 0 if it did not.

Interest groups were present in the debate over this legislation and in California seemed to have shaped that debate to some extent. As the model very weakly indicated, the party of the governor appeared to be a strong indicator of policy adoption. Party control of the legislature was a factor as well. Both governors led the charge toward linking statutory rape and teen pregnancy; both proposed new funding for programs to deter teen pregnancies. But in Georgia, Democrat Zell Miller and his floor leader were unable to convince fellow party members of the necessity for the bill. The seemingly lengthy sentence for the new conception of the crime can be probated; that is, if one is convicted with a 10–20-year sentence as the law demands, one can serve that entire sentence on probation.[47] Miller did not set up a program from the governor's office; the matter was dropped. In California on the other hand, Republican Governor Wilson did garner support from members of his own party within the legislature. While the author of the bill was a moderate Democrat, he solicited Wilson's support as well as the support of Republicans in the assembly. And in perhaps the strongest indication of the influence of the executive, those prosecuting in California are funded by the Governor's Statutory Rape Vertical Prosecution Program—not by the legislature's Teenage Pregnancy Prevention Act. Without this funding and this gubernatorial mandate, it is possible that prosecutions in California would have gone on as before and not concentrated on pregnancy at all.

Beyond Policy Adoption: Enforcing the Laws

As statutory rape laws are meant to punish sexual activity with a person under the age of consent, whether a female becomes pregnant from such an encounter should theoretically be of no importance—the crime rests on the female's incapacity, given her age, to give legal consent to sex. But pregnancy proves that the sexual activity occurred, even if one or both parties deny it. Statutory rape is notoriously difficult to prosecute because although the sexual activity that falls under it is criminalized, much of it involving adolescents is consensual. Parents usually bring the cases, and teens usually refuse to testify against their sex partners. The 10 states that have revised their laws to target pregnancies generally require that health care providers, or state welfare authorities, report illegal sexual activity to law enforcement officials. So targeting teens who apply for public assistance, for instance, removes the problem of how to prosecute the crime. The female's pregnancy corroborates that she had sex, and parents do not have to get involved because state welfare authorities report the case to the district attorney's office. What do these cases look like?

Fifteen-year-old DeAnna became pregnant, and in her fifth month went to apply for Medicaid. Her boyfriend, 22, was immediately arrested for statutory rape. He noted that he was facing a felony count which would require him to register as a sex offender if convicted: "'If I get convicted, I'm not supposed to have contact with the 'victim,' he says, holding [his girlfriend's] hand . . . he notes that, if convicted, he could be banned from many places where kids congregate—restaurants, parks, the zoo. 'It's hard to see what kind of father I can be.'" That, said the prosecutor, was not the point. "Are they sex offenders? In the sense that they like younger girls, yes" (Hardy 1996). The sheriff commented:

> What kind of message would we send if we tolerated sex between children? We would be saying, "We condone your promiscuousness, and if you get pregnant and you're 14 years old, the citizens will pay for your mistake." That is the wrong message to send. I believe 99 percent of the citizens [here] do not condone sexual activity between kids under 18. Personally, I would say 99 percent of the citizens do not condone sexual activity among unmarried people, period. There are high moral standards [here]. (Goldberg 1997)

Kevin, 18, was convicted at the felony level for statutory rape for having sex with his fiancée, Stephanie, 15. They had decided to get married after discovering she was pregnant, and he had dropped out of school to work full time in order to have health insurance for them and for the baby. His punishment included two years' probation, 100 hours of community service, counseling and parenting classes, and finishing high school or getting an equivalency degree. He also was barred from seeing the victim and had to register as a sex offender. Stephanie moved to Denver to live with relatives. When he went to trial, she read into the court record, "Thanks to the court system, I have lost the love of my life and the father of my unborn baby" (Elton 1997).

Seventeen-year-old Carrie thought she was in love with her 31-year-old religion teacher. When she got pregnant, he told her to have an abortion; instead, she tried to kill herself. At first she did not want to speak to the detective who visited her in the hospital, but then, "I loved him as much as possible . . . even though it was a very sick, twisted, manipulative kind of love. . . . I decided I had to stop him and everybody else who does this" (Gorman 2000). He went to prison.

When she was four months pregnant, 15-year-old Shontay went to the child care center at her school. Based on her paperwork, the school notified detectives, who went to Shontay's house to question her. The 22-year-old father, who was also violating his parole for robbery when engaging in sex with a minor, was sentenced to 32 months in prison. Although no longer in a relationship with the father, she nonetheless forbade him from being named in the article and said, "It's not like he forced me. . . . They [the prosecutors] ruin people's lives" (Rother 2000).

The majority of cases in California stem from reporting from medical professionals and public assistance authorities; others are reported by schools and parents. Some of the relationships are clearly coercive; others questionable; and still a third group are committed and loving. Pregnancy can prove that sexual intercourse occurred even if a teen refuses to testify. Given this, who is incarcerated depends greatly on the discretion of the local prosecutor and judge. Because the law's wording essentializes females as prey, female teens cannot stop a prosecution even if they would like to. How the female feels about her case seems to depend on how she perceives the message she is told by a victim advocate: "You girls are more easily controlled at this age . . . these guys are manipulative" (quoted in Gorman 2000). Some are resistant to this if not angered; others begin to view their relationships differently and feel used. Some cooperate; others are horrified that their partner may have to register as a sex offender.

In the 45 months after California's Statutory Rape Vertical Prosecution Program (SRVP) was put into place, 8,205 cases had been filed and 6,190 convictions obtained—a rate of 72% (Partnership for Responsible Parenting; figures from 30 June 1999). This does not reflect how many cases were reported, but based on figures for the first two years, it appears that about half of reported cases get filed. Prosecutors have concentrated most heavily on cases in which the victim was about 14–15 and the perpetrator 20 or older. However, data on the births to teen mothers suggests that such prosecutions would have little effect on deterring such births. In 1998 for instance, 59,207 California teens gave birth: 36,511 (61.7%) were 18–19; 21,630 (36.5%) were 15–17; and 1,066 (1.8%) were 10–14 (Partnership for Responsible Parenting 2000; percentages calculated by the author). Of the fathers, 10.3% were under 18, 25.6% were 18–19, and 64.2% were 20 or over. The numbers are broken down no further for those in the last group; nor is their any indication of which males were in relationships with which females. Two-thirds of these mothers were not under California's age of consent (18, as in several other states). These numbers are little different from the Urban Institute's look at the AGI statistics, finding that most teenage births are to older teens with not-so-much-older partners. Given this, it is difficult to see any direct correlation between who is targeted by California's SRVP Program and who is giving birth as a teenager.

Yet the Partnership for Responsible Parenting—Governor Wilson's four-pronged initiative against statutory rape—claimed a tremendous amount of the credit for a lower teen birthrate in California, through the SRVP Program and the public outreach campaign. Note though that over this period, birthrates for all ages decreased throughout the country. California was not unique. The outreach campaign had a $38.3 million budget for 41 months. Billboards all over California read "Sex with a minor is a major crime" in Spanish and English. The Partnership noted proudly that it conducted "both mainstream and ethnic outreach," implying that non-Hispanics are mainstream. Indeed, the Latino population in California was repeatedly noted to be a persistent problem vis-à-vis teen pregnancy rates, one constructed as "cultural" and thus perhaps a more racialized threat to the "American" family and nation. Here, the female would be the passive victim not only because of her gender but because of her ethnicity as well—she is seen as doubly incapable of autonomous choice (Volpp 2000: 108, 113). Governor Wilson may have been speaking to this when he announced, "It's not macho to get a teenager pregnant. But if you lack the decency to understand that yourself, we'll give you a year to think about it in the county jail" (quoted in Goldberg 1997).

As one might expect after seeing the repeated linkages at both the federal and state levels, information on statutory rape and teen pregnancy posted on the Partnership's Web site (www.responsibleparenting.org) is followed by statistics on how much California spends on public assistance and medi-Cal each year; how many of the state's births are out of wedlock; how families raised without a father are more at risk for a variety of psychological, economic, and often violent problems; how juvenile crime threatens Californians "each day"; and how teen mothers have a high risk of welfare dependency. The message is clear and consistent: Prosecuting statutory rape will stem the tide of teen pregnancy, an epidemic that threatens not only our moral sensibilities but also our pocketbooks and sense of personal safety.

Conclusions

Statutory rape prosecutions will probably not deter adolescent sexuality, nor end teen pregnancy or out-of-wedlock births, nor reduce the welfare rolls, nor make any impact on poverty. The causes of and contributing factors toward adolescent sexual activity, let alone poverty, are unaddressed by punitive legal measures. Yet these measures are in place because moral entrepreneurs defined adolescent sexuality and childbearing as threats to American moral and economic values, linked those activities to statutory rape and welfare dependency, and used statistics to bolster their claims. This construction of the threat was circulated (not necessarily in a top-down fashion) and stylized by the media, who must depend on others for information, and on sensation for profit. Policymakers, eager to claim credit, responded to calls for action with new laws and the invigoration of old ones. Finally, the "epidemic's" daily presence has seemed to fade away while its implementation goes on quietly, perhaps violating some civil rights of its target groups in the process.

While the PRWORA and California's SRVP Program have at their cores an overhaul of the financial distribution of public assistance and a stronger program for punishing statutory rape, respectively, they are both just as much about fighting off perceived threats—wrought by broad-scale changes particularly since the 1960s—to the economic, political, social, cultural, and moral order. Nonmarital adolescent sexuality, particularly when engaged in by the impoverished and particularly when resulting in out-of-wedlock births, has been constructed as the antithesis to this order and therefore must be contained.

With the focus on nonmarital sexuality itself, there is no discussion of broader structural problems. Debate centered on the moral limits debate on persistent inequalities of gender, race, class, and sexuality.[48] Not only does the construction of this particular moral panic about the childbearing of impoverished teens serve conservative interests vis-à-vis the regulation of nonmarital sexual activity and the dismantling of the welfare state, but it also casts anyone who differs with such a narrative as antichild, antimarriage, and anti-American. Thus, it undermines the production of counternarratives and disables any debate on the broader and more complex causes of poverty (and its gendered character), sexuality and sexual violence, and discriminatory regulatory practices.

Conclusion

The Politics of Statutory Rape Laws

This work has sought to explore how and why this particular area of sexuality—unmarried adolescent sex—has been constructed over the past 100 years as an object of social concern and a target of social control. Often, policy entrepreneurs have collapsed the categories of child and adolescent into the emotionally resonant image of a very young innocent forced into sexual activity, and have been able to link that activity to broader cultural, social, political, and economic dislocations.

For feminists, statutory rape laws were about protecting vulnerable young people, and young females, in particular, in an environment in which bright lines were still drawn between sex and rape with no continuum of coercion in between. But these same women recognized the patriarchal roots of the laws and their inscription of particular stereotypes of gender and sexuality. They sought to do away with such stereotypes through age spans which limited the number of victims to those whose relationships raised more of a presumption of coercion, and through gender-neutral language which was intended to undercut notions of gender difference and to protect all young people. But as Olsen (1984) noted, protecting women from individual abuse requires state regulation, and protecting them from that state regulation risks their exposure to individual abuse. Acknowledging difference can allow discrimination, but ignoring difference can leave women open to unacknowledged oppression (411).

For religious conservatives, statutory rape laws have served as a means by which to condemn premarital or nonmarital sexuality, and to punish homosexuality in another manner. In general, they subscribed to more traditional notions about gender—that the male is the aggressor and the female is the victim—as well as more traditional notions about sexuality—that it should take place within heterosexual marriage.

Despite these major differences, both of these groups were, at different times, instrumental in amending statutory rape laws. The implications for policies grounded in disparate constructions of gender and sexuality appear to be that policy implementation will be uneven. Indeed, the prosecutions under the laws, while definitely protective for some in unequal or manipulative relationships, have also shown themselves to be proscriptive and punitive toward unmarried sexuality that is consensual. As in the nineteenth century, law enforcement personnel charged with the day-to-day implementation of the laws may have ideas about their purposes that are different from those who advocated for them.

Constructions of the crime of statutory rape were presented by these groups as a gender-, race-, and class-neutral means of safeguarding young people, but they constructed only particular groups as being in need of state intervention. Sharing a common view of which adolescents required the most protection, they diverged significantly on the reasons why. In both the late nineteenth and late twentieth centuries, feminists sought to provide legal protection for females (and later, young males) whom they perceived to be the most disadvantaged due to race, ethnicity, and class, while conservatives were more concerned with controlling the sexuality and reproduction of those same groups.[1]

For instance, in the 1990s, a few feminists at first supported targeting the partners of pregnant teens in order to protect young women—generally non-white and non-middle-class—from exploitative sexual relationships in which they were left with a child but no emotional or financial support. But both religious and economic conservatives were at the forefront of this initiative, to send the message that the sexuality of impoverished, unmarried young people was both a moral and an economic affront to traditional American values and should be punished. In the 1970s, feminists argued for gender-neutral statutory rape laws so as to encompass young males as victims and to grant formal equality to females, making the crime one focused solely on age rather than on gender. Some conservatives were against the language because it would remove the presumption of the young female as the victim and implied that homosexual behavior that was not underage was not morally or legally wrong. But others liked the idea of gender-neutral laws as a new means by which to prosecute homosexuality, particularly as so many states were decriminalizing sodomy. Finally, most feminists were generally in favor of age spans because they would allow sex between similarly aged teens, presumably more likely to be consensual, to go unpunished. Some conservatives favored the notion so as to not punish young males too harshly for exploring their sexuality. But other feminists were concerned that an age span would leave some young women vulnerable to coercion or abuse from same-age partners; such relationships would no longer be prosecutable. Religious conservatives were not in favor of age spans, but because they wanted to retain the blanket prohibition against nonmarital adolescent sex to send a message that the proper place for sexual intercourse was solely within marriage.

In general, it was the interplay of these two sets of organized groups, coupled with legislator party affiliation, that seemed to have the most influence on changes made to statutory rape laws from the 1970s to the 1990s. This is not to suggest that policies are simply the mechanistic results of group pressure. Indeed, attention must be given to partisan lawmakers as well (Norrander and Wilcox 2001), and there is evidence that these lawmakers moderate the influence of groups (Wiggins, Hamm, and Bell 1992). A public official may choose to, but does not necessarily have to "pay close attention to what the public wants." On the other hand, a public official does have to pay close attention to what an organized, attentive, and active public wants—if he or she is to be re-elected. In the case of statutory rape, group influence coupled with partisanship appeared much more influential than did mass public opinion; NOW and other feminist groups as well as conservative Christian organizations were active and resourceful, and policymakers generally voted along party lines vis-à-vis their general alliances with these groups—Democrats with NOW, Republicans with Christian Right groups.

This finding is significant in that this study considers statutory rape a morality policy. While there are disagreements among morality policy researchers, perhaps due to the different types of questions each has asked, there appears to be a point of agreement on the influence of public opinion:

> The most strongly supported general conclusion in the morality policy literature is that policymakers are more responsible to citizen values on morality policy than on non-morality policy. These simple and salient policies on basic values create ideal conditions for democratic responsiveness. . . . Given the high salience and technical simplicity of morality policy, policymakers cannot rely on technical obfuscation and lack of interest to hide their actions from public view. They must pay close attention to what the public wants, be it out of a sense of democratic duty of electoral self interest. Whereas on typical non-salient and technical policy, there can be slippage between citizen values and public policy, on morality policy there is a much stronger and more direct correspondence. (Mooney 2001: 20)

I challenge this conclusion about the direct causal relationship between public opinion and policies that have a moral component. I do not dispute the strong effects found for correlation with public opinion; I do, however, argue that if public opinion has an effect on policy adoption and reinvention, that effect is indirect rather than direct and is channeled through organized interests.

Many of the strong correlative effects in the state politics field cannot and do not speak to causes of policy change. Indeed, in their review of the "state of state politics research" in 1995, Brace and Jewett wrote that the field is a fragmented one, slow to incorporate "widely accepted theoretical advances" in other fields. They observed, pointedly:

> The subfield would benefit from a unifying theoretical framework that could (1) integrate the various studies of state politics; (2) reconcile research concerning macro-level outcomes with theories and findings concerning micro-level behavior; and (3) capitalize on the unique comparative and contextual analytical strengths state politics research could embody. (644)

Through an empirically grounded comprehensive account of modern history of statutory rape laws, this research has sought to respond to each of these challenges. Rather than examining an amalgamation of discrete variables that would lead us to yet another specialized and nonrepeatable conclusion on what types of forces correlate with particular policy outcomes, I instead sought to bring broader theoretical insights employed in other fields of American politics into the state politics subfield. Rather than conducting one or two detailed case studies, or constructing only abstract models, I used both qualitative and quantitative methods to link everyday politics on the ground with aggregate patterns of policy outcomes and show that the two together can lead to complementary findings. And rather than conducting an analysis on the causes of a single policy change in one institution, such as the Congress, I applied my inquiry to the 50 states over a period of 30 years to take advantage of the organic opportunity presented by the states for comparative study.

The findings of this account of the adoption and implementation of modern statutory rape laws—that groups may have more influence than public opinion—has broad implications. One could argue that the American political system is indeed responsive, and is responding to those who are interested, organized, and vocal. On the other hand, there is a vast inequality of resources between groups and unorganized publics, not necessarily reflective of their actual numbers in the United States; that inequality can manifest itself in policy initiatives that may be counter to public opinion. For instance, in the 1970s feminists lobbied successfully for age-span provisions even though an overwhelming majority of people in the United States felt teen sex was "always wrong." There is also the possibility that groups may be indirectly representing, or filtering, or even leading public opinion. For instance, in the

1990s conservatives explicitly intertwined the moral and economic concerns of those on the right by linking adolescent sexuality, statutory rape, teen pregnancy, out-of-wedlock births, and welfare dependency. But through repetition, circulation, and resonance, these links were discursively naturalized as being in the center and thus garnered a great deal of support across the political spectrum.

The Politics of Gender, Sexuality, and Marriage

Statutory rape laws continue to preserve cultural narratives of gender by criminalizing and most often prosecuting activity that falls within a certain stereotype: heterosexual sex in which the male can be construed as active and the female as passive. Under today's gender-neutral laws, prosecuting activity that is labeled "deviant" for falling outside of the stereotype—homosexual sex, or heterosexual sex in which the female appears to be the dominant partner—still preserves the narrative. These last two types of prosecutions tend to garner more media attention due to their encompassing of persons deemed outside gender boundaries. But the female perpetrator and the male victim often get an amused reaction; she does not fit gender stereotypes the way male perpetrators (heterosexual or homosexual) do. And so a young male in an abusive situation with an older female might see her go unpunished, while a young male in a consensual homosexual relationship with an older male might see him have to register as a sex offender. Note also that the formal language of statutory rape laws cannot or does not encompass a female perpetrator with a female victim because the crime is one of sexual intercourse. There is no room in statutory rape laws for female sexual agency, whether she is the perpetrator or the victim; that agency would violate the boundaries of gender.

Prosecutions under the laws, particularly in their latest incarnation as a means by which to target impoverished teens who become pregnant, implicate cultural narratives of race, ethnicity, and class, as well as those of gender and sexuality. In the United States since the 1980s, the phrase *teen mother* itself has evoked a "particular image of a young, urban, poor woman of color" (Jakobsen 2001: 299). As at the turn of the twentieth century when the targets of statutory rape prosecutions were the partners of immigrant working-class females in the cities, at the turn of the twenty-first century thinly veiled references to race, ethnicity, and class have worked through the constructions of gender and sexuality in statutory rape discourses and built support for new means of controlling adolescent sexuality:

> Policy debates and public perceptions of welfare and impoverished
> Americans have focused relentlessly on the black urban poor—

blaming nonnormative family structures, sexual promiscuity, and aid-induced laziness as the root causes of poverty, and mobilizing the stereotypes of welfare queens, teen mothers, and sexually predatory young men to sustain the dismantling of the welfare state. In this way, naturalizing discourses of black cultural traits obscure the mutually constituting effects of racism, class exploitation, and sexual and gendered inequalities. (McElya 2001: 159)

Through such discourses, structural problems are individualized and public problems are privatized, with marriage constructed as the linchpin of national success or failure.[2] The underlying structures are left untouched as debate is centered on traditional morality and individual behavior—and marriage.

Statutory rape laws are predicated not as much on age as on nonmarriage; sexuality is regulated through the deployment of marriage as a form of social control (Smith 1994: 317). Seventeen states still retain fornication laws, criminalizing sex between two unmarried people of any age; they have been used recently in at least 3 of those 17 (Posner and Silbaugh 1996: 98–100; Hardy 1996; Jones 2000). While most states require that one be 18 to marry on one's own,[3] only 27 states specify a minimum age for marriage—and 10 of these exempt couples who have a child or are expecting one. In other words, only 17 states really have minimum ages for marriage, while all states have an age of consent to unmarried sex. The other 23 states allow marriage at any age with parental and/or judicial approval. But there is no such exemption for unmarried adolescent sex: Pregnancy, subsequent marriage, parental knowledge or permission, judicial discretion, or consensuality are not defenses to statutory rape prosecutions. Married teen couples are free from prosecution and assumed to be stable economic and social units; one must wonder, however, if married teenagers are even more vulnerable than the unmarried.

Indeed, in table C.1, figures derived from U.S. Census Bureau statistics show that marriages among 15–17-year-olds stand out in three ways: They have by far the lowest percentage of spouses present, by far the largest percentage of spouses absent, and a divorce rate four times as high as the next oldest age group that is the opposite of gradual increase in this number as the population ages. The 18–19-year-old age group fares only slightly better, but also has a higher percentage of absent spouses than the next oldest age group.

Marriage rates, like all vital statistics in the United States collected by the Census Bureau or the National Center for Health Statistics, are tracked by race and ethnicity rather than by income level as is done in most industrialized countries. This creates problems of overlap, such as this type of note found at the end of statistical tables: "Because Hispanics may be of any race, data in this report for Hispanics overlap slightly with the data for the Black population and

TABLE C.1 Marital Status of Persons 15 and Over, by Age, 1998

	15–17	18–19	20–24	25–29	30–34	35–39	40–44	45–54
Ever married	137,000	317,000	4,075,000	10,485,000	15,200,000	18,622,000	19,000,000	31,313,000
Married, spouse present	57,000	241,000	3,313,000	8,818,000	12,449,000	14,573,000	14,608,000	23,564,000
(percent of ever marrieds)	*(41.6)*	*(76.0)*	*(84.3)*	*(84.1)*	*(81.9)*	*(78.3)*	*(76.9)*	*(75.2)*
Married, spouse absent	51,000	61,000	390,000	699,000	939,000	1,170,000	1,041,000	1,445,000
(percent of ever marrieds)	*(37.2)*	*(19.2)*	*(9.5)*	*(6.7)*	*(6.2)*	*(6.3)*	*(5.5)*	*(4.6)*
Divorced	24,000	15,000	355,000	923,000	1,737,000	2,697,000	3,135,000	5,457,000
(percent of ever marrieds)	*(17.5)*	*(4.7)*	*(8.7)*	*(8.8)*	*(11.4)*	*(14.5)*	*(16.5)*	*(17.4)*

Note: The Census Bureau does not track these numbers or these percentages in this way. Rather than figures for "ever married," they publish figures for "never married"; I subtracted "never married" from the number of all people of that age group to obtain the number of "ever married." They also do not include the percentages I have calculated here. Rather than, for instance, calculating those divorced as a percentage of those ever married, they calculate those divorced as a percentage of all people of that age group, both never-married and ever-married. Also, the figures above do not include people widowed, so percentages do not add to 100; the number of widowed increases by age group. I include figures only through the 45–54 age group because in the age groups after this the population numbers decline, making comparisons more difficult.

Source: Data are drawn from U.S. Census Bureau (1998), Detailed Table 1: "Marital Status of Persons 15 Years and Over, by Age, Sex, Race, Hispanic Origin, Metropolitan Residence, and Region: March 1998." I use 1998 because in subsequent years, only 15–19-year-olds are tracked, and not broken out as 15–17 and 18–19 as they were in 1998.

for the Asian and Pacific Islander population. . . . 10.5 percent of the White population, 4.98 percent of the Black population, and 3.38 percent of the Asian and Pacific Islander population are also of Hispanic origin" (Kreider and Fields 2001: 6). Regardless of the sources of this tracking and of its complications, its implications are certain: Race and ethnicity themselves become explanatory factors and objects of blame. In terms of marriage, for all age groups under 55, "marriage rates for white women were more than twice those of black women with the largest difference between races in the 15–19 age group—41.2 compared with 14.8" (Clarke 1995: 4). Black women at those ages are therefore in theory more likely than white women to have children out of wedlock and therefore in theory supposedly more likely to require public assistance; this fits in with the stereotyping of impoverished women of color.

The implication is that for a teen, to be married is preferable to being unmarried. But not noted was that women who marry at ages 15–19 are more likely than any other age group to have their marriage end in divorce; about three times as likely as those who married after age 30 (Norton and Miller 1992: 7). Not noted was the high percentages of women who marry at ages 15–19 whose spouses are absent, as shown in table C.1. If the concern, again, is with protecting teens, why would early marriage not be as nationally discouraged, or made illegal, as is unmarried sexuality?

The Politics of Morality

The impact of law often lies as much in the body of discourse created in the process of its adoption as in the final legal rule itself.

—Nan Hunter

The mobilization of fear, or the beginnings of what is often referred to as a moral panic (Cohen 1972; Hall et al. 1978), does not occur in a vacuum; rather, it draws on preexisting ideologies and fears and is symptomatic of broader concerns (Thompson 1998: 20). Which claims are successful and which are not is contingent on the cultural anxieties of the moment. In the early 1900s, those fears included increasing immigration as overwhelming the numbers of American-born whites, middle-class women gaining some small measure of visibility and power through their participation in various reform movements, and young single women moving to newly industrialized cities to both live and work outside their parents' homes—each of these trends seen as subverting hierarchies of class, race, and gender. In the early 2000s, Americans who similarly feel that they have lost out due to complex structural changes are looking for something or someone to blame: the shift from a production economy to a service economy and the concurrent movement of some production overseas or to subcon-

tractors; economic, political, and social gains made by those formerly discrim-
inated against because of their race, ethnicity, gender, and sexuality; the rising
cost and potential insolvency of the welfare state.

In such a world, perceived as unstable, one can "observe an increasing obsession with the guarding of boundaries of the body, sex roles, the family, ethnic purity, and national identity—and . . . increasing anger at children who
cannot or will not fulfill their expected roles in the transmission of 'traditional
values.'" In other words, children are simultaneously "at risk" and "the risk"
themselves (Stephens 1995: 11, 13). If the family cannot sufficiently discourage
premarital or nonmarital sexuality among its children and/or protect those
children, due to some dysfunction often discursively linked to race, ethnicity,
class, or gender, then the state will step in. "Preventing sexual acts *against* the
young can be a way of regulating sexual acts *by* that population. The market for
claims in a given era is conditioned by perceptions of how far young people
have strayed from proper discipline and the threats they pose to social and sexual order" (Jenkins 1998: 225). As these claims politicize an emotive and
metaphoric language and transform collective fears into collective action, particular behaviors become regulated.

Whom do statutory rape laws serve? Young unmarried people, whose
abusive sex partners are punished. Parents, who use the laws as a means of
policing their children's sexuality and protecting them from potentially coercive relationships. Feminist groups, who have reformed formerly patriarchal
gender-specific laws that criminalized all sexual activity with an unmarried
underage female and inscribed stereotypical notions of female sexual agency
and mental capacity into law. Economic and moral conservatives, who are
able to point to the laws as a moral and legal condemnation of unmarried sexuality, and who in the initiative targeting pregnancy can attack out-of-wedlock births and welfare dependency at the same time.

Whom do statutory rape laws hurt? Consensual relationships may be
prosecuted, with the younger party unable to stop a prosecution and with
the older perhaps having to register as a sex offender. Coercive relationships, particularly within an age span, or in which a young person is just
above the age of consent, or in which the younger party is male and the
older party is female, may all go unpunished. Populations already demonized
can be targeted with little sympathy under the mobilization of particular
symbols—the predatory impoverished urban male, the homosexual "pedophile." Feminists, while instrumental in passing rape and statutory rape reform, have not been in control of the implementation of the laws, nor have
they been in control of (nor have they tried to control) statutory rape discourses over the past decade. Stereotypes of gender, sexuality, race, and class
are reinforced through which cases are prosecuted and receive attention and
which do not.

Statutory rape laws, their meanings constructed and reconstructed to reflect contemporary economic, political, social, and cultural anxieties, help some and harm others. They can be used to safeguard those who require protection, and they can be used to punish marginalized populations whose behavior has been labeled "deviant"—those who fall outside the constructed boundaries of the "traditional" married, heterosexual, middle-class American.

Appendix

Theory and Method
State Politics, Pooled Cross-Sectional Time Series, and Case Studies

This appendix reviews literature from the subfields of American national-level politics, state politics, and morality policies and discusses in depth this work's theoretical framework vis-à-vis the field of political science. It also discusses both quantitative and qualitative methodologies, the variables chosen for analysis as well as those excluded from it, and the means by which the case study states were selected.

Introduction

Statutory rape, as an issue concerning morals, appears at first as if it may not necessarily be bound by the same rules as other types of policies previously studied. Many scholars who have studied morality policies have hypothesized that the adoption and reinvention of morality policies are different from that of other types of policies. But I argue that they are not, and that the search for correlates of policy outcomes has clouded the search for a unifying theory on the potential causes of policy adoption and reinvention. To this end, I seek to integrate the theoretical concerns expressed in the study of policymaking at the national level with the advantages of studying policymaking at the state level.

State Politics and National Politics:
Common Theoretical Concerns

Studying State Politics

Studying politics at the state level can provide important insights into the field of American politics in general. Perhaps most important, it provides an arena for comparative analysis often lacking in investigations of political processes at the national level. Even more so than in the field of comparative politics, in which usually no more than a few regions or states are analyzed together, looking at a number of American states—or in this case all 50—provides a sample sufficiently large in number to test hypotheses about political behavior across varying environments.

The states are somewhat heterogeneous in their histories, populations, institutions, and political processes. "[V. O.] Key knew what too many of us ignore and that is that context matters. Individuals make choices among alternatives that are often shaped by their context, and state politics research can make important strides in clarifying context-behavior connections" (Brace and Jewett 1995: 666). The delineation and comparison of such constraints and the subsequent decisions made within them is an enormous analytical advantage to the field of state politics. Further, this context is influenced by and in turn influences local as well as national politics. Making these connections contributes to the field of American politics more generally.

Even more so today than in the past as the federal government shrinks in size, the states are "experimental laboratories of democracy."[1] As responsibility for crafting policies and administering certain programs continues to devolve to the states, it is reasonable to expect that states will vary in the ways in which they implement those policies and programs. An analysis of how and why that variation occurs is crucial to a more nuanced understanding of political behavior in the American context. Certain policy areas, such as laws concerning sexuality (which are the subject of this study), are the province of the states alone with little to no federal guidelines to follow. A federalist system requires state innovation—or a decision for inaction.

In turn, both successful and unsuccessful policymaking in the states can influence steps taken at the national level. Many, if not most, public officials at the national level have held similar posts at the state level and they do not leave these experiences behind. Indeed, "[W]hat is going on in Washington today and tomorrow may be shaped by what is going on in the American states" (Brace and Jewett 1995: 664).

Investigating subnational political processes, in short, provides an excellent opportunity through which to get at the heart of "who gets what, when, and how" in the United States. The 50 states, particularly the varying constraints within which and resources with which political actors make decisions, are a ready-made source for comparative inquiry on which political scientists can and should capitalize in order to draw out more general patterns in policymaking.

Incorporating Theoretical Insights

But the comparative state politics field suffers from a much-remarked-upon lack of theoretical integration.[2] Employing an increasing number of diverse variables to hypothesize about policy change in a host of policy areas and spanning numerous time periods has not necessarily capitalized on the opportunities, outlined above, that the study of the states can provide. Indeed, this technique has led to explanations that apply to smaller and smaller subsets of policymaking, and often to only one policy area. As there is virtually no guiding theoretical force behind the selection of variables to be tested, there is little reason to assume that one of numerous sets of correlations is more generalizable than another.

Scholars have demonstrated a variety of claims about the types of forces that correlate with policy outcomes: that such change covaries with public ideological leanings (Erikson, Wright, and McIver 1993); with group strength and the public's ideological leanings (Nice 1988, 1994); with group strength, the public's ideological leanings, and regional norms (Mooney and Lee 1995); with group strength, the public's ideological leanings, voter interest, and public officials' ideological leanings (Grogan 1994); with group strength, personal income, and the number of neighboring states that have adopted (Berry and Berry 1990); with group strength and the presence of a policy entrepreneur (Mintrom 1997). Note that each finds strong effects for organized groups. But except for the last (incorporating the efforts of policy entrepreneurs), each of these studies stops at demonstrating correlation and goes no further to try to make a causal link as to how and why policies were changed at a particular time and in a particular place.[3]

How can we know which of these correlation studies might best explain or predict the adoption process of other types of issues? It is here that broader theoretical explanations of policy change, utilized to study national-level policy change, can be brought in to the study of state politics. In the following sections, three such approaches are outlined: that policy change is most directly influenced by the power of public opinion, by political elites' internal decision making, or by interest group lobbying.

PUBLIC OPINION   Explanations of policy change based on public opinion hypothesize that vote-conscious legislators will seek to please the majority of the public by catering to the "median" voter in their district, be it local, state, or national. This Downsian (1957) model assumes that voters are arrayed on a single left–right ideological continuum. It also assumes competition between two people for a given office, and that a voter would vote for the candidate closest to him or her on the continuum. To capture the maximum number of votes, those running for office converge on the area in which the median voter should be; those voters well to the left or to the right of that point on the continuum will still vote for the candidate closest to him or her. In this way, the ideological leanings of the public are crucial to the policies passed in that particular district.

An application of this theory is Erikson, Wright, and McIver's 1993 *Statehouse Democracy*, in which they compile the results of state-level public opinion polls over a period of 13 years. They then test the public's ideological scores against public officials' ideological scores and the ideological leanings of policy outcomes. They find that these three elements are highly correlated, demonstrating that liberal states produce liberal policies and conservative states produce conservative policies.

Even if we were to assume that there is a public opinion that is "genuine" and not elite-led or manipulated, that is reasonably well-informed, and that is consistent,[4] what is the linkage mechanism? That is, how would the public's ideological stances translate themselves into new policies? One might assume that the elected officials of a given district, having lived under the same conditions as the other residents, would reflect the wishes of the majority of that district. Still, this does not point toward a causal mechanism for why a particular policy would be brought in to the legislature at a particular time.

Second, there is little reason to assume that the entire voting population is aware of and concerned about every possible issue and the way in which their representative voted on that issue; nor to assume that a large percentage of eligible voters will vote.[5] Indeed, while voter turnout at the national level is the lowest of all established industrialized democracies, turnout at the state level is even lower. It would be similarly difficult for a given public official to gather knowledge on how all potential voters feel about each issue he or she is considering. In turn, a politician would have little incentive to expend his or her political capital to provide goods to his or her constituency as a whole without knowing which of those constituents will turn out to vote. He or she would have an incentive to provide goods to those constituents more interested and more likely to vote because he or she has to be elected and reelected in order to hold office at all.[6] But the "public opinion" hypothesis is about the public as a whole rather than particular sets of voters. It does not provide a direct and traceable link between the mass public and the policymaker.

ELITES AND POLICY NETWORKS   A second set of explanations appears more "internal." Here, policy specialists (who may or may not be officeholders or staffers themselves) and other public officials create or amend policies and use their inside influence to have them passed into law. While some classified these policymaking bodies as "iron triangles" or "subgovernments" due to observations of their consensual, low-profile, ongoing activity,[7] later research showed more conflict, more partisanship, more actors, and more fluidity in this structure.[8]

John Kingdon's case studies (1997) of the process of policy changes in health and transportation illustrate the workings of such networks. Their importance, he writes, stems not only from the fact that new ideas originate with them (particularly at this point, elected officials and their staffers) and so they set the governmental agenda, but also because the policy solution chosen is dependent on the strength of the network (particularly at this point, staffers and consultants), the merit of the policy, and the network's ability to sway other inside experts and policymakers. In this second edition of his book, he adds a section about the autonomy of policymakers and hypothesizes that "government might generate its own agenda through its own processes, and its interactions with the public might involve mobilizing support, rather than reacting to public opinion, interest groups, or social movements" (230). He describes the above as a "fairly straightforward top-down model" (199).

Kingdon writes about three "streams": the political, the policy, and the problem; the greatest policy changes occur when the three join together. Turnover in office, a change in the political stream, can contribute to policy change by installing new insiders into the policy stream. This points to the notion that policymakers still have to be reelected to continue to create and pass such policies, whether or not said policies are a response to direct public demand. Kingdon notes that even if politicians are concerned with their notions of what makes good public policy and with promoting themselves as powerful to their peers, they still also have to satisfy their constituents (39–40). Further, he writes that while the agenda is also affected by outside forces such as public opinion, the policy outcome chosen from various alternatives is affected by interest group activity (19–20). This last comment presents a problem similar to that of the public opinion–public policy hypothesis: It is difficult to assume that mass public opinion is aware and concerned about the spectrum of issues and alterntives under consideration.

INTEREST GROUPS   A third set of hypotheses about the causes of policy change rests on interest group activities. As noted in the previous section, studies of the correlates of policy adoption seem consistently to find the strength of advocacy groups pertinent to a particular issue to have great explanatory power.[9] Also, the shortcomings of the previous two explanations—that a politician on his or her own cannot necessarily know which constituents are aware and concerned and will vote in the next election, and that a politician must seek reelection no matter how internally or externally motivated his or her agenda—can be somewhat reconciled when taking into account the activities of groups.

For one, the group can provide the average citizen with shortcuts of information on issues pertinent to that citizen while bringing him or her together with like-minded people. Thus, group participation can serve to help the voter become aware and concerned, as well as organized into a bloc.[10] Not only are these constituents more likely to vote, but they are more likely to vote in a similar manner. If a public official were to try to estimate which of the people in his district would vote and which would not, he or she would probably assume that those who were organized would be more prone to be aware and concerned, and thus to vote.[11] And with some information on the group, he or she would be able to better gauge how its members might vote.

Groups can also mobilize concerned citizens to contact these legislators, and can make campaign contributions and supply volunteers to particular candidates (Smith 1995). Finally, interest group elites can strengthen all of these links by promising to mobilize a given group's members to turn out to vote for that politician, or by threatening to vote for his or her opponent. With this leverage, the group can lobby for particular policy outcomes from said politician (Harvey 1998: 57).

Harvey's 1998 *Votes without Leverage* illustrates this in regard to women's organizations and their mobilization of women's votes. She finds that for the period from 1920 through the 1960s, it was the party organizations rather than interest groups who were able to promise public officials the reward of the "women's vote"; since the late 1960s in what some have termed an "era of party decline,"[12] women's organizations were able to pursue an electoral strategy more successfully than the parties themselves.[13]

Unlike the first two explanations, each of which do seem to tell part of the story of policy adoption, this hypothesis based on group activities makes a link between "inside" and "outside": Advocacy groups stand between the voting public and public officials, organizing the former and being perceived as a credible threat by the latter. There is a partisan connection here as well: Some groups tend to concentrate their lobbying efforts on one or the other major parties, not both. Because of these more explicit connections, I find this explanation to be the most compelling for a quantitative and qualitative study of policy change.

CONCLUSION: INCORPORATING A BROADER THEORETICAL FRAMEWORK   If it is true that such organizations can provide the causal link in the process of policy adoption at the national level, it stands to reason that activity on the state level would be little different. Guided by the competing hypotheses I have outlined, I test three sets of variables against each other: those measuring public opinion, those measuring the partisan leanings of "insiders," and those measuring group strength. I expect that in the case of statutory rape laws, as well as in general, it is the last which are the strongest, thus lending support to the group-based theories that have been employed to study policy change at the national level.

State Policies:
Adoption, Innovation, Diffusion, and Reinvention

This research addresses a second subfield of political science as well. Comparative state policy studies have been conducted across all 50 states in a variety of policy areas—to discern the correlates of the presence or absence of particular types of legislation, the degree of liberal or conservative ideology implied by such legislation, and the level of funding for a particular type of policy. One branch of such studies deals with policy innovation.

Earlier works in this area looked across policies in the states to generalize about whether certain states could be characterized as "innovators" or "laggards," discovering that the propensity to innovate varied from state to state.[14] Walker's work (1973) examined the geographical diffusion of the decision to adopt a policy, finding that regional proximity does make a difference and that the effect could be described as one of "spreading inkblots on a map" (1187). He found that this pattern held across policy areas.[15] In response, other works looked at temporal diffusion, finding an S-shaped learning curve in which after a particular takeoff point, most states would quickly begin to adopt until a peak is reached, then the numbers would fall off as the last few laggards adopt (Gray 1973a,b; Savage 1985).

These studies are useful in their admonition to watch for regional and temporal patterns of policy adoption, but they tell us little about how and why a state becomes a "leader." As with the subfield of state politics as a whole, it is difficult to discern if this social learning pattern is dependent mostly on the public, on party elites, on interest groups, or on some other phenomenon. This leaves us with two questions: What causes innovation? Who in one state influences whom in a neighboring state?

Later works on morality policies assumed a more dynamic process in which policies were reinvented along the temporal continuum of policy adoption. That is, as states adopted a given policy, they altered it in some ways as well. Two studies have found an "incremental and unidirectional" (Mooney and Lee 1995: 610; 1999) "linkage between date of adoption and evolving content of policy" as either becoming more generous or more restrictive as social learning occurs (Glick and Hays 1991: 837, 840). But the former note that because of the nature of morality policies, some states may never adopt and so the diffusion of adoption and reinvention might be truncated (Mooney and Lee 1995:

606). Why the assumption that the adoption and reinvention of morality policies might be different from that of other types of policies?

Morality Policies: Policy Adoption and Public Opinion

A second branch of the state policy literature looks more closely at one or two policy areas, rather than at policy adoption as a whole. In general, these writers draw distinctions between morality policies and purely economic policies. While the latter tend to evoke debate over financial interests, and their adoption has generally thought to covary with state socioeconomic variables and ideological leanings, the former raise questions over the regulation of social norms that stem from fundamental and uncompromising clashes of values.[16] Morality politics are hypothesized to be highly salient to the general public, are often simplified, and evoke strong and emotional responses. Each person may feel he or she is an "expert" on a morality policy because they do not appear complex or appear to require detailed technical knowledge of any kind. Rather, one looks to one's own moral and ethical beliefs to decide one's stance on a morality policy, and then seeks to impose that stance as the one that the polity ought to feel is "right." In short, "moral judgment . . . is guided more by feeling than by reason" (Smith 1997: 1).

Policy areas treated in this literature include abortion (Meier and McFarlane 1992, 1993; Cook, Jelen, and Wilcox 1993; Mooney and Lee 1995; Berkman and O'Connor 1993; Norrander and Wilcox 2001), disability rights (Holbrook and Percy 1992), drugs (Meier 1994), alcohol (Meier and Johnson 1990), school prayer (Moen 1984), sodomy (Nice 1988, 1994), the arts (Hofferbert and Urice 1985), living wills (Glick and Hays 1991), AIDS (Colby and Baker 1988), and the death penalty (Nice 1992, 1994; Mooney and Lee 1999, 2000, 2001). Such works have tested a variety of state demographic and political variables to determine what types of variables might influence policy adoption and policy choice. For instance, Nice (1994) found that the regulation of sodomy correlates with large Baptist populations and a general cultural conservatism; Mooney and Lee (1995) found that abortion funding policies predating *Roe v. Wade* in 1973 were most influenced by public opinion, interest group strength, and regional norms.

Much of the energy in this area has been devoted to investigating to what extent the policy adoption process is similar or different in the two types of policies.[17] As one work noted, "Issues of moral conflict are not easily assimilated into theories and models based upon economic and class interests" (Tatalovich, Smith, and Bobic 1994: 2). The verdict has generally been that morality policies and redistributive policies are determined by differing sets of variables.[18]

   The major focus of the attempt to separate out the types of policies has been public opinion and participation. A number of scholars have theorized that because of the nature of morality policies as technically simple and highly emotional, the average citizen will pay more attention, be more engaged, and have a strong opinion on that policy. As a corollary, public officials should not require outside sources of technically complex information here because "everyone" has an opinion on these issues. Thus, we should find strong effects for citizen values when examining the correlates of morality policy outcomes, because the usual advantages of interest groups (on other types of issues) are lost.[19] Public opinion, then, may "trump" interest group influence in this policy area (Mooney 2001: 11).

   However, morality issues may not divide Americans into staunchly opposed factions with a large gulf in between. On the issue of abortion in particular, which is often cited as the quintessential morality policy, the breakdown is not so black and white. Most Americans do not divide neatly into saying that the procedure should be either legal in all cases or illegal in all cases. Rather, most say it should be legal in some cases and illegal in some cases, or that it should be legal with restrictions (Cook, Jelen, and Wilcox 1993).[20] It appears that the positions taken by political elites are what force morality policies into two boxes: "Interest groups and parties, however, may cater to more extreme positions on this issue. State legislators, themselves, also may have strong preferences on abortion, and adopting a trustee role, legislators may incorporate their own preferences into public law" (Norrander and Wilcox 2001: 144). If groups represent the more extreme positions, and/or characterize a particular district or constituency as leaning in a particular direction, policymakers using group leanings as a shortcut or trusting group information on their constituencies as valid may be led to inaccurate conclusions.

   It is crucial to note that it is on the subject of abortion that the most powerful effects for public opinion have been found in this literature. However, as a recent work cautions, some of the measurements of public opinion in prominent previous works on abortion politics are somewhat incomplete.[21] For instance, state membership in the National Abortion Rights Action League, or in Catholic and evangelical Christian Churches (Berkman and O'Connor 1993) are probably more accurate measures of potential group mobilization than of the ideological leanings of that state's citizens as a whole (Norrander and Wilcox 2001: 158n. 1). A second source of public opinion on abortion studies has been the 1990 Voter Research and Surveys Exit Polls, involving 42 states (Cohen and Barrilleaux 1993; Cook, Jelen, and Wilcox 1993). But these polls cover voters in off-year elections, which have extremely low turnout rates that vary across the states and cannot be said to represent mass public opinion (Norrander and Wilcox 2000: 147). While no measurement is perfect, these types of variables in particular call into question the conclusions drawn in the morality politics literature about a strong direct effect of public opinion on morality policies.

This is not to say that the correlative effects found for public opinion in prior morality politics scholarship are spurious. It is to suggest that the way in which public opinion has been measured has its faults, and that the theoretical causal role of public opinion has not been well specified. It is also to argue that interest groups' roles as middlemen standing between public opinion and public officials, and as active drafters of and lobbyists for legislation,[22] have been slighted:

> Opinions expressed through organized interest group activities . . . may shape lawmakers' judgments on the preferences of their constituencies. Moreover, interest groups represent the attentive public, which may be more important in electoral politics than the more moderate middle. . . . [For instance], the political parties have moved away from the median voter on abortion in an effort to attract the energies and financial support of interest group activists. (Norrander and Wilcox 2001: 151)

For these types of reasons, morality policy researchers such as those quoted above are indeed beginning to question the downplaying of the role of interest groups evident in previous works. Another recent piece notes as well that, "interest groups may play a more significant role on these issues than the morality politics framework may suggest" (Haider-Markel 2001: 215).[23]

If public opinion and interest group ideologies are congruent, it appears that groups can serve as the linkage mechanism between the public and the policymakers. Group strength and public opinion leanings on abortion, for instance, correlate highly (Norrander and Wilcox 2001: 153). When the two are not congruent, note the authors of works on movie censorship (Brisbin 2001), and on the death penalty (Mooney and Lee 1999), the result may be an anti-majoritarian policy.[24]

As Norrander and Wilcox (2001) also indicate, the role of party control needs to be taken into account. State party elites tend to be more ideologically extreme than their constituents in general (Erikson, Wright, and McIver 1993). On the issue of abortion, for instance, the divide between the two major parties is similar to the divide between advocacy groups: It is more extreme than that between differing factions of the majority of Americans, and so "[s]tates with Republican majorities in the legislature may enact generally strict sets of abortion requirements, while states with Democratic majorities may protect abortion rights, *regardless of public opinion*" (Norrander and Wilcox 2001: 146; emphasis added).

If interest group characteristics and party elites are taken into account, I hypothesize, the effect found by some in the morality politics field for citizen ideological leanings/public opinion would weaken or perhaps even disappear because it is through interest group activity on partisan political elites that public opinion may have some effect. As outlined in the previous section, there is little incentive for policymakers to cater to mass public opinion, regardless of the type of policy. There are numerous incentives, on the other hand, for policymakers to be attentive to interest groups. I test these hypotheses in chapters 2, 3, and 4.

For all of these reasons, I argue that the above endeavors to separate out different types of policies are not fruitful because the search for correlation within the morality politics subfield has led to explanations that apply to small subsets of policies, and often to only one policy area. This has led researchers away from examining the causal mechanisms of policy, which is a project greatly needed in the field of comparative state politics.

Conclusion: Theory

Contrary to others in the subfield of morality politics, I contend that the nature of the policy should matter little to the broad process of policy adoption across the states. True, scholars have found that the strongest *correlates* of policy outcomes have differed across policy types—but this does not mean that the *causes* of policy adoption differ across policy types. Lowi (1998) notes when writing about morality policymaking as radicalizing other types of policymaking:

> Although these groups seem to be seeking policies that could be categorized as (largely) regulatory or redistributive, they refused to join what most of us would consider mainstream political processes, insisting instead on trying to convert political issues into moral polarities, claims into rights, legislation into litigation, grays into black and whites, and campaigns into causes and crusades. . . . [T]here is likely to be an intensification of all the political elements without necessarily transforming the patterns altogether. . . . [T]he policy at issue can remain in the same category even as its politics is being radicalized. (xvii)

Indeed, morality policies are redistributive, although they redistribute value systems rather than economic goods. Second, such policies have an economic component although it may be less visible than "pure" economic policies—morality policies must be enforced by law, which requires state resources. Third, they are regulatory, as they seek to regulate individual or group behavior.[25] Finally, I assert that the direct and immediate causes of policy change in general are rooted in group and elite activity rather than in public opinion, whether those policies appear economic or moral in nature. While public opinion may have indirect effects on policy change through groups that mediate such opinion, it is the groups themselves that represent a segment of the public more attentive, more likely to vote, and with more resources attractive to policymakers. Thus, I argue that when interest group influence and elite partisanship are accounted for, effects for public opinion will decrease.

The issue of statutory rape, as a seemingly distinctive morality policy, is particularly well-suited for challenging some of the more accepted contentions in the morality politics and state politics subfields. Within a broad theoretical framework and against a background of both quantitative and qualitative tests, this work presents a more dynamic picture of state-level decision making that can be generalized beyond particular policies and particular levels of government.

Pooled Cross-Sectional Time Series/Discrete Time Event History Analysis

In looking at policy adoption that is spread across space and over time, cross-sectional analysis alone cannot get at the variety of state policymaking processes. Utilizing data from each state from each year in an event history analysis or pooled cross-sectional time series is more efficient. The variables are tested against one another with the factors of both time and space taken into account. This method also increases the number of cases. Each state has multiple records, with each case termed a "state-year" instead of just a "state." For instance, in chapter 2 on age-span provisions, there are 686 cases of state-years rather than 50 cases of just states.

The outcomes of the tests "predict the probability that a particular type of state will adopt a policy during a particular year" in addition to determining correlates of policy adoption (Berry and Berry 1990: 399). This likelihood is the "hazard rate." State-years in which no state adopted are included as well, contributing to a more accurate calculation of a hazard rate.

For each state-year in which that state does not adopt, the dependent variable is coded as 0. In the year that that state does adopt, the dependent variable is coded as 1 and the state is dropped from the "risk set" of states that have not yet adopted. For instance, as is covered in chapter 2, the states began to adopt age-span provisions in earnest in 1971. Thus 1971 is the first year observed for each state and 1999 is the last.[26] New Jersey adopted its policy in 1978, so the total set of "New Jersey" would be years NJ71 through NJ77 coded as 0, and NJ78 coded as 1. The tests of the adoption of gender-neutral language in chapter 3 include the years 1969–1999, and the tests of the adoption of targeting the partners of pregnant teens in chapter 4 include the years 1996–1999.

As the outcome of each test is dichotomous (adopt or not adopt), scholars employing this method use logit (or probit) analysis to test the strength and direction of the independent variables. This type of logistic regression differs from linear regression in its assumptions and in its reports.[27] For one, because the dependent variable is discrete and dichotomous, plotting the variables will cluster them at 0 and 1, rather than at any points in between. Logistic regression thus assumes nonlinearity: a sigmoid or S-shaped curve, rather than a smooth line. The error terms are dichotomous rather than being normally distributed. Linear regression is not applicable because its assumptions are violated.

Second, rather than ordinary-least-squares (OLS) regression which looks for the parameter estimates that produce the smallest sum of the squared errors in the fit between the model and the data, this analysis employs maximum-likelihood estimation (MLE) which looks for the parameter estimates that give the highest likelihood of having obtained the observed sample. Unlike OLS in which the omission of an influential variable does not bias the estimates of the included variables unless it is correlated with those variables, in MLE such an omission will bias the coefficients of all included variables toward zero.

Cross-sectional time series models suffer from the problem of autocorrelation, or serial correlation. With autocorrelation, error terms at later times are correlated with error terms at earlier times, when the assumption is that they would be uncorrelated. Second, through simple inertia, events of the later years might be affected by events in the earlier years and cause autocorrelation as well. While one test for this might be to conduct a Durbin–Watson test, this is problematic. The value could be significant due to serial correlation, but also due to other reasons as well such as omitted variables. Another method of controlling the problem is to input dummy variables representing each year. I have done the latter, and find no significant effects on the models reported in chapters 2, 3, and 4.[28] Others employing this type of analysis have also found little evidence that instituting these corrections is necessary; many institute no attempts at correction at all.[29]

A third consideration when using logit is that there is little agreement on how to measure the goodness of fit of the model in a way that can tell us something about its explanatory power. Partly because of the difficulties in measurement, more attention is often paid to the significance ascribed to the individual variables rather than the overall fit. The more important theoretical reason is that we are more interested in estimating causal effects, and improving causal inferences, than the model's overall goodness of fit.[30]

The usual R^2 employed in linear regression for the percentage of the variance explained cannot be used because of the violations of the assumptions of OLS outlined above.[31] Several "pseudo-R^2s" have been developed by political scientists, but each has its own problems. None of these is agreed on, let alone universally accepted.

Some software packages produce a "percent correctly predicted" figure that cross-tabulates the number of observed "y = 0" and "y = 1" values with values predicted by the model. The problem with the comparison is that even a poorly conceived model, which yields a prediction of y = 0 (the event not occurring) or y = 1 (the event occurring) for every case, might predict a rather large percentage correctly. With logit, the number of y = 1 predictions made is equal to the number of y = 1 observations in the data, which may bias this figure as well. Finally, in an event history analysis that deals with policy adoption, the number of times the event occurs (i.e., the state adopts) is a small percentage of the overall cases. While this is not a problem in estimating causal effects, it may be a problem for the predictive capacity of the model.

Most software packages yield a "Pearson goodness-of-fit chi-square" for probit and logit that is similar to the F-test for the joint hypothesis that all coefficients except the intercept are 0. I report the percent correctly predicted and the chi-square statistic with the above caveats in mind.

Pertinent to causal effects, I report along with the coefficients of the variables a "change in probability" measure for each independent variable. This value reflects the change in the predicted probability of y = 1 (adoption) when changing the given independent variable from one standard deviation below its mean to one standard deviation above its mean, holding all other independent variables at their means (and dummy variables at .5). Since the logit curve is steepest at .5 probability, these estimates indicate the maximum potential effect of these variables (Krutz, Fleisher, and Bond 1998: 877). Because of the skew in the dependent variable noted above, due to the low probability of a state adopting in a given year, we should expect these scores to be relatively low in absolute value.[32] Still, it is these causal effects of the independent variables that are of most value in this study.

The Variables

To test the strength of the three theoretical orientations I have reviewed, I divide the variables into three major groups: those based on public opinion, on "insider" elites, and on interest groups. Thus in the qualitative (case study) and quantitative (pooled cross-sectional time series, or event history analysis) tests performed in each of the chapters, I am able to test the strength of these causal explanations against one another and draw broader conclusions. I employ six independent variables.[33]

Public Opinion/Public Demand

A number of studies of state politics, both of "morality" and "redistributive" policies, have found correlations between a state public's "liberalism" or "conservatism" and the types of policies passed in that state. Erikson, Wright, and McIver (1993) find that the liberalism or conservatism of the state electorates, based on their compilation of 13 years of public opinion polls conducted in each state, correlate strongly with state scores of liberal versus conservative policies and remained relatively stable over that period.

To test whether a state's liberal or conservative leanings correlate with more lax or more strict statutory rape policies respectively, I use Erikson, Wright, and McIver's scale as an independent variable.[34] The scale ranges from −2 to +2, the latter being the most liberal. This allows me to make assumptions about the link between a state's electorate and its policies. One might expect that a more liberal state would have a larger age-span provision, to have changed to gender-neutral language earlier rather than later, and to have not implemented a provision to target underage sexual activity resulting in pregnancy.

I did not expect to find that states classified as "liberal" necessarily produce liberal statutory rape policies, or that those classified as "conservative" necessarily produce conservative statutory rape policies. While sometimes public opinion is congruent with the direction of policy change, at other times it is not.[35] The reason for this, I suspect, is that there is no direct causal link between public opinion and policymakers. That link is provided by groups, who have particular views on policy that may or may not be the same as those of the majority of the public.

Elite "Insider" Attributes

An explanation based on policy networks, or insiders, has to take into account elite partisanship. While observations of the subgovernment model found that partisanship was less relevant in those low-profile and stable entities, those works on issue networks found them much more fluid and prone to partisan leanings.[36]

PARTY OF THE GOVERNOR   The party of the governor is important for numerous reasons. One, he or she can introduce legislation or set the tone on the type of legislation to be produced. Two, he or she can use the veto. Three, he or she can appoint task forces on various issues. In the 1970s, for instance, a number of governors created executive offices dealing with women's issues; others worked closely with external feminist task forces on rape and domestic violence. These governors were more prone to be members of the Democratic

Party, which had a much closer relationship with liberal women's groups than did the Republican Party. These women's groups, in return, were more prone to work within and vote for the Democratic Party than the Republican Party. The variable is drawn from the *Statistical Abstract of the United States*, and coded 1 for Democrat, 2 for Independent, and 3 for Republican.

PARTY OF THE LEGISLATURE   Legislation is drafted and fought over in this arena. Party control affects who is chairing committees in which legislation is introduced and either pushed forward or put aside; it is in committee that bill content is crafted. Partisanship virtually determines the vote on the floor. The variable is drawn from the *Statistical Abstract of the United States*, and coded 1 for unified Democratic legislatures, 2 for those under mixed control, and 3 for those under Republican control.

ELECTORAL COMPETITION   Key suggested in 1949 that high electoral competition could lead to more policy adoptions, and that those adopted would be more liberal. Normally risk-averse legislators would be more responsive to their constituencies due to the risk of defeat in these areas of higher voter participation, and further, they would be more responsive to have-nots and produce more liberal policies in fear of lower socioeconomic classes actually turning out to vote. While the theory has been refined, most empirical tests of this hypothesis have shown that competitive areas tend to produce more liberal policies.[37] If interest groups are to be effective in promising voter mobilization for a particular legislator in exchange for him or her pushing through the group's policy preferences, it follows that the environment must be competitive for the legislator to expend his or her political capital on behalf of the group.

    The Ranney index, created in 1976, had been the most utilized measure of competitiveness at the state level. But it is more accurately a measure of the strength of the Democratic Party in state government, with a midpoint at which Democratic and Republican strength in a given state are close to even. In 1993, Holbrook and Van Dunk created an alternate measure at the district level, incorporating the percentage of popular vote won by the winning candidate, the winning candidate's margin of victory, whether the seat was safe, and whether the seat was contested. It is this measure that I incorporate into the model.

Interest Group Activity

I hypothesize that group activity is the driving force behind policy change, and that group strength will explain much of the variance in state statutory rape laws. Given the topic and the history of statutory rape laws detailed in chapter 1, I look at the National Organization for Women (NOW) and the Christian Right.

NATIONAL ORGANIZATION FOR WOMEN   NOW was formed in 1966 to effect equality for women. Its interests vis-à-vis statutory rape law lie in protecting young women while still allowing for their ability to make choices, in raising consciousness about and prosecuting sexual abuse of any kind, and in promoting gender-neutral language in the law. The organization was instrumental to the reform of both forcible rape laws and statutory rape laws.[38] It is important to note as well that, in general, NOW is an organization more ideologically congruent with the Democratic Party than with the Republican Party—thus I assume that party control of state government works together with or moderates group strength.[39]

One must bear in mind that feminists are split on the issue of statutory rape and that this could affect the results. However, I expected a state with a large number of NOW members to have a larger age span, to have changed to gender-neutral language earlier, and to have not implemented a pregnancy-prevention policy.

The raw figures on NOW membership were provided to me by the organization's national headquarters, and were broken down by state. I computed with these raw figures and the actual population a measure of membership per 100,000 of the population.

This measurement of group membership is a proxy of group influence which assumes that group size correlates highly with group strength. This assumption can be a problem,[40] particularly with some measurements of groups used in the past in the state politics literature such as church membership. Membership in a Catholic parish, for instance, does not necessarily correlate with organized political action linked to the beliefs of the parish. NOW, however, is a lobbying organization with a particular program of political action. For the purposes of this study, I assume that states which have a proportionately larger number of dues-paying members are states in which the organization is stronger. There are of course limits to this assumption, but this is the best available measure of feminist strength.

THE CHRISTIAN RIGHT   To measure the strength of the Christian Right, I use a five-point scale of Christian Right influence on a state's Republican Party computed by Green, Guth, and Wilcox (1998) from two sets of interviews of Republican elites.[41] The points on the index are weak, modest, contested, strong, and great. In some ways, such a measure is more accurate than one of sheer group size, because it is a closer measurement of actual influence. This group–party link mirrors the assumptions that I have made about NOW's relationship with the Democratic Party. I expected to find that states with stronger influence would have smaller age spans that were put into effect later, would have changed to gender-neutral language later, and would have been more prone to implement a pregnancy-prevention measure.

Excluded Variables

I do not incorporate sociodemographic variables into the qualitative and quantitative tests. In short, they can tell us little about the causal links of policy change, but correlate highly with the political variables that then skew the effects of the latter.

This work seeks to target the types of variables that could be the actual sources of policy change in a particular place at a particular time—in other words, I use variables that represent agents of change and that link to various theoretical explanations for policy change. The state politics literature, and the morality politics literature, have been much more concerned with examining variables that strongly correlate with policy outcomes. However, most of these variables are latent and static, and cannot actually cause policy change although their presence or absence may correlate with it. As one scholar has asked, "How is it that income, industrialization, and the like affect public policy? Certainly these conditions cannot influence public policy on their own" (Ringquist 1993: 82). This question highlights a shortcoming in much of the state politics literature: A linkage mechanism—an agent—is missing.

Examples of such variables are percentage of the population that is black and/or Hispanic, education level and income level, urbanization level, "political culture," church membership (generally, previous scholars have separately measured Catholics, Baptists, and Fundamentalists), the percentage of women in the workforce, whether the state is prone to be an "innovator," and the number of neighboring states that have adopted previous to the state in question. While testing these types of variables can help to characterize states and perhaps illuminate after the fact why specific states seem more likely than others to have obtained certain policy outcomes, one cannot draw broader theoretical conclusions about how and why policy adoption occurs at a particular time. These "background" variables might have indirect effects by influencing the configuration of active political variables such as the six I include. But asserting that a high level of education across a state's population correlates with a particular policy change tells us nothing of who might have conceived of the legislation, who drafted it, who brought it to the attention of particular legislators, which legislators may have pushed such a change through, which party tended to vote for or against that bill in the legislature, or who as governor signed or vetoed the bill. It is these types of causal links that this research seeks to piece together.

Second, if I were to include these types of variables, they might act not as controls but as contaminants for the political variables. One could assume, for instance, that the percentage of the population that is Baptist would contaminate the Christian Right variable because of high correlation, or that the education and income levels of the population would contaminate the NOW variable for the same reasons. Thus, I performed all of the tests both with and without these variables.

CHURCH MEMBERSHIP   Gusfield in his 1963 (2d ed. 1986) study of prohibition, Meier in his 1994 study of alcohol-related policies, and Nice in his 1994 study of sodomy laws found that a large number of Baptists or Fundamentalists and a smaller number of Catholics correlate with stricter policies. I, too, would expect that Baptists would correlate with more conservative policies (a smaller age span, a later change to gender-neutral language, and a pregnancy prevention measure) and Catholics with slightly more liberal policies (the opposite). For Catholics and Baptists as a percentage of a state's population, data are from Quinn, et al. (1982).

RACE   I included the state's percentage of blacks and Hispanics because of the way minorities have been linked to adolescent sexuality; indeed, the teen mother has been historically coded as nonwhite.[42] I would expect that states with higher percentages of minorities would be more prone to having stricter statutory rape laws: smaller age spans, a later change to gender-neutral language, and a pregnancy-prevention measure; states with smaller minority populations would be more prone to having more liberal laws. The data on race are drawn from the *Statistical Abstract of the United States*. I then derived from these raw numbers (raw number of blacks and number of Hispanics[43]), and that of the total population of the state, the percentage of blacks and Hispanics in the state.

INCOME AND EDUCATION   Some studies of morality policies at the state level dismiss socioeconomic variables such as income and education since morality policies do not always have a visible economic component.[44] Others have found a relationship between these variables and other types of policies considered more redistributive in nature.[45] Historians and sociologists have found some relationship between those of higher incomes and education and taking a more liberal stance on matters of morality, and those with lower incomes and less education taking a more conservative stance. The latter have been more prone to use the law as a means of social control, while the former have been more prone to deal with sexual matters privately.[46] Thus I would expect states with higher per capita incomes and education levels to have more liberal policies: larger age spans between teens in order to prosecute the older one for statutory rape, earlier gender-neutral language, and no provision targeting the partners of pregnant teens.

These data are from the *Statistical Abstract of the United States*. The raw numbers on per capita income were given in both current and constant dollars. Using the consumer price index deflator figures from the U.S. Department of Labor's Bureau of Labor Statistics, I converted these numbers into 1982–1984 constant dollars (1982–1984 = 100). The measure for educational attainment is the percentage of the state's population with a bachelor's degree or more.

RATE OF BIRTHS TO TEEN MOTHERS (AGED 15–19)   One potential and very visible outcome of adolescent sexual activity is a young female's pregnancy, and even more so her becoming a "teen mother." While the rate of births to teen mothers was at a historic high in the 1950s rather than in more recent times as many public officials have asserted, there is a difference: Today's teens are much more likely to be unmarried than their predecessors.[47] Particularly in recent years, public officials and interest groups at both national and state levels have persistently linked unmarried pregnant teens and a general breakdown of morals. Further, they have repeatedly spoken of adolescent sexuality as almost invariably leading to teen pregnancy.[48] The third set of changes to statutory rape laws that targets the partners of pregnant teens rests explicitly on this assumption.

I would expect that a state which has a higher rate of births to teen mothers as percentage of all births would be more prone to having more conservative statutory rape laws: a smaller age span, a later change to gender-neutral language, and policies targeted at the partners of pregnant teens. The data on births to teen mothers are from the *Statistical Abstract of the United States*. In those years which only gave the teen birthrate per 1,000 rather than the percentage of births to teenage females as a percentage of all births, I divided this number by the number of the entire birthrate per 1,000 for that state to come up with the percentage of births to teens.

INNOVATION   Savage (1978) computed a scale of innovation as a general trait of the states, which ranges from 0 to 2.[49] He categorized 181 policies in areas ranging from labor to taxation to civil rights to crime, from the late nineteenth century through the late twentieth century. About one-half of the states showed consistency over that 100-year period. I use his more pertinent measure of 69 policies compiled into his "Later Twentieth Century Index." Many works on morality policies have included this measure.[50] One could assume that an "innovative" state would be more prone to innovate in the area of morality as well.

NEIGHBORING STATES   Following Berry and Berry's 1990 study of lottery policy adoptions (which sought to measure regional effects on the tendency to adopt at a particular time), as many others have done I drew up a variable called "neighbors."[51] For a given year, this is the number of states contiguous to the case-state that have adopted. I included Hawaii and Alaska in this measure, although they did not, and code each year as 0 for those states. This measure is probably the most problematic of all of these—because of the simple pattern of diffusion, it is bound to have strong effects as more and more states adopt. If a true relationship, it still tells us nothing about whom the adoption "next door" is pressuring to adopt in a given state.

Results of Adding These Variables to the Model

With the added variables, the fit of the models improved,[52] and the most highly significant variables became neighbor adoption,[53] the percentage of the population that is black (high levels negatively correlated with policy adoption), college education and income level (high levels of each positively correlated with policy adoption), the teen birthrate (a higher teen birthrate positively correlated with the adoption of age-span provisions, but negatively correlated with pregnancy-prevention provisions, which is somewhat ironic), and party of the legislature and the governor (democratic control positively correlated with policy adoption). NOW, the Christian Right, and citizen ideology—potential causes of policy change—became virtually insignificant.

As expected, NOW strength correlates highly with income and education, at about 0.7. Including measures of income and education weakens the significance level of the former. Teen birthrate correlates negatively with NOW at about −0.5 and also becomes significant as the NOW variable becomes insignificant. But it is the NOW leader that can draft a bill, bring it to the legislature, and lobby for its passage; the "teen birthrate" and the "income level" of a given state cannot. This variable points to policy change through its organized contributions of labor, votes, and information to its allies in the Democratic Party; the measurements of the other variables do not necessarily translate into political activity.

Also as expected, church membership pulls from the Christian Right variable: Baptists correlate positively with Christian Right strength at about 0.6; Catholics correlate negatively with Christian Right strength at about −0.5. Both the percentage of the population that is black, and the teen birthrate, correlate positively with Christian Right strength at about 0.5. These four variables are measures of identification among a state's populace that may or may not translate into some kind of unified action vis-à-vis policymakers. The Christian Right variable, however, is a direct measure of the influence of an active and organized segment allied with the Republican Party that both turns out to vote and provides resources to candidates and policymakers.

Ideology, too, is highly correlated with Baptists at −0.7 (a higher Baptist population correlates with a more conservative electorate), and with Catholics at 0.6 (the opposite). Ideology correlates positively with the income variable at 0.5.

One interpretation of these results is to say that any effects found for the group and public opinion variables tested alone will be spurious, and it is the above results that should be trusted. Including these variables still show some effects for the partisanship of "insider" elites, which speaks to one of the three major theories of policy change.

But to accept these results is to create two serious sets of concerns. The incorporation of these variables corrupts the political variables and introduces multiple correlations into the model that make it difficult to separate out which variables may be controlling for the effects of which others. There is no reason to assume that these sociodemographic variables are "pure" while the political variables are somehow flawed. The second, and more important, reason is theoretical. To include these variables repeats the much-criticized problem in the state politics literature: that it is concentrated on correlation with inactive variables such as these that cannot in and of themselves push policy change in a particular place at a particular time. They also cannot tell us anything about policy change in general that can be applied to other policy areas at other levels of government. With these concerns in mind, I omit these variables from the quantitative and qualitative tests.

Combining Pooled Cross-Sectional Time Series Analysis with Comparative Case Studies

Substantive and detailed case study material serves two purposes: One is to uphold the hypotheses generated by the theoretical framework (Peters 1998: 150); the second is to more clearly illustrate the process of policy change when the quantitative results appears ambiguous (King, Keohane, and Verba 1994: 5). This type of data delineates the nuances of policymaking that quantitative analysis is unable to fully capture: specific actors operating under specific constraints. Indeed, the state politics literature may be missing "politics" in the attempt to make broader points about covariation (Stonecash 1996). This work uses both types of analysis to compensate for the problems of each when used in isolation.

Case studies can complement the evidence for one's causal inferences as inferred through quantitative work, and also can explain unexplained deviations from the quantitative model. As Walker (1973) noted early on, political scientists studying state policy adoption through quantitative analysis are able to explain only a "modest amount of the variance . . . in so immense and elaborate a system. The presence of a single aide on a legislative staff who is enthusiastic about a program, or the chance reading of an article by a political leader can cause states to adopt new programs" (1189). Some events simply cannot be quantified.

Second, using case studies as a form of analyzing political phenomena does not have to suffer from a lack of rigor. Too often, cases are chosen based on the value of the dependent variable because that case might be particularly interesting or appear as a puzzling outlier. But viewing the cases as units on whom independent variables can be measured and described, one can choose one's cases based on the values of the explanatory variables and thus be as unbiased as possible in relation to the values of the dependent variables.

I chose three cases based on the variables measuring group strength: NOW membership and Christian Right influence (see table A.1). Note that they both compare and contrast on their values of the NOW variable (New Jersey: high, California: high, Georgia: low) and the Christian Right variable (New Jersey: low, California: middle/high, Georgia: high). In terms of citizen ideology, Georgia is conservative and the other two states are liberal. Party control is relatively constant for all three states over the period in question.

If public opinion were the cause of policy change, Georgia's adoption patterns should be different from that of the other two states, which should be similar to one another. If group strength were the cause of policy change, New Jersey and California should adopt similar provisions, or California and Georgia should adopt similar provisions depending on the division of power between NOW and the Christian Right in that particular state. As the results of this research pointed toward this last scenario, we can more confidently rule out the influence of public opinion because of the dissimilarities of California and Georgia on their values of citizen ideological leanings.

The values of the three states on all three dependent variables are different, enabling me to analyze the hypotheses fairly by testing variance of outcome. Yet the values on the dependent variable do not necessarily vary consistently with the hypotheses to be tested. Thus I do not bias my results toward success, and appear to account for the typical as well as the exceptional (King, Keohane, and Verba 1994: 137; Peters 1998: 71, 148).

Table A.1   Case Study States—Values on Independent and Dependent Variables

	NOW Members (% of population)	Christian Right	Party Control of the Legislature	Party of the Governor	Ideology	Age-Span Ptovision	Gender-Neutral Language	Pregnancy-Prevention Program
CA	High	Contested	D	D/R	Liberal	1993: 3 years	Late	Yes
GA	Low	Strong	D	D	Conservative	1995: 3 years	Late	No
NJ	High	Weak	D	D/R	Liberal	1978: 4 years	Early	No

Conclusion

This research incorporates six political variables that correspond to three major explanations of policy change: that such change is caused primarily by public opinion, by insider elites, and/or by interest groups. The political variables were chosen based on their relevance to the broader theoretical orientation of this research, to the field of state politics, and to the subject of statutory rape. By exploring these variables through pooled cross-sectional time series analysis and qualitative case study work, I present both a more abstract and more precise explanation of policy adoption. In other words, I link the macro and the micro in testing competing hypotheses of policy change for three sets of changes to statutory rape laws in the 50 states.

Notes

Introduction

1. Georgia is one of 10 states that expressly allows marriage at any age if the female is pregnant or if the two are the parents of a child born out of wedlock (GA Code Ann 19-3-37).

2. See, for example, McCann (1994) on this sociolegal approach to law; see also Duggan (2000) and Walkowitz (1992) on circulation and repetition as shaping material institutions and practices. See Kintz (1997) on resonance.

3. For example, Meier and McFarlane (1992), Meier and Johnson (1990), and Nice (1988); also Mooney and Lee (1995), Smith (1999), and Oakley (1999). The appendix reviews the pertinent literature from the subfields of American national-level politics and policymaking, state politics and policymaking, and morality politics and policymaking and details this work's theoretical and methodological frameworks and contribution to these literatures.

4. For example, Berry and Berry (1990), Mintrom (1997), Singer and Willett (1993), Mooney and Lee (1995), Meier and McFarlane (1992), Smith (1999), and Oakley (1999). See the appendix for a more detailed discussion of pooled cross-sectional time series, or event history analysis, using a logit model; this is the model employed here.

5. For a review of theories of policymaking, and for descriptions of the variables utilized in the logit model and in case studies, see the appendix.

6. California, Georgia, and New Jersey were chosen based on their comparable and contrasting values on the key explanatory independent variables, not on the dependent variables. For instance, two of the three states (California and New Jersey) are comparable on a measure of public opinion, but not on a measure of interest group strength. California and Georgia are comparable on interest group strength, but not on public opinion. This allows similarities or differences in policy outcomes to be more easily traceable to one variable or another. Further, these three states are also regionally representative of the United States. See the appendix for more detail.

7. On this "fine line," see, for example, Pivar (1973), Nathanson (1991), Kenney (1992), and Oberman (2000).

8. *Michael M. v. Superior Court of Sonoma County* (1981). This case is discussed in more detail in chapters 3 and 4.

Chapter 1: Statutory Rape Laws in Historical Context

1. What was called "statutory rape" through the late twentieth century is now variously titled in the fifty states. The names include statutory rape, rape in the *n*th degree (as distinct from forcible rape which is usually first degree, statutory rape was often classified as second-, third-, or fourth-degree rape), sexual assault in the *n*th degree (same), sexual battery in the *n*th degree (same), statutory sexual seduction, sexual abuse of a minor, child sexual abuse, child molestation, child rape, and indecency with a child. I will continue to call the offense statutory rape throughout this work—because that is how they are popularly and most often referred to, and also to clarify that this book seeks to unpack assumptions about and constructions of the agency and sexuality of teens (not young children) as manifested in debates over the adoption and implementation of statutory rape laws.

2. I use the words *perpetrator* and *victim* throughout as per the language of the laws; it is not a reflection on whether I believe a particular sexual relationship is consensual or not.

3. More anecdotally, an average of 470 females under 14 marry in Texas each year; in Kentucky from 1994 to 1996, 1,300 females 15 or younger were married, 71 of them 12 or 13 (Volpp 2000: 93, 109).

4. See Cocca (2002c).

5. Statute of Westminster I, 3 Edw., c. 13 (1275); see also Eidson (1980: 762).

6. Statute of Westminster II, 13 Edw., c. 34 (1285).

7. 18 Eliz., ch. 7 §4 (1576).

8. See table 1.1 in this chapter.

9. See also hooks (1984), Davis (1983), and Odem (1995).

10. Most states have taken their fornication statutes off the books. Seventeen states have retained them (Posner and Silbaugh 1996: 98–100): Arizona, Florida, Georgia, Idaho, Illinois, Massachusetts, Michigan, Mississippi, New Mexico, North Carolina, North Dakota, Oklahoma, South Carolina, Utah, Virginia, West Virginia, and the District of Columbia.

11. Mississippi's law was repealed by Laws 1998, ch. 549 §6. Through 1997, Miss. Code Ann. statute 97-3-67 could be used to prosecute only, "Any person who shall have carnal knowledge of any unmarried person of previously chaste character." In Texas, the law was changed in 1993. Tex. Penal Code Ann. §21.11 Indecency with a Child formerly read: "It is a defense to prosecution under this section that the child was at the time of the alleged offense 14 years or older and had, prior to the time of the alleged offense, engaged promiscuously in 1) sexual intercourse, 2) deviate sexual intercourse, 3) sexual contact, or 4) indecent exposure."

12. This is not to say that "all" middle-class women or "all" feminists at the time had this concern; I use "middle class" here to stand in for those feminist social purity activists extremely interested in and worried about the morality and domesticity of the working class, and with enough leisure time to dedicate themselves to trying to reform

working-class social values and conduct. Those engaged in these campaigns were very prominent in the first wave of feminism; those who disagreed with their ideas about gender and sexuality were much less organized and their ideas much less developed (see DuBois and Gordon 1984: 31). While joining in some areas with the women campaigning for suffrage (who also had divisions among them), they also had numerous points of disagreement with the suffragists. These types of divisions within feminism persist today.

13. See also Peiss (1986) and Walkowitz (1980).

14. On passionlessness, see Cott (1978). Also, note the fears of and hysteria around the "white slave traffic"—middle-class men abducting young working-class women and forcing them into prostitution—and the resulting federal Mann Act of 1910, which criminalized transporting an unmarried woman over a state line; see Langum (1994). See also Odem (1995), Kunzel (1993), Peiss (1986), Stansell (1987), Larson (1997), Walkowitz (1980, 1992), and DuBois and Gordon (1984).

15. See, for example, Bederman (1995), Roberts (1997), and Lancaster and DiLeonardo (1997); see generally, the writings of Ida B. Wells collected in *On Lynchings* (2002).

16. On silence in black communities as a protectionist mechanism, see Giddings (1992), Morrison (1992), and Cohen (1999).

17. WCTU organizer, 1891, quoted in Larson (1997).

18. Larson (1997) citing Helen Gardner's 1895 *A Battle for Sound Morality: The History of Recent Age-of-Consent Legislation in the United States, Part II.*

19. See Odem (1995), Alexander (1995), Kunzel (1993), Larson (1997), Schlossman and Wallach (1985), and Stansell (1987).

20. As at the turn of the century, this does not include "all" feminists. From about the 1970s, feminists have been bitterly divided over one branch's (radical feminists') alignment with conservative religious forces on some issues, while the other branches (for instance, liberal feminists, sex radical feminists, lesbian feminists) would not undertake such an alliance.

21. This is not to say that "nothing" happened in the area of sex crimes legislation from the 1910s until the 1970s. In the 1950s, for instance, a wave of "sexual psychopath" laws was passed. Philip Jenkins (1998: 72) cites the phrase *child molester* as appearing for the first time in *Reader's Digest* in 1953. See his *Moral Panic* for more detail on this time period.

22. See Spohn and Horney (1992: 20–22), Marsh, Geist, and Caplan (1982: 11, 19), Bienen (1980a: 177–180), and Searles and Berger (1987).

23. There is no defense for consensuality, in theory because an underage person is not mature enough to truly give consent to any sexual activity. There are, however, other defenses to a charge of statutory rape. Some states allow the mistake-of-age defense in which the perpetrator has compelling reason to believe that the victim is of age. Other states with age-span provisions allow a perpetrator whose age is very close to the age of the victim to be free from prosecution. Finally, all states exempt married partners from prosecution.

24. See Bienen (1980a: 177–180) and Searles and Berger (1987: 25–27).

25. In many states, same-age relationships can still be prosecuted as a misdemeanor; in several states as a felony.

26. Oberman is citing an interview with one of the feminist attorneys who revised the statute in Illinois.

27. As noted in the first note in this chapter, the crime is also known as statutory sexual seduction, rape in the *n*th degree (as distinct from forcible rape which is usually first degree, statutory rape was often classified as second-, third-, or fourth-degree rape), sexual abuse in the *n*th degree, sexual abuse of a minor, child sexual abuse, child rape, and indecency with a child.

28. Note that adolescents have other rights of consent, such as to marriage (in most states with parental or judicial permission; in some states if the female is pregnant), to abortion, to treatment for sexually transmitted diseases, to drug treatment.

29. See, for instance, Mead (1986) and Murray (1984). Also Lewis in Moynihan (1968) on the culture of poverty.

30. 450 US 464–502 (1981). This case is discussed in detail in chapter 3.

31. See Alan Guttmacher Institute (1994).

32. See, for example, the Urban Institute (1997).

33. Goodman quoting sociologist Elijah Anderson.

34. P.L.104-193, "Personal Responsibility and Work Opportunity Reconciliation Act of 1996." Title I Temporary Assistance to Needy Families, August 22, 1996.

35. P.L. 104-193, sec. 402(a) (1), (v), and (vi).

36. Connecticut, Delaware, Florida, Georgia, Idaho, Pennsylvania, Tennessee, Texas, Virginia, and Wisconsin.

37. For exceptions, see Donovan (1997) and Elders and Albert (1998).

38. States that require a parent's consent for abortions performed on minors must allow for that teenager to seek "judicial bypass" of that requirement, meaning that the teen can appeal to a judge in lieu of her parents. The judicial consent and the parental consent are viewed equally by the law.

39. See Elders and Albert (1998).

40. On these points, see Nathanson (1991) and Duggan (2000).

Chapter 2: Robbing the Cradle

1. See chapter 1 for a historical and more extensive discussion of statutory rape laws as rooted in a cultural narrative of gender vis-à-vis sexuality: that heterosexual males are the active and aggressive party, and heterosexual females the submissive and passive party. The male was punished so that the female was protected. There was no room in statutory rape law for female sexual agency because that agency violated the heteronormative boundaries of gender. Girls at the turn of the twentieth century who testified that their activity was consensual were often prosecuted under delinquency statutes, and consensuality is still not accepted as a defense to a statutory rape prosecution. The only defense is that the two parties were married at the time of the sexual act. In other words, the sexual activity of the "underage" who are unmarried is criminal; the sexual activity of the "underage" who are married is legal.

2. This age span represents the range of first intercourse for many teens in the 1990s; numbers range from 40% to 70% for this age group. See, for example, Alan Guttmacher Institute (1999a).

3. See, for example, Hall et al. (1978), Jenkins (1998), and Thompson (1998).

4. See also Marsh, Geist, and Caplan (1982) and Spohn and Horney (1992).

5. Some states have also implemented additional definitions of the crime of statutory rape that specify that the perpetrator be in a position of power, or have supervisory authority, over the victim. Others grade the punishment more harshly if such a relationship exists. Still others have no such provision. Such definitions are intended to get at coercion based on power relations rather than on force, and can include activity between parents and children, stepparents and stepchildren, foster parents and foster children, guardians and wards, and prison guards and inmates. My concern in this book, however, is generally with the criminalization of unmarried teens' sexual activity because every state criminalizes it.

6. The provisions require that one partner be a certain number of years older than the other for the crime of statutory rape to be prosecuted at the felony level, but in many states, same-age relationships can still be prosecuted as a misdemeanor, and in several states as a felony. This illuminates what may be the substantive purpose of statutory rape laws as noted in note 1, often obscured with rhetoric about protecting the young and vulnerable, and that is to discourage nonmarital sexuality. See chapter 1 for more detail on the history of the laws.

7. See chapter 1 for greater detail.

8. Bienen (1980a) cites one study that finds that the rate of "false" reports is the same for those over and under 16.

9. As noted, there is no defense for consensuality, in theory because an underage person is not mature enough to truly give consent to any sexual activity. The only universal defense to statutory rape is marriage—that is, that the two parties are married to one another, which makes their activity legal. There are other defenses to statutory rape as well that are not accepted in every state. Some states allow the mistake-of-age defense in which the perpetrator had a compelling reason to believe that the victim is of age. Like the marriage exemption, this lends support to the notion that it is not the age of and protection of the victim that is of great concern in and of itself. Also, as mentioned, some states with age-span provisions allow a perpetrator whose age is very close to the age of the victim to be free from prosecution. Third, until 1998, a few southern states also had a "promiscuity defense," namely, that if it could be proven that the (female) victim was not a virgin, no crime had been committed. This follows on statutory rape's roots as a crime that sought to protect not a young female per se, but her virginity, so as to make her more marriageable. See chapter 1 for more detail.

10. Following Mooney and Lee's work (1995: 601 fn 2) on pre–*Roe v. Wade* abortion regulation reform, I begin the analysis in the first year in which sustained policy adoptions began. Alabama had reformed its abortion law several years before other states began doing so in earnest in 1966. Thus Mooney and Lee use 1966 as the first year of analysis and exclude Alabama from the analysis. In the case of statutory rape reform, New York adopted an age-span provision in 1950 (and revised its age-span provision in 1965, still several years before the other states), more than twenty years before significantly continuous activity began across the states in 1971. In this chapter, therefore, I examine 49 states for the period 1971–1999 and exclude New York.

11. For example, Walker (1969), Gray (1973a), and Mooney and Lee (1995).

12. The three states were selected based on their comparable and contrasting values of the independent variables (NOW strength, Christian Right strength, citizen ideological leanings, and party control of the legislature and governorship), rather than their values on the dependent variable. See the appendix for further information on the methods by which the case study states were chosen.

13. §2A: 138-1. The age of consent had been raised from 10 to 16 in 1887. 1905 ch. 159 §115.

14. Interview with Leigh Bienen, 23 September 1999.

15. For example, Mooney and Lee (1995), Haider-Markel and Meier (1996), Mooney (2000), Lowi (1988), Norrander and Wilcox (2000), and Epstein and Kobylka (1992). One recent exception is Vergari (2000).

16. Ga. Code Ann. 16-6-3. This corroboration requirement remains in the current law.

17. This was inspired by a case near Towery's district, which garnered heavy news coverage. Two parents went away for a vacation and left their small children alone for several days. Towery remarked, "It was just appalling. . . . I do remember that because it sent me through the roof, and that's when I decided to raise the penalties for cruelty" (interview with Towery, 30 August 1999).

18. Langford had introduced statutory rape reform in 1994 as well, but it did not make it out of the Judiciary Committee on which he sat (interview with Langford, 8 September 1999).

19. Interview with Mary Beth Westmoreland, 30 August 1999.

20. Interview with J. Tom Morgan, DeKalb County district attorney, 30 August 1999.

21. This offense criminalizes soliciting, enticing, or taking any person under 16 to any place for the purpose of indecent acts or child molestation. It basically punishes any sexual proposition or sexual contact by any person of any age with any person under 16, at the felony level. As one district attorney noted, this criminalized teenage petting or oral sex by a mandatory ten years in prison, while those convicted of statutory rape, or vaginal intercourse, often received a probated sentence of one year (interview with J. Tom Morgan, 30 August 1999).

22. Barnes would become governor of Georgia; at the time, Zell Miller was the governor (interview with Langford, 8 September 1999).

23. Interview with Towery, 30 August 1999.

24. Like the sentences for statutory rape I have mentioned, this sentence can be probated as well. It is not mandatory. Thus in cases of consensual sex, the sentence had basically symbolic value (interview with J. Tom Morgan, 30 August 1999). This part of the act was proposed by then-Governor Zell Miller, and moved through by his floor leaders, as a means of getting at older men who impregnated underage teens. See chapter 4 for more details of this policy initiative.

25. Cal. Penal Code §261.5

26. Note that although this provision is gender-neutral, it does not name the perpetrator as necessarily the older party; one might assume this was intended to allow the prosecution of males who were younger than their female partners. See chapter 3 for detail of how the law was made gender-neutral in California.

27. Beckerman's stepson was not named as a victim in the case, however. One article says that he "saw the neighbor, Faye Abramowitz, have sex with his friend and watched pornographic movies at her home" (Moody 1993). He was sent to counseling.

28. Senate Floor, Comm. Rep. CA SB 22. This committee was important to the policy adoption discussed in chapter 4 as well, linking statutory rape and teen pregnancy.

29. See chapter 1 for more detail.

30. As noted in note 10, New York is excluded because of its 1950 adoption.

31. See the appendix for a discussion of the variables used here, as well as excluded variables and pooled cross-sectional time series in general.

32. The dummy "New England" variable includes Connecticut, Massachusetts, New Hampshire, and Vermont. I did this out of concern that these New England states' tendency to have adopted age spans very late if at all was skewing the effects of the group variables in particular. Each has high membership in NOW, little Christian Right influence, and a liberal citizenry. Each also adopted progressive rape reform in the 1970s—except for age-span provisions. This may be because such states have a tendency to leave on the books the more traditional versions of morality-based laws in general. On New England's history vis-à-vis morality policies, see, for example, Evans, (1997), Karlsen (1987), Eldridge (1997), and Cott et al. (1996). This action to contain the effects of these exceptional cases improves the ability to explain the policymaking process on this issue in the majority of states.

33. I dichotomize the dependent variable as "two- to three-year age span" versus "four- to six-year age span" because the feminists agitating for age-span provisions were generally concerned with protecting teenagers (particularly teenage females) from being coerced or manipulated into sexual activity by a person more powerful than they. A span of two to three years tends to include teens who are more likely to be similarly situated; for instance, one or two grades apart in high school, sharing similar experiences and similar peers. A four- to six-year span, on the other hand, is more reflective of people differently situated: an adult and a teen, a college student and a high school student, a high school student and a junior high school student. It is this type of power differential that was of concern to feminist lobbyists.

34. State-level polls asking about the same policy issues over time are most usable on the subject of abortion. Norrander and Wilcox (2001) found that on that subject, citizen responses are basically congruent to group activity and it is difficult to disaggregate the two. They also point out that group leanings are more extreme than that of the public on this issue. On statutory rape, though, note that none of the legislators in the case studies undertook to poll the public themselves.

35. I realize that a one-tailed test at the .10 level is lenient. However, recent articles report this significance level with caveats. I do the same. See Stream (1999) and Hojnacki and Kimball (1999).

36. Note, though, that NOW could have been influential in some states at an elite level without necessarily having a large membership base. And recall that in California the organization has a large membership but was uninterested in using its influence on the issue of statutory rape laws in the 1990s. It is these types of "exceptions" that point out the necessity of case study work to supplement the quantitative findings.

37. See also, for example, Pierce and Miller (2001).

38. Rozell and Wilcox (1998) and Norrander and Wilcox (2001).

39. Most states have taken their fornication statutes off the books. Seventeen states have retained them (Posner and Silbaugh 1996: 98–100): Arizona, Florida, Georgia, Idaho, Illinois, Massachusetts, Michigan, Mississippi, New Mexico, North Carolina, North Dakota, Oklahoma, South Carolina, Utah, Virginia, West Virginia, and the District of Columbia.

Chapter 3: Prosecuting Mrs. Robinson

1. In many states, the crime is defined as one of "sexual intercourse," which implies heterosexual sex. Other states are more vague and classify the crime as "unlawful sexual conduct," which given the gender-neutral language allows for the punishment of homosexual activity as well.

2. Unlike chapter 2 on age-span provisions, there is no reliable measure of public opinion on gender-neutral laws of any kind, let alone gender-neutral statutory rape laws. In general, pushing for gender-neutral language can be considered liberal in nature; resistance to such language is a more conservative viewpoint often based on ideas about the proper roles of males and females.

3. This was but one part of a sweeping effort at reforming rape laws nationwide. See Bienen (1980a: 177–180) and Searles and Berger (1987: 25–27). See chapter 1 for details of this rape reform movement.

4. Note that the debate as characterized below is about the sexual activity of teens, not about the sexual abuse of small children.

5. See Cocca (2002c).

6. Interview with Leigh Bienen, 23 September 1999.

7. There are various reasons for states to act in anticipation of court decisions. One major reason is to avoid being sued by its own citizens and thus be forced to allocate resources to defend the state from such a lawsuit (and also to have to follow through with the appeal process if the state loses at the initial level). Amending the law in question avoids such an expense of time and personnel.

8. (1977, CA1 NH) 564 F2d 602, cert. denied 436 US 950, 56 L Ed 2d 793, 98 S Ct 2858.

9. There was another circuit case dealing with statutory rape law, in 1980. But while the case came from Arizona, the law in question was the federal statutory rape statute (18 USCA 2241 and 2243) dealing with U.S. territories. That statute came into play because the female in question was Native American (*US v. Hicks* [1980, CA9 Ariz] 625 F2d 216).

10. Indeed, a recent study (Smith 1999) on the propensity of legislatures to adopt refusal-of-treatment laws found that state courts had virtually no influence on legislative adoption.

11. *Craig v. Boren*, 429 US 190 (1976). This level of scrutiny is termed "intermediate scrutiny." Laws involving "suspect classifications" such as race receive strict scrutiny, which burdens the state to show that the classification is necessary to achieve compelling state interest; economically based laws generally receive minimal scrutiny,

which burdens the challenger to show that the classification has no rational relationship to achieving a permissible state objective.

12. As noted in note 8, the Supreme Court "denied cert." to this case; that is, at least six of the nine justices declined to hear the appeal.

13. See McCollum (1982: 358–359) and Eidson (1980: 786). Also see 450 US 464 at 474.

14. It is somewhat ironic that while statutory rape laws were historically concerned with white females' chastity, as discussed in chapter 1, they are construed by the Supreme Court as attempts to circumscribe teenage (read: poor, black) motherhood. The use of statutory rape laws as a deterrent to engaging in sexual activity in which a young female becomes pregnant is the subject of chapter 4.

15. See, for instance, In Re T.A.J., a 1998 case from California, in which the defense challenged the law (unsuccessfully) on the basis of privacy rights.

16. Kansas was the first state to adopt a gender-neutral provision in 1969. I thus begin the analysis of the 50 states in 1969, and continue it through 1999 by which time only Alabama had not yet incorporated gender-neutral language in its rape statutes.

17. Powell v. State, 510 SE.2d18 (1998). The best-known previous challenge was appealed to the U.S. Supreme Court in Bowers v. Hardwick, 478 US 186 (1986).

18. See Walker (1969), Gray (1973a), and Mooney and Lee (1995).

19. See the appendix for a fuller explanation of how these particular states were chosen based on the values of the independent variables. New Jersey, Georgia, and California adopted both age-span provisions and gender-neutral language in the same year, and so some of the events recounted in this chapter will be familiar. These three states are in the minority of states in this pattern of simultaneous policy adoption. Seven states only adopted one of the two provisions, 26 states adopted these two provisions in different years, and 17 adopted in the same year. These are 3 of the 17. Because I chose the case study states based on their values on the independent variables rather than their values on the dependent variable so as not to skew my results toward success, it is merely by chance that these three states adopted the two provisions simultaneously. If one were to split hairs, one could say that New Jersey adopted the two provisions at separate times due to its legislature returning to its statutory rape law after the public outcry over the briefly lowered age of consent, and so passed its actual age-span provision slightly later than the gender neutrality.

20. §2A: 138-1. The penalty was a fine, imprisonment at hard labor of not more than 15 years, or both. As noted in chapter 2, the fine had been raised to $5000 from the 1905 statute's $2000 (1905 Ch. 159 §115). The age of consent had been raised from 10 to 16 in 1887.

21. Note that the four-year age span was removed in 1979 before the act took effect, in cases when the victim is under 13, and an offense was added that criminalized sexual penetration with a victim under 16 when the perpetrator is at least four years older. This is detailed in chapter 2.

22. Interview with Bienen, 23 September 1999.

23. Ibid.

24. During the debate over the statutory rape reform bills, two court cases in New Jersey upheld gender-specific language—State v. Thompson, 162 NJ Super 302, 392

A2d 678 (1978); and *State v. Hill*, 170 NJ Super 485, 406 A2d 1334 (1979). The legislature chose to act anyway.

25. *In the Interest of B.L.S.*, 264 Ga. 643, 449 SE2d 823, 94 Fulton Cty DR 3737 (1994). It had also done so in 1979 in *Barnes v. State*, 244 Ga 302, 260 SE2d 40. Also in 1995, the age of consent was raised from 14 to 16, and an age span of three years was implemented.

26. Interview with Steve Langford, 8 Sepetember 1999; and interview with Matt Towery, 30 August 1999.

27. New York followed this pattern as well. It struck down the gender-specific forcible rape law as unconstitutional in 1984 in *People v. Liberta*, but distinguished it from statutory rape law and left the latter gender-specific.

28. Statutory rape laws as a deterrent to teen pregnancy is discussed in more detail in chapter 4 and in Cocca (2002a).

29. 25 Cal 3d 608, 601 P2d 572, 159 Cal Rptr 340 (1979), cert. granted 100 S Ct 2984, aff'd, 450 US 464 (1981).

30. 25 Cal 3d 608 at 615, 621–25. See also Eidson (1980: 787).

31. Coda: The statutory rape charges against Michael were dropped. The Supreme Court remanded the case to Sonoma County Superior Court for trial. But Michael could not be found. Finally, in 1984—at which time he was 24-years-old, married, and a father—he was arrested for a parole violation. At that point, Sharon could not be found and the prosecutor dropped the case (UPI 1984).

32. See Cocca (2002c).

33. See the appendix for a discussion of the variables used here, as well as excluded variables and pooled cross-sectional time series in general. Note that I have classified Idaho as a state with a gender-neutral statute with a five-year age span because of the wording of its crime of "sexual battery" which is a high-grade felony carrying a maximum sentence of life in prison. Idaho also has a "rape" statute that criminalizes penetration of a female under 18 by the perpetrator's penis; clearly gender-specific. It also, though, has a "male rape" statute criminalizing the forcible rape of males by males. With this and sexual battery, women can be charged and males are acknowledged as victims. Thus I include Idaho as a gender-neutral adopt-state.

34. When I contacted the chapter and state development director of NOW to obtain the state membership numbers from the organization, I explained my project to her. She acknowledged that NOW played a central role in rape law reform, particularly in the 1970s, but cautioned me that state membership might not capture that relationship. She explained that in some states in which NOW membership is high in proportion to the population, there have been members of the legislature—particularly chairs of judiciary committees—completely unsympathetic to their goals. On the other hand, in some states in which NOW's membership base is proportionately low, sympathetic committee chairs pushed their draft legislation through. This was particularly true in the 1970s during the bulk of the reform movement, and at which time there were fewer female legislators (interview with Barbara Hays, 22 April 1999).

35. For example, Oakley (1999), Pierce and Miller (2001), and Smith (1999).

36. See also Cocca (2002a).

37. Alabama, Arkansas, Arizona, California, Illinois, Kansas, Minnesota, New York, and Wisconsin.

38. It is somewhat difficult to generalize about statutory rape prosecutions because of the methods by which arrest and conviction records on the crime are collected; in short, they are often bundled in with several other "morals" offenses like indecent exposure, or sometimes bundled with forcible rape. Having said this, the National Judicial Reporting Program survey for 1998 that breaks down crimes by the sex of the offender found that of persons convicted for "Sexual Assault" (including forcible rape) felonies 97% were male and 3% were female (Durose, Levin, and Langan 2001). A Bureau of Justice Statistics survey that combines datasets reports that of all offenders in state prison for "Other sexual assault," 98.8% were male and 1.2% were female (Greenfeld 1997). The chief of the sex crimes division in Cook County, Illinois, has said that less than 5% of pending felony cases had female perpetrators; he could only remember two or three cases of women in positions of power charged with the crime (Stevens 1998). In terms of probated sentences, a Georgia Department of Corrections spokesman said that of the approximately 800 people on probation in that state for statutory rape, 18 are women—about 2% (Jones 2000). In short, the number of women prosecuted for statutory rape does not appear to have skyrocketed since the adoption of gender-neutral language. However, according to a recent (FBI) Uniform Crime Reporting Program study, the number of male victims has risen to include about 14% of all types of sexual assaults reported to law enforcement (Snyder 2000). This indicates that while those prosecuted are still overwhelmingly male, a not insignificant number of them were prosecuted for same-sex activity.

39. On this link, see, for example, Jenkins (1998).

40. Later, Manzie was charged with additional crimes so that he is to serve 70 years; many of the charges against Simmons were dropped when Manzie—who received an additional six-month sentence for his refusal—would not testify against Simmons. Simmons is to serve five years for endangering the welfare of a child (Hanley 1999a,b).

41. This is not to say that medicalized language is not used to describe pedophilia—it virtually always is. Recent examples include *New York Times* articles such as "Sex Offenders Test Parole Officers" (Purdy 1997a), "Wave of New Laws Seeks to Confine Sex Offenders: Mental Hospitalization" (Purdy 1997b), and "New Therapy Offers Promise in Treatment of Pedophiles" (Leary 1998). My point is that such language tends to be coupled with describing the [male] offenders as "violent," "dangerous," and "abusive."

42. After several years of searching LEXIS and Westlaw, with no date restrictions, for caselaw (all federal and state cases) and for secondary legal and news items (all U.S. news and wire services, all major world news outlets, all law reviews, all bar journals), I have found no such cases. Altering search terms in a myriad of combinations and varying the levels of specificity of the searches has made no difference. Interviews with district attorneys have been fruitless as well.

43. I have found no cases fitting these descriptions either.

44. O'Neill later said that the girls "made lots of it up," that he never used any object for penetration, that the girls probably knew that he did not have a penis, and that perhaps they were embarrassed about the events (Minkowitz 1995: 140).

45. After testimony from the females (one of whom later appeared on the *Jerry Springer Show*), and from transgender activists, O'Neill was sentenced to 90 days in prison, 6 years of probation, which included counseling, and mandatory reporting of all

contacts with females under the age of consent or that might lead to sexual intimacy (www.brentpayton.com/trans/sean_oneill_sentenced_to_90_days.txt).

46. Indeed, a Florida case saw an older male prosecuted for one instance of sex with a 15-year-old male (which was videotaped by a third party) who testified that he had consented to the sex. The perpetrator was given a sentence of 150 years and 30 years probation. He appealed the sentence, and the appeals court wrote that departing so far from statutory rape sentencing guidelines was deserved because the perpetrator "sees nothing wrong with his conduct" because "the minor male does not feel victimized;" the court therefore found him not amenable to rehabilitation and as posing a danger to society (*Jory v. State of Florida*, 647 So.2d 152 at 153, 1994). They were unconvinced by the defendant's argument that "he had done nothing illegal and that state's pursuit of case stemmed from lifestyle prosecution, a classic example of homophobia" (at 152). The dissenting judge agreed with the perpetrator, and wrote "Florida's sexual battery laws are gender neutral. As such, courts should apply them equally and fairly to all defendants, however distasteful a defendant's lifestyle may be to a particular judge or panel of judges" (at 156). See also note 38.

Chapter 4: From "Welfare Queen" to "Exploited Teen"

1. California, Connecticut, Delaware, Florida, Idaho, Pennsylvania, Tennessee, Texas, Virginia, and Wisconsin. This may make no difference to studying policy adoption. On the other hand, it is possible that some or all of these 10 states are atypical in some way vis-à-vis the other 40 states.

2. The Alan Guttmacher Institute (AGI) is a nonpartisan organization that collects and analyzes data on sexual activity, contraception, abortion, and childbearing. Other adolescent self-reports vary: about two-thirds to three-quarters of teens report having had sexual intercourse. The figure cited in the text from AGI is about the average of that range.

3. The phrase *welfare queen* itself is perhaps more accurately one that others have ascribed to Reagan as having used. He did, while running for President, describe in stump speeches a woman with "80 names, 30 address, 12 social security cards," who was "collecting welfare, under each of her names." Regardless of the initial source of the coining of the phrase, it has circulated continuously in both elite and mass discourses on welfare.

4. See also Lindberg et al. (1997).

5. AGI (1999a). Compiled from 1995 National Survey of Family Growth and 1995 National Survey of Adolescent Males.

6. See the bibliography for examples of the literally hundreds of articles that make this link, and also tend to quote the AGI "two-thirds" statistic.

7. P.L. 104-193, "Personal Responsibility and Work Opportunity Reconciliation Act of 1996." Title I Temporary Assistance to Needy Families, 22 August 1996.

8. Note also that the teenage birthrate, as a "per-1,000-population" figure, is different from looking at the percentage of all births that are to teenagers. The teenage birthrate may rise and fall with the overall birthrate and thus not be of comparative significance. An example would be the high teenage birthrate in the baby-boom period

of the 1950s; the overall birthrate was very high as well, so we can draw few conclusions about teenagers from that figure. Looking at the percentage of all births that are births to teenagers is more informative in drawing specific conclusions about teenagers, but those figures are not often used in public discourses on teenage pregnancy even though the Department of Health and Human Services does collect them.

9. See chapter 1 for more details.

10. Lieberman Amendments 4899–4900, 142 Congressional Record S8222-01, 18 July 1996; and Amendments 4946–4947, 142 Congressional Record S8395-04, 22 July 1996.

11. 142 Congressional Record S8395-04, 22 July 1996.

12. Note that in the spring of 2002, President George W. Bush's administration had to extend the PRWORA; it was set to expire after five years. On this exact section, the 2002 report entitled "Working toward Independence" says that the Bush proposal will "clarify the meaning of the TANF goal to encourage the formation and maintenance of *healthy* two parent *married* families *and responsible fatherhood*" (20; emphasis added). The Bush administration also proposes to require states to "describe efforts to promote marriage as part of their state plan through explicit descriptions of their family formation and healthy marriage efforts; numerical performance goals; and annual reporting of state achievement" (20).

13. Representative Eva Clayton (D-NC), 142 Congressional Record H5737-02, 30 May 1996.

14. Senator Rick Santorum (R-PA), 142 Congressional Record S8076-02, 18 July 1996.

15. 142 Congressional Record S8366-01, 19 July 1996.

16. 142 Congressional Record S8395-04, 22 July 1996.

17. At www.now.org, thousands of press releases, legislative updates, and informational pieces on various issues are stored. I have looked through each page having to do with welfare reform, and sexuality in general, and youth in general. In addition, I have contacted the organization at both the national and the state levels to ask about their position on the matter of statutory rape, teen pregnancy, and welfare reform. Each time, I have been assured that the priorities of the organization have not changed and that it is concerned with protecting all women from harm.

18. The current Bush administration's 2002 "Working toward Independence" proposal to extend the PRWORA, virtually echoes this language in its section entitled "Encourage Abstinence and Prevent Teen Pregnancy." That section begins,

> The sexual revolution that began in the 1960s has left two major problems in its wake. The first is the historic increase in non-marital births that have contributed so heavily to the Nation's domestic problems including poverty, violence, and intergenerational welfare dependency. The second is the explosion of sexually transmitted diseases that now pose a growing hazard to the Nation's public health. (22)

The importation of this language from a very conservative publication, and its repetition in a government document about a law often cited as bipartisan, discursively naturalize such ideas as centrist and commonsensical.

19. In the adopt-states, this recommendation became a requirement.

20. Note the use of the word *alleged* to describe the father's identity as reported by the mother; the assumption is apparently that if she became pregnant, she might be promiscuous as well.

21. California, Delaware, Florida, Idaho, and Tennessee adopted in 1996; Connecticut, Pennsylvania, Texas, Virginia, and Wisconsin adopted in 1997. One cannot make much of a claim about either a temporal or a geographic pattern from looking at these 10 states over two years.

22. "Governor's Initiative, 1996–97," 1 April 1996.

23. Assembly Bill (AB) 1490, chap. 789 (1996). Although it is titled "1995," it was not passed until 1996; thus I assign California 1996 as its adopt year. See Cal. Penal Code §261.5.

24. I have attempted repeatedly and in a number of different ways to contact Caldera and two men who were his key consultants during this time period and have been unsuccessful. I do, however, have Caldera's 500-page well-organized and detailed bill file that he kept throughout his campaign for the Teenage Pregnancy Prevention Act. It includes secondary material on which he based the bill, press releases from his office and from the governor's office, various drafts of the bill, reports from each of the committees that saw the bill, letters in support and opposition, memoranda within his office and those to and from other committees, correspondence within and outside of the legislature, and secondary material covering the progress of the bill. I also have the governor's bill file, which is an additional 50 or so pages.

25. Quoting Michael Males, then a doctoral student at the University of California at Irvine.

26. Caldera did not begin corresponding directly with Governor Wilson until the summer, at which point he told Wilson that he was "delighted to learn recently" that the governor was supportive of funding statutory rape prosecutions to combat teen pregnancy. This seems difficult to believe, but points to the notion that the two had not spoken about it in the past (letter, 1 August 1995).

27. AB 1490 Bill Text Introduced by Caldera, 24 February 1995.

28. While this was occurring, Senate Leader Bill Lockyer (D-Hayward; he became attorney general of California in November 1998) introduced a bill for a state-funded media campaign targeting adult men in order to reduce teen pregnancy. It was to include electronic and print ads and billboards as well as educational materials to be passed out by schools and community groups. The money would come from Governor Wilson's proposed $32 million to prevent pregnancy.

29. AB 1490 Amended by Caldera, 6 April 1995.

30. See chapters 2 and 3 for detail on the 1993 amendments to the California statutory rape law.

31. Press Release, Governor Wilson's Office, "Wilson Urges Passage of Criminal Justice Reforms; Applauds District Attorneys for the Fight against Crime," 27 June 1995.

32. Ibid.

33. News Release, Louis Caldera's Office, "Teenage Pregnancy Prevention Bill Passes Assembly Public Safety Committee," 9 January 1996.

34. Amendment, 6 April 1995 and AB 1490 Senate Committee on Criminal Procedure Hearing, 14 May 1996.

35. One could also interpret this as making the collection of funds easier. If a district attorney were to lose the criminal case because he or she could not prove the perpetrator guilty beyond a reasonable doubt, it might be easier to pursue the case in civil court in which one need only prove the perpetrator guilty by a preponderance of the evidence. A portion of the money would be rolled over to the "Underage Pregnancy Prevention Fund." The ACLU alone objected to this lowering of the standard of proof.

36. Letters: Planned Parenthood, 9 August 1996; ACLU, 9 August 1996; National Council of Jewish Women, 6 August 1996; and Los Angeles Free Clinic, 7 August 1996.

37. Assembly Bill 1490 Amended by Caldera, 20 August 1996.

38. According to a letter to the author from Elizabeth McGovern, NOW legislative advocate, January 6, 2000, NOW may have supported Wilson's statutory rape vertical prosecution program, although there is no written record of that. McGovern herself was not employed by NOW at the time. According to McGovern, the woman who was the president of the California chapter of NOW at the time, Elizabeth Toledo, "doesn't remember whether NOW had a position. However, another past president, Linda Joplin, who has been actively involved with the organization for many years, believes that the California chapter of NOW did have a support position on Wilson's Statutory Rape Vertical Prosecution program." There is no record of any NOW activity on Caldera's bill; nor did conversations with NOW members elicit any recollection of such activity.

39. Letter to Mike Machado, 13 September 1996.

40. For more on the construction of an epidemic of teen pregnancy as caused by statutory rape, see Cocca (2002a).

41. At the time of my interviews, Baker was the attorney general of Georgia. He advised me to speak to DeKalb County District Attorney J. Tom Morgan as someone who would be more knowledgeable about the subject of statutory rape and about what types of cases were being prosecuted.

42. Interview with Steve Langford, D-LaGrange, 8 September 1999.

43. Ibid. Act 965, SB 210 and Act 876, HB 1316.

44. Interview with J. Tom Morgan, district attorney, DeKalb County, Georgia, 30 August 1999.

45. Ibid. In the 1998 gubernatorial election, Morgan recalled, the Republican candidate for lieutenant governor urged that type of aggressive prosecution in order to stem teen pregnancy. He lost. On the implementation side, prosecutors in Georgia were unconvinced of the connection between prosecuting statutory rape and reducing teenage pregnancies. Morgan, who along with other district attornies across the state had been courted about the issue and the need for more prosecutions, reacted to the purported link by saying, "That is the dumbest thing I ever heard" (interview with Morgan). In California, the situation was the opposite among these legal professionals: They were interviewed repeatedly as spokespeople for the new policy, and prosecuted about 10 times more statutory rape cases than in previous years.

46. See the appendix for a discussion of the variables used here, as well as excluded variables and pooled cross-sectional time series in general.

47. Interview with Morgan, 30 August 1999.

48. For a fuller-length treatment of this theme, see Duggan (2000).

Conclusion

1. On this point, in other areas of sexuality, see also D'Emilio and Freedman (1997), Stansell (1987), Walkowitz (1992), Odem (1995), Alexander (1995), and Kunzel (1993).

2. On these points, see Duggan (2000: 35, 65) and Best (1990: 175, 180).

3. In Nebraska one may be 17; in Mississippi the male may be 17 and the female may be 15; in Ohio the male must be 18 but the female may be 16. See Posner and Silbaugh (1996).

Appendix

1. See Nice (1994: 12), quoting Adrian (1976: 56); also Savage (1978: 219) and Berry and Berry (1990: 400, quoting Elazar 1972).

2. See, for example, Brace and Jewett (1995) and Jewell (1982). At a roundtable about theoretical approaches to the study of state politics at the meeting of the American Political Science Association in Atlanta in August 1999, much of the discussion was devoted to this problem, and participants called for more work to be done on theoretical concerns and on causal inferences. In particular, Jan Leighley cited the need to examine the mechanisms by which policy is made by the chosen independent variables, and to address the theories of concerns of other subfields; Rick Hofferbert noted that political scientists need to get away from the "Casablanca style" of research in which we simply "round up the usual suspects [independent variables]" to test them.

3. I am speaking here of the segment of the comparative state politics literature that consists mainly of 50-state quantitative studies and employs no case study research. The case study research in the state politics field suffers from its own problems; namely, that it is often used to study one or two states and is not linked in any comprehensive way with more abstract tests that might show more general patterns. This is why I combine these two methods.

4. See, for example, Lippmann (1922), Campbell et al. (1960), Converse (1964), Margolis and Mauser (1989), Stimson (1991), Page and Shapiro (1992), and Zaller (1992).

5. See, for example, Campbell et al. (1960), Abramson, Aldrich, and Rohde (1995), Rosenstone and Hansen (1993), and Wolfinger and Rosenstone (1980).

6. On the necessity of reelection seeking in general, see Mayhew (1974), Jacobson (1992), Fiorina (1989), Fenno (1978), and Arnold (1990).

7. For example, Lowi (1979).

8. For example, Heclo (1978) and Berry (1989).

9. For example, Mooney and Lee (1995), Nice (1988, 1994), Grogan (1994), Berry and Berry (1990), Mintrom (1997), and Haider-Markel (2001).

10. While a person alone might muse (correctly, mathematically speaking) that his or her vote will make little or no difference to the outcome of any election, knowing that others would vote in the same manner could overcome the willingness to be a "free rider" and merely rely on the efforts of others to receive benefits. This could reach a point of diminishing returns if the group is very large; thus, the individual group mem-

ber could assume that numerous others are voting his or her preference. But perhaps a person in such a group would receive social approval (solidary benefits) from voting along with others in the group. This notion of solidary benefits as helping to overcome Olson's collective action problem (1968) was first proposed by Wilson (1973) and has been illustrated in, for example, Chong (1991) with the civil rights movement. See also Margolis and Mauser (1989), Popkin (1991), and Page and Shapiro (1992) on using a group's stance as an informational shortcut for how to vote. See Wattenberg (1996) on groups organizing votes and Mayhew (1974) and Arnold (1990) on politicians catering to groups. On political action committees and their influence, see Grenzke (1989), Berry (1997), and Conway and Green (1995).

11. See, for instance, Verba and Nie (1972) on group identification and forms of participation, and on black turnout; and Radcliff and Davis (2000) on union membership as affecting turnout.

12. Wattenberg (1991, 1996), Aldrich (1995), Jacobson (1992), Rosenstone, Behr, and Lazarus (1996), and Berry (1997). Along with candidate-centered voting and an increasing willingness among the public to find the parties irrelevant, as well as electoral rules virtually ensuring the failure of a third party, structural changes in Congress providing more access points to outsiders have also contributed to a rise in the number and importance of groups: Berry (1989, 1997), Schlozman and Tierney (1983), Grenzke (1989), Salisbury (1990), Cigler (1991), and Cigler and Loomis (1995). On groups vis-à-vis hearings on court appointments, see Maltese (1995), Silverstein (1994), and DeGregorio and Rosotti (1995); in the courts, see Epstein and Kobylka (1992).

13. This latter period is particularly pertinent to this book, as I hypothesize that the strength of NOW (and the strength of Christian conservatives, on the opposite side of the ideological spectrum) is crucial to the adoption of specific statutory rape policies.

14. See Walker (1969), Gray (1973a,b), and Savage (1978).

15. See also Walker (1969) and Savage (1985).

16. See Meier (1994), Nice (1994), Mooney and Lee (1995), Tatalovich and Daynes (1988), Gusfield (1986), and Moen (1984).

17. See, for example, Meier and McFarlane (1992), Meier and Johnson (1990), Mooney and Lee (1995), Glick and Hays (1991), and Tatalovich and Daynes (1988).

18. See, for example, Meier and McFarlane (1992: 691), Mooney (2001), Oakley (1999), and Meier (2001).

19. See Mooney and Lee (2001), Haider-Markel and Meier (1996), Meier (1994), and Nice (1992).

20. This impacts on another finding by morality policy scholars that there is little compromise on morality policy as there is on other types of policies (Mooney and Lee 1995; Lowi 1988). The case of abortion shows that there can be, and I find that the case of statutory rape shows the same.

21. Norrander and Wilcox (2001). Note too that these authors have been writing about the subject of abortion for years and are among those who have found strong effects for public opinion themselves.

22. There is some evidence as well that a bill supported by groups has a better chance of passing than one without such support. See Wiggins, Hamm, and Bell (1992: 90).

23. See also Glick and Hutchinson (2001).

24. See also Margolis and Mauser (1989) on elites rather than public opinion as determining policy outcomes; and Page and Shapiro (1989), noting that public policy moves against, or ignores, public opinion at least one-third of the time.

25. On these points, see Tatalovich and Daynes (1981).

26. Berry and Berry (1990: 398) surmise that at least in theory no state is at risk of adopting until another one has. See also Mintrom (1997).

27. This explication of logit and probit is derived from Aldrich and Nelson (1984), Cramer (1991), Greene (1990), and Kennedy (1998).

28. The goodness of fit is slightly higher; the coefficients and the standard errors of the six main variables are little different both in their values and in their relationship to one another. The results reported in chapters 2, 3, and 4 do not include the annual dummies; I follow Mooney and Lee (1995) in dropping them from the analysis.

29. For example, Mooney and Lee (1995); others who institute no corrections are Meier and McFarlane (1992), Oakley (1999), Smith (1999), Spriggs, Maltzman, and Wahlbeck (1999), and King and Meernik (1999).

30. See, for instance, King (1986, 1991) and Luskin (1991) on how well-fitting models may tell us little to nothing about causal effects and about the real world. Also see Spriggs, Maltzman, and Wahlbeck (1999).

31. Cox and Wermuth (1992) determined that the largest possible value of R^2 in a linear probability model with a dichotomous outcome is 0.36, no matter how strong the influence of the predictors.

32. Mooney and Lee (1995: 620) note this problem as well.

33. The section following discusses variables excluded from the analysis.

34. The static nature of this variable is an issue, even though the authors demonstrate stability over time. The best alternate measure is that of Berry et al. (1998), which covers the years 1960–1997 (the original article covered the years 1960–1993; an update through 1997 was provided to me by one of the authors). However, Erikson, Wright, and McIver's measure is a product of public opinion polls, a direct measure. Berry et al.'s measure is a product of an ideology score for the district's incumbent, the estimated ideology score for a challenger or hypothetical challenger to the incumbent, and election results. These district-level results are compiled to produce a score for the whole state. That this measures citizen ideology is based on the Downsian theorem (1957) that voters on a left–right continuum will vote for the candidate closest to himself or herself on that continuum. We cannot know how "close" the voter is to the candidate, and we cannot know the ideological predilections of nonvoters who are an increasing segment of the American population (particularly in off-year elections). By using the Erikson, Wright, and McIver measure I sacrifice variability over time, but using polls brings the measure closer to citizen preferences than does the proxy of election results.

35. See, for example, Page and Shapiro (1992), who find that public opinion and policy are congruent about two-thirds of the time and opposite about one-third.

36. On subgovernments, see Lowi (1979); on networks, see Berry (1989).

37. Dye (1966), Holbrook and Percy (1992), Haider-Markel and Meier (1996), and Oakley (1999). An exception: Mooney and Lee (1995) found that high party competition caused avoidance of innovation for pre–*Roe v. Wade* abortion reform.

38. See, for example, Lichtenstein (1975), Bienen (1980a), and Searles and Berger (1987).

39. See, for example, Wiggins, Hamm, and Bell (1992).

40. See, for example, Brace et al. (1989).

41. I also computed a measure of Christian Right influence from the Christian Coalition's 1998 "Scorecard," supplied to me by the organization. For 15 issues in the House and 11 in the Senate, it records the votes of every congressperson and computes the percentage of those votes on which the congressperson voted "for" the Coalition's viewpoint. I compiled and averaged these scores to come up with two state averages: one for the House and one for the Senate. These measures did not perform very well in tests because the coefficients for the House and for the Senate sometimes pointed in different directions. This was probably due in part to basing the figures for the Senate on only two people. The Green, Guth, and Wilcox scale is more on target for the purposes of this research anyway, as it is measured at the state- rather than national-level legislature.

42. See Luker (1996), Lawson and Rhode (1993), Solinger (1992), Roberts (1997), and Cohen (1999).

43. Hispanic is an ethnic, not a racial, categorization. Hispanics can be black or white. However, Hispanics are often constructed as nonwhite, regardless of the nature of the category. Their very measurement, when no other ethnic group is statistically tracked in such a way or so consistently, is indicative of their constructed status as a distinct group.

44. For example, Mooney and Lee (1995).

45. See generally, Dye (1966) and Hwang and Gray (1991).

46. See, for example, Odem (1995), Alexander (1995), Gusfield (1963), Kunzel (1993), and Peiss (1986). Also, Nice (1994) finds a relationship between low education/income and stricter morality policies.

47. See, for example, Luker (1996) and Lawson and Rhode (1993).

48. Chapter 4 discusses this in great detail; also see Luker (1996), Lawson and Rhode (1993), and Solinger (1992).

49. He also ranks the states against one another. I tried to use this measure as well; it performed no better and no worse than that of the index.

50. Oakley (1999), Nice (1988), and Mooney and Lee (1995: 611) were exceptions and found that this measure includes proportionately too many nonmorality-based policies and thus would add little to the discussion of morality policies

51. Smith (1999), Stream (1999), Oakley (1999), and Mintrom (1997).

52. The Pearson goodness-of-fit chi-square of these models ranged from .019 two-tailed to .094 two-tailed. In the following paragraphs, I cite approximations of the correlations based on all three tests; the numbers were very similar but not identical given that different years were covered; states adopted the three types of policies at different times.

53. I dropped the neighbor variable and ran the regressions again without it, because it clearly drew so much from each of the others. The results that follow are those without this variable.

Bibliography

AAP Information Services Pty, Ltd. 1998. "Teacher Who Raped Boy Says He Initiated Meeting." *AAP Newsfeed* (Western Australian Regional), 5 February.

Abcarian, Robin. 1995. "For Every Teen Mother, There Has to Be a Father." *Los Angeles Times*, 25 January.

Abramson, Paul, John Aldrich, and David Rohde. 1995. *Change and Continuity in the 1992 Elections*. Washington, DC: CQ Press.

Adams, Gina, Karen Pittman, and Raymond O'Brien. 1993. "Adolescent and Young Adult Fathers: Problems and Solutions." In *The Politics of Pregnancy: Adolescent Sexuality and Public Policy*, edited by Annette Lawson and Deborah Rhode, 216–237. New Haven, CT: Yale University Press.

Agence France Presse. 1998. "Seven Years Behind Bars for Women Teacher Convicted of Raping Boy Teen." [General News Item, var. pub.], 6 February.

"Aide Faces Sex Charge in Case Involving Student." 1998. *New York Times*, 18 June.

Aldrich, John. 1995. *Why Parties?* Chicago: University of Chicago Press.

Aldrich, John, and Forrest Nelson. 1984. *Linear Probability, Logit, and Probit Models*. Thousand Oaks, CA: Sage.

Alan Guttmacher Institute. 1994. *Sex and America's Teenagers*. New York: Alan Guttmacher Institute.

———. 1997. "Welfare Reform, Marriage and Sexual Behavior." New York: Alan Guttmacher Institute.

———. 1998. "Teenage Pregnancy and the Welfare Reform Debate." New York: Alan Guttmacher Institute.

———. 1999a. "Teen Sex and Pregnancy." (September). New York: Alan Guttmacher Institute.

———. 1999b. "Teenage Pregnancy: Overall Trends and State-by-State Information." (April). New York: Alan Guttmacher Institute.

———. 1999c. "U.S. Teenage Pregnancy Statistics." (June). New York: Alan Guttmacher Institute.

Alexander, Ruth. 1995. *The "Girl Problem": Female Sexual Delinquency in New York, 1900–1930.* Ithaca, NY: Cornell University Press.

Allison, Paul. 1984. *Event History Analysis.* Newbury Park, CA: Sage.

Alter, Jonathan. 1994. "The Name of the Game is Shame." *Newsweek*, 12 December.

Alvarez, Lizette. 1998. "G.O.P. Bill to Back Parental Consent Abortion Laws." *New York Times*, 21 May.

Amelio, Anthony M. 1995. "Florida's Statutory Rape Law: A Shield or a Weapon?—A Minor's Right of Privacy under Florida Statute §794.05." 26 *Stetson Law Review* 407.

American Bar Association, Center on Children and the Law. 1997. "Sexual Relationships between Adult Males and Young Teen Girls: Exploring the Legal and Social Responses." Chicago: American Bar Association.

American Law Institute. 1985a. *Model Penal Code and Commentaries Part II §210.0–213.6.* Philadephia: American Law Institute.

———. 1985b. *Model Penal Code Complete Statutory Text.* Philadephia: American Law Institute.

———. 1995. *Model Penal Code, Article 213. Sexual Offenses.* Eagan, MN: West Group.

Andre-Clark, Alice Susan. 1992. "Note: Whither Statutory Rape Laws: Of Michael M., the Fourteenth Amendment, and Protecting Women from Sexual Aggression." *Southern California Law Review* 65: 1933–1992.

Applebome, Peter. 1998. "No Room for Children in a World of Little Adults." *New York Times*, 10 May.

Arnold, Douglas. 1990. *The Logic of Congressional Action.* New Haven, CT: Yale University Press.

Ash, Jim. 1996. "Kurth Bill to Revise Rape Law." *Florida Today*, 20 March.

Associated Press. 1993. "Surgery Blamed in Coach Sex Scandal Motive." *Sacramento Bee*, 16 June.

———. 1995. "Wilson Touts Tough on Crime Positions." *AP Wire Services*, 27 June.

———. 1996. "Teen Sex Laws among 77 Effective Today." *Florida Today*, 29 September.

———. 1997a. "Boy Who Had Sex with Teacher Says Pregnancy Was Planned." *Columbian* (Vancouver, WA), 22 August.

———. 1997b. "Far-Right Ex-Lawmaker, Father of Teacher in Sex Case; Ex-Congressman John Schmitz Raised Daughter according to Strict Catholic Teachings." *News Tribune*, 11 August.

———. 1997c. "Teacher Pleads Guilty to Sex with 13-Year Old Male Student." *Columbian* (Vancouver, WA), 7 August.

———. 1997d. "Teacher's Husband: 'I Want Her to Get Help'; Wife, Who Had Sex with Student, Is 'Still Living in Fantasy Land,' Man Says." *News Tribune*, 25 August.

———. 1998a. "At YM Magazine, It's a Girl's World." AP Online, 29 June.

———. 1998b. "Convicted Rapist Has House Shot At." *New York Times*, 1 July.

———. 1998c. "Ex-Teacher, Convicted of Rape, Arrested." *Columbian* (Vancouver, WA), 3 February.

———. 1998d. "'Fixation' with Teenager Costs Ex-Teacher 7½ Years in Prison." *Chicago Tribune*, 7 February.

———. 1998e. "Molester Kept Out of Oregon Community." AP Online, 7 August.

Ayres, B. Drummond. 1996. "Marriage Advised in Some Youth Pregnancies." *New York Times*, 9 September.

Bachrach, Peter, and Morton Baratz. 1962. "The Two Faces of Power." *American Political Science Review* 56: 947–952.

Baer, Judith. 1996. *Women in American Law: The Struggle toward Equality from the New Deal to the Present*. 2d ed. New York: Holmes and Meier.

Bailey, Beth. 1988. *From Front Porch to Back Seat: Courtship in Twentieth-Century America*. Baltimore: Johns Hopkins University Press.

Bailey, Eric. 1996. "New Law Levies Sizable Fines for Intercourse with Minors; Crime Bill Signed Monday by Governor Wilson Established a Legislative Fund for Anti-Teenage Pregnancy Prevention Programs." *Los Angeles Times* (Orange County ed.), 24 September.

Bartels, Larry. 1997. "Specification Uncertainty and Model Averaging." *American Journal of Political Science* 41, no. 2 (April): 641–674.

Bartlett, Katharine, and Rosanne Kennedy, eds. 1991. *Feminist Legal Theory: Readings in Law and Gender*. Boulder, CO: Westview.

Beck, Nathaniel, and Jonathan N. Katz. 1995. "What to Do (and Not to Do) with Time-Series Cross-Section Data." *American Political Science Review* 89, no. 3 (September): 634–647.

Bederman, Gail. 1995. *Manliness and Civilization: A Cultural History of Gender and Race in the United States, 1880-1917*. Chicago: University of Chicago Press.

Beisel, Nicola. 1997. *Imperiled Innocents: Anthony Comstock and Family Reproduction in Victorian America*. Princeton, NJ: Princeton University Press.

Berestein, Leslie. 1996. "Underage Sex Also a Civil Crime." *Orange County Register*, 24 September.

Berkman, Michael, and Robert O'Connor. 1993. "Do Women Legislators Matter? Female Legislators and State Abortion Policy." *American Politics Quarterly* 21, no. 1 (January): 102–124.

Berlant, Lauren, and Lisa Duggan, eds. 2001. *Our Monica, Ourselves: The Clinton Affair and the National Interest.* New York: New York University Press.

Berry, Jeffrey. 1989. "Subgovernments, Issue Networks, and Political Conflict." In *Remaking American Politics,* edited by Richard Harris and Sidney Milkis, 239–260. Boulder, CO: Westview.

———. 1997. *The Interest Group Society.* Boston: Addison-Wesley.

Berry, William, and Frances Stokes Berry. 1990. "State Lottery Adoptions as Policy Innovations: An Event History Analysis." *American Political Science Review* 84, no. 2 (June): 395–415.

Berry, William, Evan Ringquist, Richard Fording, and Russell Hanson. 1998. "Measuring Citizen and Government Ideology in the American States, 1960–93." *American Journal of Political Science* 42, no. 1 (January): 327–348.

Best, Joel. 1990. *Threatened Children: Rhetoric and Concern about Child-Victims.* Chicago: University of Chicago Press.

Bienen, Leigh. 1976. "Rape I." *Women's Rights Law Reporter* 3 (winter): 45–57.

———. 1977. "Rape II." *Women's Rights Law Reporter* 3 (spring/summer): 90–137.

———. 1980a. "Rape III: National Developments in Rape Reform Legislation." *Women's Rights Law Reporter* 6, no. 3 (spring/summer): 170–213.

———. 1980b. "Rape IV." Supplement to Summer 1980 volume. New Brunswick, NJ: Rutgers Law School.

———. 1998. "Defining Incest. [Symposium: Throwing Away the Key: Social and Legal Responses to Child Molesters. Part II: Social, Cultural, and Legal Context.]" *Northwestern University Law Review* 92 (summer): 1501–1580.

Billig, Lewis. 1995. "We Must Enforce Statutory Rape Laws." *San Diego Union-Tribune,* 6 April.

Booke, James. 1996. "An Old Law Chastises Pregnant Teenagers." *New York Times,* 28 October.

Bossing, Lewis. 1998. "Now Sixteen Could Get You Life: Statutory Rape, Meaningful Consent, and the Implications for Federal Sentencing Enhancement." *New York University Law Review* 73 (October): 1205–1250.

Boston Globe Staff. 2002. "Church Allowed Abuse by Priest for Years." *Boston Globe,* 6 January.

"Boyfriend, 15, Is Charged in Fatal Beating of Child." 1999. *New York Times,* 2 July.

Brace, Paul, Youssef Cohen, Virginia Gray, and David Lowery. 1989. "How Much Do State Interest Groups Influence State Economic Growth?" *American Political Science Review* 83, no. 4 (December): 1297–1308.

Brace, Paul, and Aubrey Jewett. 1995. "The State of State Politics Research." *Political Research Quarterly* 48, no. 3 (September): 643–681.

Brisbin, Richard. 2001. "From Censorship to Ratings: Substantive Rationality, Political Entrepreneurship, and Sex in the Movies." In *The Public Clash of Private Values: The Politics of Morality Policy*, edited by Christopher Z. Mooney, 91–112. New York: Chatham House.

Bronner, Ethan. 1998. "Two Teen Mothers to Sue over Honor Society Expulsion." *New York Times*, 6 August.

Brooke, James. 1996. "An Old Law Chastises Pregnant Teen-Agers." *The New York Times*, 28 October.

Broom, Jack, and Carol Ostrom. 1998a. "LeTourneau Appeared Ready to Flee; She Gets 7½ Years—Vehicle Contained Passport, $6,200, Baby Clothes, and Her Rape Victim." *Seattle Times*, 6 February.

———. 1998b. "LeTourneau Likely to Serve Time in Prison—Most Rearrested Sex Offenders Get Full Term." *Seattle Times*, 5 February.

Bruni, Frank. 1997. "In an Age of Consent, Defining Abuse by Adults." *New York Times*, 9 November.

Bumiller, Kristin. 1988. *The Civil Rights Society: The Social Construction of Victims*. Baltimore: Johns Hopkins University Press.

Butler, Judith. 1994. "Interview [Gayle Rubin]: Sexual Traffic." *differences* (summer/fall): 62–99.

Califia, Pat. 1981. "Man/Boy Love and the Lesbian/Gay Movement." In *The Age Taboo: Gay Male Sexuality, Power, and Consent*, edited by Daniel Tsang, 133–146. Boston: Alyson Publications.

———. 1994. *Public Sex: The Culture of Radical Sex*. San Francisco: Cleis.

"California Encourages Males to Take Responsibility in Pregnancy Prevention and Fatherhood." 1998. *Business Wire*, 5 October.

Campbell, Angus, Philip Converse, Warren Miller, and Donald Stokes. 1960. *The American Voter*. New York: Wiley.

Campbell, Colin. 1997. "Mistake or Lack of Information as to Victim's Age as Defense to Statutory Rape." *American Law Reports* 46: [n.p.].

Carby, Hazel. 1992. "Policing the Black Woman's Body in an Urban Context." *Critical Inquiry* 18 (summer): 738–755.

Carmines, Edward, and James Stimson. 1980. "The Two Faces of Issue Voting." *American Political Science Review* 74: 78–91.

Carroll, Matt. 2002. "A Revered Guest: A Family Left in Shreds." *Boston Globe*, 6 January.

Cavallaro, Rosanna. 1996. "Criminal Law: A Big Mistake: Eroding the Defense of Mistake Fact About Consent in Rape." *Journal of Criminal Law and Criminology* 86: 815–860.

Chamallas, Martha. 1988. "Consent, Equality, and the Legal Control of Sexual Conduct." *Southern California Law Review* 61: 777–861.

Chauncey, George. 1994. *Gay New York: Gender, Urban Culture, and the Making of the Gay Male World, 1890–1940*. New York: Basic Books.

Chesney-Lind, Meda, and Randall Shelden. 1998. *Girls, Delinquency, and Juvenile Justice*. 2d ed. Belmont, CA: West/Wadsworth.

Chong, Dennis. 1991. *Collective Action and the Civil Rights Movement*. Chicago: University of Chicago Press.

Cigler, Allan. 1991. "Interest Groups: A Subfield in Search of an Identity." In *Political Science: Looking to the Future*, edited by William Crotty, 99–135. Evanston, IL: Northwestern University Press.

Cigler, Allan, and Burdett Loomis. 1995. *Interest Group Politics*. Washington, DC: CQ Press.

Clarke, S. C. 1995. "Advance Report of Final Marriage Statistics, 1989 and 1990." *Monthly Vital Statistics Report* 43, no. 12 (suppl.). Hyattsville, MD: National Center for Health Statistics.

Cocca, Carolyn. 2002a. "From 'Welfare Queen' to 'Exploited Teen': Welfare Dependency, Statutory Rape, and Moral Panic." *National Women's Studies Association Journal* 14, no. 2 (summer): 56–79.

———. 2002b. "The Politics of Statutory Rape Laws: Adoption and Reinvention of Morality Policy in the States, 1969–99." *Polity* 35, no. 1 (fall): 51–72.

———. 2002c. "Prosecuting Mrs. Robinson? Gender, Sexuality, and Statutory Rape Laws." *Michigan Feminist Studies* 16 (summer): 61–84.

Cohen, Cathy. 1999. *The Boundaries of Blackness: AIDS and the Breakdown of Black Politics*. Chicago: University of Chicago Press.

Cohen, Jeffrey and Charles Barrilleaux. 1993. "Public Opinion, Interest Groups, and Abortion Policy in the American States," in *Abortion: The Shifting Political Landscape*, Malcolm Goggin, ed. Beverly Hills: Sage, pp. 203-21.

Cohen, Stanley. 1972. *Folk Devils and Moral Panics*. London: MacGibbon and Kee.

Colby, David, and David Baker. 1988. "State Policy Responses to the AIDS Epidemic." *Publius* 18 (summer): 113–130.

Connerton, Kelly C. 1997. "The Resurgence of the Marital Rape Exemption: The Victimization of Teens by Their Statutory Rapists." 61 *Albany Law Review* 237.

Connor, Tracy. 1998. "Judge Throws Book at Cradle-Robbing Teacher." *New York Post* (Metro ed.), 7 February.

Converse, Philip. 1964. "The Nature of Belief Systems in Mass Publics." In *Ideology and Discontent*, edited by David Apter, 206–261. New York: Free Press.

Conway, M. Margaret, and Joanne Connor Green. 1995. "Political Action Committees and the Political Process in the 1990s." In *Interest Group Politics*, 4th ed., edited by Allan Cigler and Burdett Loomis, 155–174. Washington, DC: CQ Press.

Cook, Elizabeth Adell, Ted Jelen, and Clyde Wilcox. 1993. "State Political Cultures and Public Opinion About Abortion." *Political Research Quarterly* 46 (December): 771–781.

Cook, Fay Lomax, and Edith Barrett. 1992. *Support for the American Welfare State: The Views of Congress and the Public.* New York: Columbia University Press.

Cooper, Michael. 1999. "Drifter Says He Had Sex with Up to 300." *New York Times,* 29 July.

Cott, Nancy. 1978. "Passionlessness: An Interpretation of Victorian Sexual Ideology, 1790–1850." *Signs* 4 (winter): 219–236.

Cott, Nancy, Jeanne Boydston, Ann Braude, Lori Ginzberg, and Molly Ladd-Taylor, eds. 1996. *Root of Bitterness: Documents of the Social History of American Women.* 2d ed. Boston: Northeastern University Press.

Cox, David and Nanny Wermuth. 1992. "A Comment on the Coeffecient of Determination for Binary Responses." *American Statistician* 46: 1-4.

Cramer, J. S. 1991. *The Logit Model: An Introduction for Economists.* London: Edward Arnold.

Crenshaw, Kimberlé. 1991. "Mapping the Margins: Intersectionality, Identity Politics, and Violence against Women of Color." *Stanford Law Review* 43: 1241–1299.

———. 1992. "Whose Story Is It, Anyway? Feminist and Anti-Racist Appropriations of Anita Hill." In *Race-ing Justice, En-gendering Power: Essays on Anita Hill, Clarence Thomas, and the Construction of Social Reality,* edited by Toni Morrison, 402–440. New York: Pantheon.

Daly, Matthew. 1998. "Statutory Rape Unit Ineffective, Critics Say Much-Touted Program Is Understaffed, Results in Few Convictions." *Hartford Courant,* 10 April.

"Damage to Boys Who Are Prey for Older Women: Women Who Abuse Young Boys Often Escape the Heavy Jail Terms Handed Down to Men Who Are Caught Abusing Young Girls." 1998. *Scottish Daily Record,* 6 February.

Dangerous Bedfellows, ed. 1996. *Policing Public Sex.* Boston: South End Press.

Davis, Angela. 1983. *Women, Race, and Class.* New York: Vintage.

DeGregorio, Christine and Jack E. Rossotti. 1995. "Campaigning for the Court: Interest Group Participation in the Bork and Thomas Confirmation Process," in *Interest Group Politics* , 4th edition, ed. Allan J. Cigler and Burdette A. Loomis. Washington: CQ Press: 215-238.

DeLaMothe, Cassandra. 1996. "*Liberta* Revisited: A Call to Repeal the Marital Exemption for All Sex Offenses in New York's Penal Law." *Fordham Urban Journal* 23: 857–892.

Delgado, Richard, and Jean Stefancic. 1994. *Failed Revolutions: Social Reform and the Limits of Legal Imagination*. Boulder, CO: Westview.

D'Emilio, John, and Estelle Freedman. 1997. *Intimate Matters: A History of Sexuality in America*. 2d ed. Chicago: University of Chicago Press.

Diamond, Sara. 1989. *Spiritual Warfare: The Politics of the Christian Right*. Boston: South End Press.

Diamond, Sara. 1995. *Roads to Dominion: Right Wing Movements and Political Power in the United States*. New York: Guilford.

Donnino, William. 1997. "Practice Commentary: McKinney's Consolidated Laws of New York Annotated, Penal Law, Chapter 40 of the Consolidated Laws, Part 3 Specific Offenses, Title H Offenses Against the Person Involving Physical Injury, Sexual Conduct, Restraint and Intimidation, Article 130 Sex Offenses." Eagan, MN: West Publishing.

Donovan, Patricia. 1997. "Can Statutory Rape Laws Be Effective in Preventing Adolescent Pregnancy?" *Family Planning Perspectives* 29, no. 1 (January/February): 30–34.

Downs, Anthony. 1957. *An Economic Theory of Democracy*. New York: Harper.

———. 1972. "Up and Down with Ecology: The Issue-Attention Cycle." *Public Interest* 28: 38–50.

DuBois, Ellen, and Linda Gordon. 1984. "Seeking Ecstasy on the Battlefield: Danger and Pleasure in Nineteenth-Century Feminist Sexual Thought." In *Pleasure and Danger: Exploring Female Sexuality*, edited by Carole Vance, 31–49. London: Pandora-HarperCollins.

Duggan, Lisa. 2000. *Sapphic Slashers: Sex, Violence, and American Modernity*. Durham, NC: Duke University Press.

Duggan, Lisa, and Nan Hunter, eds. 1995. *Sex Wars: Sexual Dissent and Political Culture*. New York: Routledge.

Duggan, Lisa, Nan Hunter, and Carole Vance. 1995. "False Promises." In *Sex Wars: Sexual Dissent and Political Culture*, edited by Lisa Duggan and Nan Hunter, 43–67. New York: Routledge.

Durose, Matthrew, David Levin, and Patrick Langan. 2001. "Felony Sentences in the State Courts, 1998." Bureau of Justice Statistics Bulletin (October). Washington, DC: U.S. Department of Justice.

Dye, Thomas R. 1966. *Politics, Economics, and Public Policy: Policy Outcomes in American States*. Chicago: Rand McNally.

———. 1979. "Politics vs. Economics: The Development of the Literature on Policy Determinism." *Policy Studies Journal* 7: 652–662.

Edelman, Murray. 1988. *Constructing the Political Spectacle*. Chicago: University of Chicago Press.

"[Editorial]: Mary Kay LeTourneau Is Not Just a Convicted Child Rapist. She's a Liar . . ." 1998. *Seattle Times*, 5 February.

"Editorial: Sex, Honor, and Grade Point Averages." 1998. *New York Times*, 7 August.

Egan, Timothy. 1998. "Contact with Young Lover Lands Ex-Teacher in Prison." *New York Times*, 7 February.

Eidson, Rita. 1980. "The Constitutionality of Statutory Rape Laws." *UCLA Law Review* 27: 757-815.

Elders, M. Joycelyn, and Alexa Albert. 1998. "Adolescent Pregnancy and Sexual Abuse." *Journal of the American Medical Association* 280, no. 7: 648–649.

Eldridge, Larry, ed. 1997. *Women and Freedom in Early America*. New York: New York University Press.

Ellwood, Daniel. 1988. *Poor Support: Poverty in the American Family*. New York: Basic Books.

Elton, Catherine. 1997. "Jail Baiting: Statutory Rape's Dubious Comeback." *New Republic* 217, no. 16 (October 20): 12.

Epstein, Lee, and Joseph Kobylka. 1992. *The Supreme Court and Legal Change: Abortion and the Death Penalty*. Chapel Hill: University of North Carolina Press.

Erikson, Robert, Gerald Wright, and John McIver. 1989. "Political Parties, Public Opinion, and State Policy in the United States." *American Political Science Review* 83, no. 3 (September): 729–750.

———. 1993. *Statehouse Democracy: Public Opinion and Policy in the American States*. New York: Cambridge University Press.

Erwin, Diana Griego. 1994. "Why No Crime When Men Exploit Girls?" *Sacramento Bee*, 1 September.

———. 1996. "Getting Tougher on Statutory Rape." *Sacramento Bee*, 28 March.

Estrich, Susan. 1986. "Rape." *Yale Law Journal* 95: 1087–1184.

Evans, Sara. 1979. *Personal Politics: The Roots of Women's Liberation in the Civil Rights Movement and the New Left*. New York: Vintage.

———. 1997. *Born for Liberty: A History of Women in America*. 2d ed. New York: Free Press.

"Excerpts from Today's Hearing." 1998. *Seattle Times*, 6 February.

Faderman, Lillian. 1981. *Surpassing the Love of Men: Romantic Friendship and Love between Women from the Renaissance to the Present*. New York: William Morrow.

———. 1991. *Odd Girls and Twilight Lovers: A History of Lesbian Life in Twentieth Century America*. New York: Penguin.

Fairbanks, David. 1977. "Religious Forces and 'Morality' Policies in the American States." *Western Political Quarterly* 30 (September): 411–417.

Federal Bureau of Investigation, U.S. Department of Justice. 1994. *Uniform Crime Reports for the United States*. Washington, DC: U.S. Government Printing Office.

Feminist Majority Newsletter 8, no. 2. 1996. Retrieved 14 November 1999 from http://www. feminist.org.

Fenno, Richard. 1978. *Homestyle.* Boston: Little, Brown.

Fielder, Jim. 1998. "Lovesick." *Mirabella* (June): 168–174.

Fineman, Martha. 1995. *The Neutered Mother, The Sexual Family.* New York: Routledge.

Fiorina, Morris. 1989. *Congress: Keystone of the Washington Establishment.* New Haven, CT: Yale University Press.

Fisch, Joseph. 1998. "Sentencing in Crimes against Children." *New York Law Journal* 219, no. 14. (January 22): [n.p.].

Fitten, Ronald, and Nancy Bartley. 1997. "Ex-Teacher Pleads Guilty in Rape of Boy." *Seattle Times*, 7 August.

Foster, Dick. 1994a. "Girl, 15, Finds 'Boyfriend' is a Woman." *Rocky Mountain News*, 5 November.

———. 1994b. "Woman, Accused of Playing Boyfriend to Girls, to Stand Trial." *Rocky Mountain News*, 24 December.

Foucault, Michel. 1995. *Discipline and Punish.* Translated by Alan Sheridan. New York: Vintage.

———. 1990. *The History of Sexuality:* Vol. 1, *An Introduction.* Translated by Robert Hubley. New York: Vintage.

———. 1991. "Governmentality." In *The Foucault Effect: Studies in Governmentality*, edited by Graham Burchell, Colin Gordon, and Peter Miller, 87–104. Hempstead, NY: Harvester Wheatsheaf.

Francescani, Christopher. 1999. "Sex and the City Teen: An Old Taboo Is Suddenly a Popular Practice." *New York Post*, 25 July.

Freeman, Alan D. 1982. "Anti-Discrimination Law: A Critical Review." In *The Politics of Law: A Progressive Critique*, edited by David Kairys, 96–116. New York: Pantheon.

Freeman, Jody. 1989–1990. "The Feminist Debate over Prostitution Reform: Prostitutes' Rights Groups, Radical Feminists, and the Impossibility of Consent." *Berkeley Women's Law Journal* 5: 75–109.

Frohmann, Lisa. 1997. "Convictability and Discordant Locales: Reproducing Race, Class, and Gender Ideologies in Prosecutorial Decisionmaking." *Law and Society Review* 31, no. 3: 531–556.

Fuentes, Luisa. 1994. "Note: The Fourteenth Amendment and Sexual Consent: Statutory Rape and Judicial Progeny." *Women's Rights Law Reporter* 16: 139–152.

Gallup Center. Various Years. *The Gallup Poll Monthly.*

Gallup Organization. 1998. "Special Reports: Global Study of Family Values. An International Gallup Poll: Family Values Differ Sharply Around the World." Available at http//:www.gallup.com/Special_Reports/family.htm.

Gaventa, John. 1980. *Power and Powerlessness: Quiescence and Rebellion in an Appalachian Valley.* Urbana: University of Illinois Press.

Geraci, Joseph, ed. 1997. *Dares to Speak: Historical and Contemporary Perspectives on Boy-Love.* Norfolk, UK: Gay Men's Press.

Geronimus, Arline. 1997. "Teenage Childbearing and Personal Responsibility: An Alternative View." *Political Science Quarterly* 112, no. 3: 405–430.

Giddings, Paula. 1992. "The Last Taboo." In *Race-ing Justice, En-gendering Power: Essays on Anita Hill, Clarence Thomas, and the Construction of Social Reality*, edited by Toni Morrison, 441–470. New York: Pantheon.

Gilbert, Susan. 1998. "New Light Shed on Normal Sex Behavior in a Child." *New York Times*, 7 April.

Gilens, Martin. 1996. "'Race Coding' and White Opposition to Welfare." *American Political Science Review* 90, no. 3: 593–604.

Giles, Darrell. 2001. "Boy Dad's Plea; Let Me Marry Jailed Teacher." *Herald Sun*, 6 April.

Glick, Henry, and Scott Hays. 1991. "Innovation and Reinvention in State Policymaking: Theory and the Evolution of Living Will Laws." *Journal of Politics* 53, no. 3 (August): 835–850.

Glick, Henry, and Amy Hutchinson. 2001. "The Rising Agenda of Physician Assisted Suicide: Explaining the Growth and Content of Morality Policy." In *The Public Clash of Private Values: The Politics of Morality Policy*, edited by Christopher Z. Mooney, 55–70. New York: Chatham House.

Goggin, Malcolm. 1993. "Understanding the New Politics of Abortion: A Framework and Agenda for Research." *American Politics Quarterly* 21, no. 1 (January): 4–30.

Goldberg, Stephanie. 1997. "Jailbait: Politicians Dust Off Old Sex Laws to Combat Teenage Pregnancy." *Playboy* 44, no. 1 (January 1): [n.p.].

Goldhaber, Michael, and Jerry Markon. 1997. "Net Fling Leads to Rape Charge; Man Arrested after Allegedly Having Sex with Minor He Met Online." *Newsday*, 19 December.

Goode, Erica. 1999. "Study on Child Sex Abuse Provokes Political Furor: Conservatives Criticize Psychology Report." *New York Times*, 13 June.

Goodman, Ellen. 1995. "In Defense of Adolescent Girls (Jailbait)." *Boston Globe*, 19 February.

———. 1996a. "A Criminal Record or a Wedding Band?" *Boston Globe*, 12 September.

———. 1996b. "Targeting the Men Who Prey on Teen-Age Girls" *Boston Globe*, 8 February.

———. 1996c. "Victims of War on Sin." *Boston Globe*, 14 July.

———. 1998. "Law Can't Force Child, Parent Talks." *Albany (NY) Times Union*, 10 July.

Gordon, Linda. 1988. *Heroes of Their Own Lives: The Politics and History of Family Violence*. New York: Viking.

———. 1990a. "Family Violence, Feminism, and Social Control." In *Women, the State, and Welfare*, edited by Linda Gordon, 178–199. Madison: University of Wisconsin Press.

———. 1990b. "The New Feminist Scholarship on the Welfare State." In *Women, the State, and Welfare*, edited by Linda Gordon, 9–36. Madison: University of Wisconsin Press.

———. 1994. *Pitied but Not Entitled: Single Mothers and the History of Welfare*. Cambridge: Harvard University Press.

Gorman, Anna. 2000. "Sex with Minors Can Have Major Consequences." *L.A. Times*. Jan. 30.

Gorman, Tom. 1993. "After the Sex Scandal Youths Who Were Asked To Have Sex with Coach's Wife Now Focus on Lobbying for Changes in Rape Law." *Los Angeles Times*, 25 July.

Gray, Virginia. 1973a. "Innovation in the States: A Diffusion Study." *American Political Science Review* 67, no. 4 (December): 1174–1185.

———. 1973b. "Rejoinder to 'Comment' by Jack L. Walker." *American Political Science Review* 67, no. 4 (December): 1192–1193.

Green, John, James Guth, and Clyde Wilcox. 1998. "Less Than Conquerors: The Christian Right in State Republican Parties." In Anne Costain and Andrew McFarland eds., *Social Movements and Political Institutions*. Lanham, MD: Rowman and Littlefield: 117-135.

Greene, William. 1990. *Econometric Analysis*. New York: Macmillan.

Greenfeld, Lawrence. 1996. "Sex Offenses and Offenders." Bureau of Justice Statistics Bulletin (March). Washington, DC: U.S. Department of Justice.

Gregg, B. G. 1999. "State Targets Predators of Kids on Web." *Detroit News*, 9 February.

Grenzke, Janet. 1989. "PACs and the Congressional Supermarket: The Currency is Complex." *American Journal of Political Science* 33: 1–24.

Grogan, Colleen. 1994. "Political-Economic Factors Influencing State Medicaid Policy." *Political Research Quarterly* 47, no. 3 (September): 589–622.

Gross, Jane. 1997a. "Left Out in Isolated Town: Runaways Exposed to HIV." *New York Times*, 31 October.

———. 1997b. "Trail of Arrests, HIV Fears, and a Woman's Tale of Love." *New York Times*, 29 October.

Gruen, Lori, and George Panichas, ed. 1997. *Sex, Morality, and the Law.* New York: Routledge.

Guerrina, Britton. 1998. "Mitigating Punishment for Statutory Rape." *University of Chicago Law Review* 65 (fall): 1251–1277.

Gulotta, Thomas, Gerald Adams, and Raymond Montemayor, eds. 1993. *Adolescent Sexuality.* Thousand Oaks, CA: Sage.

Gunning, Sandra. 1996. *Race, Rape, and Lynching.* New York: Oxford University Press.

Gusfield, Joseph. 1986. *Symbolic Crusade.* 2d ed. Urbana: University of Illinois Press.

Gutierrez, Ramon. 1991. *When Jesus Came, the Corn Mothers Went Away.* Stanford, CA: Stanford University Press.

Hagle, Timothy, and Glenn Mitchell II. 1992. "Goodness of Fit Measures for Probit and Logit." *American Journal of Political Science* 36, no. 3 (August): 762–784.

Haider-Markel, Donald. 2001. "Morality Policy and Individual-Level Political Behavior: The Case of Legislative Voting on Lesbian and Gay Issues." In *The Public Clash of Private Values: The Politics of Morality Policy,* edited by Christopher Z. Mooney, 115–129. New York: Chatham House.

Haider-Markel, Donald, and Kenneth J. Meier. 1996. "The Politics of Gay and Lesbian Rights: Expanding the Scope of the Conflict." *Journal of Politics* 58, no. 2 (May): 332–349.

Hall, Stuart, Chas Critcher, Tony Jefferson, John Clarke, and Brian Roberts. 1978. *Policing the Crisis: Mugging, the State, and Law and Order.* New York: Holmes and Meier.

Handler, Joel. 1995. *The Poverty of Welfare Reform.* New Haven, CT: Yale University Press.

Handler, Joel, and Yeheskel Hasenfeld. 1997. *We the Poor People: Work, Poverty, and Welfare.* New Haven, CT: Yale University Press.

Hanigsberg, Julia. 1995. "An Essay on the Piano, Law, and the Search for Women's Desire." *Michigan Journal of Gender and Law* 3: 41–75.

Hanley, Robert. 1997a. "Days Before Slaying, Parents of Suspect Pleaded for Help." *New York Times,* 4 October.

———. 1997b. "Questions About a Sting That Used a Teen-Ager: Slain Boy's Parents Consider Suing Officials." *New York Times,* 28 December.

———. 1999a. "Killer Will Not Turn Against Man Accused of Abusing Him." *New York Times,* 23 July.

———. 1999b. "Pedophile Admits He Abused Young Killer." *New York Times,* 23 July.

Harari, Susan, and Maris Vinovskis. 1993. "Adolescent Sexuality, Pregnancy, and Childbearing in the Past." In *The Politics of Pregnancy: Adolescent Sexuality and Public Policy,* edited by Annette Lawson and Deborah Rhode, 23–58. New Haven, CT: Yale University Press.

Hardy, Quentin. 1996. "Prosecuting Teen Pregnancy: In Idaho, a Different Approach." *Newsday*, 17 July.

Harris, Louis, and Associates. Various Years. *The Harris Poll.*

Hartman, Saidiya. 1997. *Scenes of Subjection: Terror, Slavery, and Self-Making in Nineteenth Century America.* New York: Oxford University Press.

Harvey, Anna L. 1998. *Votes without Leverage: Women in American Electoral Politics, 1920–1970.* New York: Cambridge University Press.

Heclo, Hugh. 1978. "Issue Networks and the Executive Establishment." In *The New American Political System*, edited by Anthony King, 87–124. Washington, DC: American Enterprise Institute.

Herbert, Bob. 1999. "America's Littlest Shooters." *New York Times*, 2 May.

Hernandez, Raymond. 1999. "A New Threat in Collecting Child Support." *New York Times*, 21 March.

Hero, Rodney, and Caroline Tolbert. 1996. "A Racial/Ethnic Diversity Interpretation of Politics and Policy in the States of the U.S." *American Journal of Political Science* 40, no. 3 (August): 851–871.

Hersch, Patricia. 1998. *A Tribe Apart: A Journey into the Heart of American Adolescence.* New York: Fawcett Columbine.

Herzik, Eric. "The Legal-Formal Structuring of State Politics: A Cultural Explanation." *Western Political Quarterly* 38, no. 3: 413–423.

Hewitt, Bill, Lorenzo Benet, Jonny Dodd, Leslie Berestein, Elizabeth Leonard, and Jamie Reno. 1998. "Out of Control: A Strange Story Gets Stranger as an Ex-Teacher, Madly in Love with a 14-Year-Old, Is Expecting a Second Child Believed to Be His." *People Weekly*, 30 March, 44–49.

Higginbotham, Evelyn Brooks. 1992. "African American Women's History and the Metalanguage of Race." *Signs* 17, no. 2 (winter): 251–274.

Higgins, Tracy. 1995. "'By Reason of Their Sex': Feminist Theory, Postmodernism, and Justice." *Cornell Law Review* 80: 1536–1594.

Hill, Kim Quaile. 1994. *Democracy in the Fifty States.* Lincoln: University of Nebraska Press.

Hill, Kim Quaile, Jan Leighley, and Angela Hinton-Andersson. 1995. "Lower-Class Mobilization and Policy Linkage in the U.S. States." *American Journal of Political Science* 39, no. 1 (February): 75–86.

Hofferbert, Richard, and John Urice. 1985. "Small-Scale Policy: The Federal Stimulus versus Competing Explanations for State Funding of the Arts." *American Journal of Political Science* 29 (May): 308–329.

Hojnacki, Marie, and David Kimball. 1999. "The Who and How of Organizations' Lobbying Strategies in Committee." *Journal of Politics* 61, no. 4 (November): 999–1024.

Holbrook Thomas, and Stephen Percy. 1992. "Exploring Variation in State Laws Providing Protections for Persons with Disabilities." *Western Political Quarterly* 45: 201–220.

Holbrook, Thomas, and Emily Van Dunk. 1993. "Electoral Competition in the American States." *American Political Science Review* 87, no. 4 (December): 955–962.

Holmes, Steven. 1998. "Birth Rate for Unmarried Black Women Is at a 40-Year Low." *New York Times*, 1 July.

hooks, bell. 1984. *Feminist Theory: From Margin to Center*. Boston: South End Press.

Hsu, Gracie. 1996. "Statutory Rape: The Dirty Secret Behind Teen Sex Numbers." *Family Policy* 9, no. 3 (June): 1–16.

Hull, Tupper. 1990. "Rape Bill Targets Women Offenders." *San Francisco Examiner*, 12 June.

Hunt, Alan. 1993. *Explorations in Law and Society*. New York: Routledge.

Hunter, Nan. 1995. "Marriage, Law, and Gender: A Feminist Inquiry." In *Sex Wars: Sexual Dissent and Political Culture*, edited by Lisa Duggan and Nan Hunter, 107–122. New York: Routledge.

Hunter, Nan D., and Sylvia A. Law. 1997. "Brief *Amici Curiae* of Feminist Anti-Censorship Taskforce et al., in *American Booksellers Association v. Hudnut*." In *Sex, Morality, and the Law*, edited by Lori Gruen and George Panichas, 199–222. New York: Routledge.

Hwang, Sung-Don, and Virginia Gray. 1991. "External Limits and Internal Determinants of State Public Policy." *Western Political Quarterly* 44: 277–299.

Iglesias, Elizabeth. 1996. "Rape, Race, and Representation: The Power of Discourse, Discourses of Power, and the Reconstruction of Heterosexuality." *Vanderbilt Law Journal* 49: 868–922.

Ingram, Carl. 1995. "State Leads Nation in Rate of Teen-Age Births, Study Says." *Los Angeles Times*, 22 March.

Jacobs, Andrew. 1999. "School Official Charged with Molesting Student: Stuyvesant Assistant Principal Is Accused." *New York Times*, 22 May.

Jacobs, John. 1996. "The Politics of Statutory Rape." *Sacramento Bee*, 12 May.

Jacobson, Gary. 1992. *The Politics of Congressional Elections*. 3d ed. New York: HarperCollins.

Jakobsen, Janet R. 2001. "'He Has Wronged America and Women': Clinton's Sexual Conservatism." In Lauren Berlant and Lisa Duggan eds, *Our Monica, Ourselves* (New York: New York University Press.): 291-314.

James, Caryn. 1998. "Revisiting a Dangerous Obsession." *New York Times*, 31 July.

Jenkins, Philip. 1998. *Moral Panic: Changing Concepts of the Child Molester in Modern America*. New Haven, CT: Yale University Press.

Jewell, Malcolm. 1982. "The Neglected World of State Politics." *Journal of Politics* 44 (August): 446–454.

Joffe, Carole. 1993. "Sexual Politics and the Teenage Pregnancy Prevention Worker in the United States." In *The Politics of Pregnancy: Adolescent Sexuality and Public Policy*, edited by Annette Lawson and Deborah Rhode, 284–300. New Haven, CT: Yale University Press.

Johnson, Cathy Marie, and Kenneth Meier. 1990. "The Wages of Sin: Taxing America's Legal Vices." *Western Political Quarterly* 43 (September): 577–596.

Johnson, Janet Buttolph, and Richard Josyln. 1995. *Political Science Research Methods.* 3d ed. Washington, DC: CQ Press.

Jones, Andrea. 2000. "Statutory Rape Charges Likely to Rise with Teen Sex." *Atlanta Journal-Constitution*, 31 August.

Jordan, Hallye. 1996. "Panel Toughens Teen Pregnancy Penalties." *San Jose Mercury News*, 16 January.

Kaiser Family Foundation. 1997. "State Reports: Virginia: Richmond to Crack Down on Rape." *Daily Kaiser Family Foundation Reproductive Health Report*, 9 April.

Karlsen, Carol. 1987. *The Devil in the Shape of a Woman: Witchcraft in Colonial New England.* New York: Vintage.

Kataoka, Mike. 1993. "Ex-Hemet Quarterbacks Sue Coach Brown, Wife." *The Press-Enterprise* [Riverside, CA], 14 September.

Kathlene, Lyn. 1995 "Alternative Views of Crime: Legislative Policymaking in Gendered Terms." *Journal of Politics* 57: 696–723.

Keane, Kevin. 1998. "Governor Adds Resources to Fight Teen Pregnancy." Tommy Thompson, Governor of Wisconsin, Press Release: June 12. Available at www.wisgov.state.wi.us/98pr/Teen%20pregnancy.htm.

Kelley, Donna, and Bill Hemmer. 1998. "Dr. Joyce Brothers Discusses Teacher–Student Sex Scandal and Clinton Investigation." *CNN Morning News*, 6 February.

Kennedy, Peter. 1998. *A Guide to Econometrics.* Cambridge: MIT Press.

Kenney, Sally. 1992. *For Whose Protection: Reproductive Hazards and Exclusionary Policies in the United States and Britain.* Ann Arbor: University of Michigan Press.

Kenney, Sally, and Helen Kinsella, eds. 1997. *Politics and Feminist Standpoint Theories.* Binghamton, NY: Haworth Press.

Key, V. O. 1949. *Southern Politics in State and Nation.* New York: Vintage.

Kiernan, Louise. 1995. "The Criminal Charge: Statutory Rape Law Gets Murkier with Age." *Chicago Tribune*, 28 July.

Kilborn, Peter. 1997. "Sex-Abuse Cases Sting Pentagon, but the Problem Has Deep Roots." *New York Times*, 10 February.

Kincaid, James. 1992. *Child-Loving: The Erotic Child and Victorian Culture.* New York: Routledge.

———. 1998. *Erotic Innocence: The Culture of Child Molesting.* Durham, NC: Duke University Press.

King, Gary. 1986. "How Not to Lie with Statistics: Avoiding Common Mistakes in Quantitative Political Science." *American Journal of Political Science* 30, no. 3 (August): 666–687.

———. 1991. "'Truth' is Stranger than Prediction, More Questionable than Causal Inference." *American Journal of Political Science* 35, no. 4 (November): 1047–1053.

King, Gary, Robert Keohane, and Sidney Verba. 1994. *Designing Social Inquiry: Scientific Inference in Qualitative Research.* Princeton, NJ: Princeton University Press.

King, Kimi Lynn, and James Meernik. 1999. "The Supreme Court and the Powers of the Executive: The Adjudication of Foreign Policy." *Political Research Quarterly* 52, no. 4 (December): 801–824.

Kingdon, John. 1997. *Agendas, Alternatives, and Public Policies.* 2d ed. New York: Harper-Collins.

Kintz, Linda. 1997. *Between Jesus and the Market: The Emotions That Matter in Right-Wing America.* Durham, NC: Duke University Press.

Kitrosser, Heidi. 1997. "Meaningful Consent: Toward a New Generation of Statutory Rape Laws." *Virginia Journal of Social Policy and the Law* (winter): 287–338.

Klass, Tim. 1998. "LeTourneau Gets 7½ Years in Prison." *Columbian* (Vancouver, WA), 6 February.

Klassen, Albert, Colin Williams, Eugene Levitt, and Hubert O'Gordon, eds. 1989. *Sex and Morality in the U.S.: An Empirical Inquiry under the Auspices of the Kinsey Institute.* Middletown, CT: Wesleyan University Press.

Klein, Joe. 1996. "The Predator Problem." *Newsweek*, 29 April, 32.

Kohn, Alan. 1992. "Underage Unwed Father Held Obligated to Support Child." *New York Law Journal* 208, no. 85 (October): 1, col. 3.

Kreider, Rose, and Jason Fields. 2001. "Number, Timing, and Duration of Marriages and Divorces: Fall 1996." *Current Population Reports*, P70-80. Washington, DC: U.S. Census Bureau.

Krutz, Glen, Richard Fleisher, and Jon Bond. 1998. "From Abe Fortas to Zoe Baird: Why Some Presidential Nominations Fail in the Senate." *American Political Science Review* 92, no. 4 (December): 871–881.

Kunzel, Regina. 1993. *Fallen Women, Problem Girls: Unmarried Mothers and the Professionalization of Social Work, 1890–1945.* New Haven, CT: Yale University Press.

Lancaster, Roger, and Micaela DiLeonardo, eds. 1997. *The Gender Sexuality Reader: Culture, History, Political Economy.* New York: Routledge.

Landry, D. J., and J. D. Forrest. 1995. "How Old Are U.S. Fathers?" *Family Planning Perspectives* 27: 159–165.

Langum, David. 1994. *Crossing over the Line: Legislating Morality and the Mann Act.* Chicago: University of Chicago Press.

Larson, Jane. 1997. "'Even a Worm Will Turn at Last': Rape Reform in Late Nineteenth-Century America." *Yale Journal of Law and the Humanities* (winter): 1–71.

Law, Sylvia. 1984. "Rethinking Sex and the Constitution." *University of Pennsylvania Law Review* 132: 955–1040.

Lawson, Annette. 1993. "Multiple Fractures: The Cultural Construction of Teenage Sexuality and Pregnancy." In *The Politics of Pregnancy: Adolescent Sexuality and Public Policy*, edited by Annette Lawson and Deborah Rhode, 101–125. New Haven, CT: Yale University Press.

Lawson, Annette, and Deborah Rhode, eds. 1993. *The Politics of Pregnancy: Adolescent Sexuality and Public Policy.* New Haven, CT: Yale University Press.

Leary, Warren. 1998. "New Therapy Offers Promise in Treatment of Pedophiles." *New York Times*, 12 February.

Lefkowitz, Melanie, and Sean Gardiner. 2001. "Sex Charge for Teacher." *Newsday*, 22 June.

Lemos, Phil. 1998. "New Blood vs. Experience in 19th House District Always Climbing Uphill, Farr Seeks His 10th Term." *Hartford Courant*, 29 October.

Lesher, Dave. 1996. "State Faces a Tough Battle Against Teenage Pregnancy." *L.A. Times*, Jan. 30.

Levesque, Roger. 1997. "Dating Violence, Adolescents, and the Law." *Virginia Journal of Social Policy and the Law* 4: 339–397.

Levin-Epstein, Jodie. 1997. *State TANF Plans: Out-of-Wedlock and Statutory Rape Provisions.* Washington, DC: Center for Law and Social Policy.

Levy, Michael. 1999. "The Politics of Sex: The Age of Consent Debate in the Houses of Parliament." Paper presented at the annual meeting of the American Political Science Association, 1–5 September, Atlanta, Georgia.

Lewin, Tamar. 1998. "Birth Rates for Teen-Agers Declined Sharply in the 90s." *New York Times*, 1 May.

Lewis, Oscar. 1968. "The Culture of Poverty." In *On Understanding Poverty: Perspectives from the Social Sciences*, edited by Daniel P Moynihan, 187–200. New York: Basic Books.

Lewis, Rochelle. 1987a. "New Law is Sought to Make Rape Charges Gender-Neutral." *Albany (NY) Times Union*, 4 May.

———. 1987b. "Women Can Be Charged with Statutory Rape." *Gannett News Service*, 9 July.

Lichtenstein, Grace. 1975. "Rape Laws Undergoing Changes to Aid Victims." *New York Times*, 4 June.

Lindberg, Laura Duberstein, Freya Sonenstein, Leighton Ku, and Gladys Martinez. 1997. "Age Difference between Minors Who Give Birth and Their Adult Partners." *Family Planning Perspectives* 29, no. 2 (March/April): 61–66.

Lippmann, Walter. 1922. *Public Opinion*. New York: Harcourt Brace.

Lopez, Pablo. 1998. "Sex with Teenagers a Crime, Not Love: Prosecutors Armed with More State Funding Aggressively Going after Statutory Rape Cases." *Fresno Bee*, 3 May.

Lowe, Ed. 1997. "After the Rage, Uncertainty." *Newsday*, 11 April.

Lowi, Theodore. 1979. *The End of Liberalism*. 2d ed. New York: Norton.

———. 1988. "New Dimensions in Policy and Politics." In *Moral Controversies in American Politics: Cases in Social Regulatory Policy*, edited by Raymond Tatalovich and Byron Daynes, xiii–xxvii. Armonk, NY: M. E. Sharpe.

Lucero, Bruce. 1998. "Parental Guidance Needed." *New York Times*, 12 July.

Luker, Kristen. 1984. *Abortion and the Politics of Motherhood*. Berkeley and Los Angeles: University of California Press.

———. 1996. *Dubious Conceptions: The Politics of Teenage Pregnancy*. Cambridge: Harvard University Press.

Lukes, Steven. 1974. *Power: A Radical View*. London: Macmillan.

———, ed. 1986. *Power*. New York: New York University Press.

Luskin, Robert. 1991. "Abusus Non Tollit Usum: Standardized Coefficients, Correlations, and R^2s." *American Journal of Political Science* 35, no. 4 (November): 1032–1046.

Lynch, Michael. 1998. "Enforcing 'Statutory Rape'?" *The Public Interest* 132 (summer): 3–16.

MacIntyre, Sally, and Sarah Cunningham-Burley. 1993. "Teenage Pregnancy as a Social Problem: A Perspective from the United Kingdom." In *The Politics of Pregnancy: Adolescent Sexuality and Public Policy*, edited by Annette Lawson and Deborah Rhode, 59–73. New Haven, CT: Yale University Press.

MacKinnon, Catharine. 1989. *Toward a Feminist Theory of the State*. Cambridge: Harvard University Press.

———. 1991. "Reflections on Sex Equality under Law. *Yale Law Journal* 10: 1281–1328.

Maguire, Kathleen, and Ann Pastore, eds. [U.S. Department of Justice, Bureau of Justice Statistics]. 1995. *Sourcebook of Criminal Justice Statistics*. Washington, DC: U.S. Government Printing Office.

Maltese, John Anthony. 1995. *The Selling of Supreme Court Nominees*. Baltimore, MD: Johns Hopkins University Press

"Man, 28, Pleads Guilty to Sex with Underage Girl." 1998. *Albany (NY) Times Union*, 25 May.

Mansnerus, Laura. 1999a. "Teenager Who Killed Boy Defends Molester as Good Role Model." *New York Times*, 13 October.

———. 1999b. "'Thinking About You': Sam Manzie's First Words in a Letter to the Man Convicted of Molesting Him." *New York Times*, 17 October.

Margolis, Michael, and Gary Mauser, eds. 1989. *Manipulating Public Opinion*. Orlando, FL: Harcourt.

Marin, Rick. 1999. "Those New Teen Age Movies Fogged My Glasses." *New York Times*, 20 March.

Marsh, Jeanne, Alison Geist, and Nathan Caplan. 1982. *Rape and the Limits of Law Reform*. Boston: Auburn House.

Martineau, Pamela. 1995. "Caldera Proposes Tougher Penalties for Statutory Rape Resulting in Pregnancy." *Civic Center News Source*, 11 April.

Mattei, Laura R. Winsky. 1998. "Gender and Power in American Legislative Discourse." *Journal of Politics* 60, no. 2: 440–461.

Matthews, Jon. 1995. "Media Campaign against Teen Pregnancies Urged." *Sacramento Bee*, 22 March.

———. 1996. "Panel Oks Bill Targeting Men Who Impregnate Minors." *Sacramento Bee*, 15 May.

Mayer, William. 1993. *The Changing American Mind: How and Why Public Opinion Changed between 1960 and 1988*. Ann Arbor: University of Michigan Press.

Mayhew, David. 1974. *Congress: The Electoral Connection*. New Haven, CT: Yale University Press.

Maynard, Roy. 1999. "The End of Innocence." *World*, 30 January.

McCann, Michael. 1994. *Rights at Work: Pay Equity Reform and the Politics of Legal Mobilization*. Chicago: University of Chicago Press.

McCollum, James. 1982. "Case Development: Constitutional Law—Statutory Rape—Gender-Based Classification Regarding Statutory Rape Law Is Not Violative of the Equal Protection Clause of the Fourteenth Amendment: *Michael M. v. Superior Court*." *Howard Law Journal* 25: 341–365.

McCullough, Marie. 1997. "Statutory Rape Laws Lack Conviction." *York (PA) Daily Record*, 4 May.

McElya, Micki. 2001. "Trashing the Presidency: Race, Class, and the Clinton/Lewinsky Affair." In *Our Monica, Ourselves*, edited by Lauren Berlant and Lisa Duggan, 156–174. New York: New York University Press.

McFadden, Kay, and Melanie McFarland. 1998. "National Media Followed LeTourneau Closely—Networks, Cable Channels, All Turned Out for Today's Hearing." *Seattle Times*, 6 February.

McFadden, Robert. 1997a. "Suspect in New Jersey Strangling Was Reportedly Sex-Case Victim." *The New York Times*. 3 October.

———.1997b. "Days Before Slaying, Parents of Suspect Pleaded for Help." *The New York Times*. 4 October.

———. 1997c. "Questions About a Sting that Used a Teen-Ager." *The New York Times*. 28 December.

McKenna, M.A.J. 1996. "State's Worst-in-Nation Ranking Target of Prevention Campaign." *The Atlanta Journal-Constitution*, Jan. 20.

McNamara, Douglas. 1998. "Sexual Discrimination and Sexual Misconduct: Applying New York's Gender Specific Sexual Misconduct Law to Consenting Minors." 14 *Touro Law Review* 479.

Mead, Lawrence M. 1986. *Beyond Entitlement: The Social Obligations of Citizenship*. New York: Free Press.

Meier, Kenneth J. 1994. *The Politics of Sin: Drugs, Alcohol, and Public Policy*. Armonk, NY: M. E. Sharpe.

———. 2001. "Sex, Drugs, Rock, and Roll: A Theory of Morality Politics." In *The Public Clash of Private Values: The Politics of Morality Policy*, edited by Christopher Z. Mooney, 21–36. New York: Chatham House.

Meier, Kenneth J., and Cathy Johnson. 1990. "The Politics of Demon Rum: Regulating Alcohol and Its Deleterious Consequences." *American Politics Quarterly* 18, no. 4 (October): 404–429.

Meier, Kenneth J., and Deborah McFarlane. 1992. "State Policies on Funding of Abortions: A Pooled Time Series Analysis." *Social Science Quarterly* 73, no. 3 (September): 690–698.

———. 1993. "The Politics of Funding Abortion: State Responses to the Political Environment." *American Politics Quarterly* 21, no. 1 (January): 81–101.

Meier, Robert, and Gilbert Geis. 1997. *Victimless Crimes?* Los Angeles: Roxbury.

"Men Who Impregnate Girls." 1996. *Sacramento Bee*, 19 April.

Mendel, Dan. 1995. "Highlights of the California Budget." *San Diego Union-Tribune*, 3 August.

Miller, Susannah. 1994. "Recent Developments: The Overturning of Michael M.: Statutory Rape Law Becomes Gender-Neutral in California." *UCLA Women's Law Journal* 5: 289–298.

Mink, Gwendolyn. 1990. "The Lady and the Tramp: Gender, Race, and the Origins of the American Welfare State." In *Women, the State, and Welfare*, edited by Linda Gordon, 92–122. Madison: University of Wisconsin Press.

Minkowitz, Donna. 1995. "On Trial: Gay? Straight? Boy? Girl? Sex? Rape?" *Out* (October): 99–101, 140–146.

Mintrom, Michael. 1997. "Policy Entrepreneurs and the Diffusion of Innovation." *American Journal of Political Science* 41, no. 3 (July): 738–770.

Moen, Matthew. 1984. "School Prayer and the Politics of Life Style Concern." *Social Science Quarterly* 65: 1070–1081.

Moody, Lori. 1993. "Underage Sex: A Double Standard? Those Closely Affected Want Rape Laws to Be Gender Neutral." *Los Angeles Daily News*, 4 March.

Mooney, Christopher Z. 2001. "Introduction: The Public Clash of Private Values: The Politics of Morality Policy." In *The Public Clash of Private Values: The Politics of Morality Policy*, edited by Christopher Z. Mooney, 3–18. New York: Chatham House.

Mooney, Christopher, and Mei-Hsien Lee. 1995. "Legislating Morality in the American States: The Case of Pre-Roe Abortion Regulation Reform." *American Journal of Political Science* 39, no. 3 (August): 599–627.

———. 1999. "Morality Policy Re-Invention: Death Penalty Policy in the American States." *Annals of the American Academy of Political and Social Science* 566: 80–92.

———. 2000. "The Influence of Values on Consensus and Contentious Morality Policy: U.S. Death Penalty Reform, 1956–82." *Journal of Politics* 62: 223–239.

———. 2001. "The Temporal Diffusion of Morality Policy: The Case of Death Penalty Legislation in the American States." In *The Public Clash of Private Values: The Politics of Morality Policy*, edited by Christopher Z. Mooney, 170–183. New York: Chatham House.

Moore, Teresa. 1995. "Study Slams State Crackdown on Deadbeat Parents." *San Francisco Chronicle*, 23 March.

Morrison, Toni, ed. 1992. *Race-ing Justice, En-gendering Power: Essays on Anita Hill, Clarence Thomas, and the Construction of Social Reality.* New York: Pantheon.

Moynihan, Daniel P. 1968. *On Understanding Poverty: Perspectives from the Social Sciences.* New York: Basic Books.

Muller, Judy, and Peter Jennings. 1998. "Former Teacher Sent Back to Jail for Seeing Boy; Evidence the Pair Might Flee with Their Baby." *World News Tonight with Peter Jennings* [ABC], 6 February.

Muller, Judy, and Mark Mullen. 1998. "Why Teacher Won't Stay Away from Child Lover; Seeking Motivation for Mary LeTourneau's Actions." *ABC World News This Morning*, 6 February.

Muller, Judy, and Deborah Roberts. 1998. "Teacher Sex Scandal; Mary Kay LeTourneau Back in Court Today." *Good Morning America* [ABC], 6 February.

Munger, Frank. 1998. "Immanence and Identity: Understanding Poverty through Law and Society Research." *Law and Society Review* 32, no. 4: 931–968.

Murolo, Priscilla. 1997. *The Common Ground of Womanhood: Class, Gender, and Working Girls' Clubs, 1884–1928*. Champaign: University of Illinois Press.

Murray, Charles. 1984. *Losing Ground: American Social Policy, 1950–1980*. New York: Basic Books.

Nagin, Daniel, Greg Pogarsky, and David Farrington. 1997. "Adolescent Mothers and the Criminal Behavior of Their Children." *Law and Society Review* 31, no. 1: 137–162.

Nagler, Jonathan. 1994. "Scobit: An Alternative Estimator to Logit and Probit." *American Journal of Political Science* 38, no. 1 (February): 230–255.

Nathanson, Constance. 1991. *Dangerous Passage: The Social Control of Sexuality in Women's Adolescence*. Philadelphia: Temple University Press.

National Law Journal Staff. 1995. "Sex Impersonation Charged." *National Law Journal*, 9 January.

Navarro, Mireya. 1996. "States Hope Statutory Rape Crackdown Will Fight Teen Pregnancy." *New York Times*, 19 May.

Nayo, Lydia. 1995. "Once I Was 15 and Pregnant." *Los Angeles Times*, 12 April.

Nelson, Thomas, Roasalee Clawson, and Zoe Oxley. 1997. "Media Framing of a Civil Liberties Conflict and Its Effect on Tolerance." *American Political Science Review* 91, no. 3: 567–583.

Newman, Maria. 1998. "Teachers More Reluctant to Touch in the Classroom." *New York Times*, 24 June.

Nice, David. 1988. "State Deregulation of Intimate Behavior." *Social Science Quarterly* 69 (March): 203–211.

———. 1992. "The States and the Death Penalty." *Western Political Quarterly* 45 (December): 1037–1048.

———. 1994. *Policy Innovation in State Government*. Ames: Iowa State University Press.

Nikos, Karen. 1993. "Effort to Make Statutory Rape Law Apply to Women Gaining Support." *Sacramento Bee*, 22 February.

Norman, James. 1979. "I'm Trying to Help Teens, Claims the Sex-At-13 Woman." *The New York Post*, 30 April.

Norman, James. 1979. "Lawmakers Get New Rape Bills." *New York Post*, 30 April.

Norman, James, and Joanne Wasserman. 1979. "Sex Law Shock: Now Women in N.J. Can Face Rape Charges." *New York Post*, 7 May.

Norrander, Barbara, and Clyde Wilcox. 2001. "Public Opinion and Policymaking in the States: The Case of Post-Roe Abortion Policy." In *The Public Clash of Private Values: The Politics of Morality Policy*, edited by Christopher Z. Mooney, 143–160. New York: Chatham House.

North American Man/Boy Love Association. 1981. "The Case for Abolishing Age of Consent Laws." In *The Age Taboo: Gay Male Sexuality, Power, and Consent*, edited by Daniel Tsang, 92–106. Boston: Alyson.

Norton, Arthur, and Louisa Miller. 1992. "Marriage, Divorce, and Remarriage in the 1990s." *Current Population Reports P23-180.* Washington, DC: U.S. Census Bureau.

Nowack, Sandy. 2000. "A Community Prosecution Approach to Statutory Rape: Wisconsin Pilot Policy Project." *DePaul Law Review* 50: 865–895.

Nownes, Anthony, and Patricia Freeman. 1998. "Interest Group Activity in the States." *Journal of Politics* 60, no. 1 (February): 86–112.

Oakley, Maureen Rand. 1999. "Explaining the Adoption of Morality Policy Innovations: The Case of Fetal Homicide Policy." Paper presented at the annual meeting of the American Political Science Association, 1–5 September, Atlanta, Georgia.

Oberman, Michelle. 1994. "Turning Girls into Women: Reevaluating Modern Statutory Rape Law." *Journal of Criminal Law and Criminology* 85: 15–78.

———. 2000. "Regulating Consensual Sex with Minors: Defining a Role for Statutory Rape." *Buffalo Law Review* 48: 703–784.

———. 2001. "Girls in the Master's House: Of Protection, Patriarchy, and the Potential for Using the Master's Tools to Reconfigure Statutory Rape Law." *DePaul Law Review* 50: 799–826.

Odem, Mary E. 1995. *Delinquent Daughters: Protecting and Policing Adolescent Female Sexuality in the United States, 1885–1920.* Chapel Hill: University of North Carolina Press.

Olsen, Frances. 1984. "Statutory Rape: A Feminist Critique of Rights Analysis." *Texas Law Review* 63: 387–432.

Olson, Mancur. 1968. *The Logic of Collective Action.* Cambridge: Harvard University Press.

"On the Hill Two Teens Take Case to Senate." 1999. *Rocky Mountain News,* 16 March.

"Orange County Crackdown on Statutory Rape Proceeds." 1996. *West's Legal News* 2864 (April 3).

Opinion Research Service. Various Years. *American Public Opinion Index.*

Page, Benjamin, and Robert Shapiro. 1992. *The Rational Public.* Chicago: University of Chicago Press.

"Parole Revoked, Ex-Teacher Sent to Prison in Teen Sex Case." 1998. *Washington Post,* 7 February.

Pearce, Diana. 1990. "Welfare Is Not *for* Women: Why the War on Poverty Cannot Conquer the Feminization of Poverty." In *Women, the State, and Welfare*, edited by Linda Gordon, 265–278. Madison: University of Wisconsin Press.

———. 1993. "'Children Having Children': Teenage Pregnancy and Public Policy from the Woman's Perspective." In *The Politics of Pregnancy: Adolescent Sexuality and Public Policy*, edited by Annette Lawson and Deborah Rhode, 46–58. New Haven, CT: Yale University Press.

Peiss, Kathy. 1986. *Cheap Amusements: Working Women and Leisure in Turn-of-the-Century New York*. Philadelphia: Temple University Press.

Perkins, Kathryn Dore. 1994. "Outrage Seen in Adults Fathering Teens' Babies." *Sacramento Bee*, 24 April.

Perry, Tony. 1996. "Getting Tough on Teenage Pregnancies; Laws; With the Failure of Education and Counseling Programs, Governor Boosts Prosecution of Men Who Have Sex with Underage Girls." *Los Angeles Times*, 7 January.

Peters, B. Guy. 1998. *Comparative Politics: Theory and Methods*. New York: New York University Press.

Peterson, Karen. 1998. "Woman's Obsession for Boy Crosses Many Lines." *USA Today*, 5 February.

Phoenix, Ann. 1993. "The Social Construction of Teenage Motherhood: A Black and White Issue?" In *The Politics of Pregnancy: Adolescent Sexuality and Public Policy*, edited by Annette Lawson and Deborah Rhode, 74–100. New Haven, CT: Yale University Press.

Pierce, Patrick, and Donald E. Miller. 2001. "Variations in the Diffusion of State Lottery Adoptions: How Revenue Dedication Changes Morality Politics." In *The Public Clash of Private Values: The Politics of Morality Policy*, edited by Christopher Z. Mooney, 160–169. New York: Chatham House.

Pierson, Paul. 1994. *Dismantling the Welfare State? Reagan, Thatcher, and the Politics of Retrenchment*. New York: Cambridge University Press.

Pivar, David. 1973. *Purity Crusade*. Westport, CT: Greenwood.

Platt, Anthony. 1969. *The Child Savers: The Invention of Delinquency*. Chicago: University of Chicago Press.

"Plea Deal Made in Sex Assaults." 1995. *Denver Post*, 29 November.

Ploscowe, Andrea. 1994. "Book Review: The Intrafeminist Controversy over Pornography and Sex Crimes." *Criminal Law Forum* 5: 749–761.

Poovey, Mary. 1988. *Uneven Developments*. Chicago: University of Chicago Press.

Popkin, Samuel. 1991. *The Reasoning Voter*. Chicago: University of Chicago Press.

Posner, Richard, and Katharine Silbaugh. 1996. *A Guide to America's Sex Laws*. Chicago: University of Chicago Press.

"Predatory Teacher Deserves No Break." 1997. *News Tribune*, 27 August.

"Press Charges: Statutory Rape Occurs with Alarming Frequency in California." 1995. *Santa Barbara News Press*, 4 May.

"Put the Heat on Predators: Adult Men Impregnate, Abandon Too Many Girls." 1995. *San Diego Union Tribune*, 12 April.

"Pupil Romp: Teacher Caught with Boy, 14; Teacher Mary Kay Le Tourneau Who Was Jailed after Bedding a 12 Year Old Pupil Has Been Caught with the Same Toy Boy Just Weeks after She Was Freed." 1998. *Scottish Daily Record*, 5 February.

Purdum, Todd. 1998. "Death of Sex Offender Tied to Megan's Law." *New York Times*, 9 July.

Purdy, Matthew. 1997a. "Sex Offenders Test Parole Officers: Predators are Reined In; 'I Watch Him Like a Hawk.'" *New York Times*, 8 June.

———. 1997b. "Wave of New Laws Seeks to Confine Sexual Offenders: Mental Hospitalization." *New York Times*, 29 June.

Quadagno, Jill. 1994. *The Color of Welfare: How Racism Undermined the War on Poverty.* New York: Oxford University Press.

Quinn, Bernard, Herman Anderson, Martin Bradley, Paul Goetting, and Peggy Shriver. 1982. *Churches and Church Membership in the United States, 1980.* Atlanta: Glenmary Research Center.

Radcliff, Benjamin, and Patricia Davis. 2000. "Labor Organization and Electoral Participation in Industrial Democracies." *American Journal of Political Science* 44, no. 1 (January): 132–141.

Ramirez, Anthony. 1998. "After All These Years, 'Lolita' Still Disturbs." *New York Times*, 2 August.

Ramos, Victor Manuel. 1997. "Rape Suspect: Girl Lied over Age; Met 14-Year-Old through Internet." *Newsday*, 20 December.

Ranney, Austin. 1976. "Parties in State Politics." In *Politics in the American States*, 3d ed., edited by Herbert Jacob and Kenneth Vines, 51–92. Boston: Little, Brown.

Rashbaum, William. 2000. "A Bronx Man, 35, Is Charged with the Sexual Abuse of Boys." *New York Times*, 25 February.

Reagan, Leslie. 1997. *When Abortion Was a Crime: Women, Medicine, and the Law in the United States.* Berkeley and Los Angeles: University of California Press.

Regan, Milton C. Jr. 1995. "Spousal Privilege and the Meanings of Marriage." *Virginia Law Review* 81: 2045–2134.

Reid, Cheryl, and Debbie Cafazzo. 1997. "Teacher Pleads Guilty to Sex with Boy, 13: Woman, 35, Recently Gave Birth to Highline Student's Baby; Sex-Deviancy Treatment Sought." *News Tribune*, 8 August.

Rendon, Jim. 1997. "Jail Baited." *Metroactive* (December): 18–24.

Rhode, Deborah. 1993. "Adolescent Pregnancy and Public Policy." In *The Politics of Pregnancy: Adolescent Sexuality and Public Policy*, edited by Annette Lawson and Deborah Rhode, 301–335. New Haven, CT: Yale University Press.

Rice, Tom, and Alexander Sumberg. 1997. "Civic Culture and Government Performance in the American States." *Publius* 27, no. 1 (winter): 99–114.

Rich, Adrienne. 1980. "Compulsory Heterosexuality and Lesbian Existence." *Signs* 5: 24–75.

Ringquist, Evan. 1993. "Does Regulation Matter: Evaluating the Effects of State Air Pollution Programs." *Journal of Politics* 55: 1022–1045.

Rivera, Jenny. 1994. "Domestic Violence against Latinas by Latino Males: An Analysis of Race, National Origin, and Gender Differentials." *Boston College Third World Law Journal* 14: 231–257.

Roan, Shari. 1995a. "The Birth Control Bust." *Los Angeles Times*, 11 July.

———. 1995b. "The Invisible Men." *Los Angeles Times*, 10 July.

Roane, Kit. 1998. "Woman, 35, Faces Charge of Rape of Boy." *New York Times*, 27 March.

Roberts, Dorothy. 1997. *Killing the Black Body: Race, Reproduction, and the Meaning of Liberty*. New York: Pantheon.

Rodman, Hyman. 1984. *The Sexual Rights of Adolescents*. New York: Columbia University Press.

Roper Center. Various Years. *The Public Perspective: A Roper Center Review of Public Opinion and Polling*.

———. 1998. "Pre-Teens, Parents, Find Little Time for Talk. Connection Gap Seen as Kids, Parents, Split on Priorities." Available at www.roperstarch.com.

Rosenberg, Gerald. 1991. *The Hollow Hope: Can Courts Bring About Social Change?* Chicago: University of Chicago Press.

Rosenstone, Steven, Roy Behr, and Edward Lazarus. 1996. *Third Parties in America*. 2d ed. Princeton, NJ: Princeton University Press.

Rosenstone, Steven, and John Mark Hansen. 1993. *Mobilization, Participation and Democracy in America*. New York: Macmillan.

Rother, Caitlin. 2000. "Truth, Consequences for Teen Mother." *San Diego Union-Tribune*, 12 April.

Rozell, Mark, and Clyde Wilcox. 1998. *Interest Groups in American Campaigns: The New Face of Electioneering*. Washington, DC: CQ Press.

Rubin, Gayle. 1975. "The Traffic in Women." In *Toward an Anthropology of Women*, edited by Rayna Rapp, 157–210. New York: Monthly Review Press.

———. 1981. "Sexual Politics, the New Right, and the Sexual Fringe." In *The Age Taboo: Gay Male Sexuality, Power, and Consent*, edited by Daniel Tsang, 108–115. Boston: Alyson.

———. 1984. "Thinking Sex: Notes for a Radical Theory of the Politics of Sexuality." In *Pleasure and Danger: Exploring Female Sexuality*, 2d ed., edited by Carole Vance, 267–319. London: Pandora/HarperCollins.

Saad, Linda. 1998. "Americans Growing More Tolerant of Gays." Available at http//:www.gallup.com/POLL_ARCHIVES/961214.

Sachs, Susan. 1998. "A Chilling Crime and a Question: What's in a Child's Mind?" *New York Times*, 16 August.

Salisbury, Robert. 1990. "The Paradox of Interest Groups in Washington: More Groups, Less Clout." In *The New American Political System*, edited by Anthony King, 203–229. Washington, DC: American Enterprise Institute.

Sandowski, Elizabeth. 1979. "Trenton's Policy on Sexuality is Laissez-Faire." *New York Times*, 30 December.

Sanko, John. 1999. "Owens Signs Bill on Statutory Rape." *Rocky Mountain News*, 17 April.

Santana, Arthur, and Charles Brown. 1998. "Traffic Tie-Up Expected for LeTourneau Hearing." *Seattle Times*, 5 February.

Savage, Robert. 1978. "Policy Innovativeness as a Trait of American States." *Journal of Politics* 40, no. 1 (February): 212–224.

———. 1985. "Diffusion Research Traditions and the Spread of Policy Innovation in a Federal System." *Publius* 15: 1–27.

Scarponi, Diane. 1999. "State Agency [CT] Seeks More Ways to Catch Statutory Rapists." *Associated Press Newswires*, 25 February.

Scheingold, Stuart. 1974. *The Politics of Rights*. New Haven, CT: Yale University Press.

———. 1991. *The Politics of Street Crime: Criminal Process and Cultural Obsession*. Philadelphia: Temple University Press.

Schlossman, Steven, and Stephanie Wallach. 1985. "The Crime of Precocious Sexuality." *Harvard Educational Review* 48: 65–94.

Schlozman, Kay Lehman and John Tierney. 1983. "More of the Same: Washington Pressure Group Activity in a Decade of Change." *Journal of Politics* 45: 351–375.

Schmitt, Eric. 1996. "War Is Hell. So Is Regulating Sex." *New York Times*, 17 November.

Schur, Edwin. 1980. *The Politics of Deviance: Stigma Contests and the Uses of Power*. Englewood Cliffs, NJ: Prentice-Hall.

Sciolino, Elaine. 1997a. "The Army's Problems with Sex and Power." *New York Times*, 4 May.

————. 1997b. "Sergeant Convicted of Eighteen Counts of Raping Female Subordinates." *New York Times*, 30 April.

Searles, Patricia, and Ronald Berger. 1987. "The Current Status of Rape Reform Legislation: An Examination of State Statutes." *Women's Rights Law Reporter* 10, no. 1 (spring): 25–43.

Sedgwick, Eve. 1985. *Between Men*. New York: Columbia University Press.

Seelye, Katharine, and James Brooke. 1999. "Protest Greets N.R.A. Meeting in Denver." *New York Times*, 2 May.

Shanley, Mary Lyndon, Carole Pateman, and Mary Stanley, eds. 1991. *Feminist Interpretations and Political Theory*. University Park: Pennsylvania State University Press.

Shapiro, Robert, Kelly Patterson, Judith Russell, and John Young. 1987. "The Polls—Public Assistance." *Public Opinion Quarterly* 51: 120–130.

Shin, Annys. 1998. "A New Twist on an Old Law." *Ms.* 8, no. 6 (May/June): [n.p.]

Silverstein, Mark. 1994. *Judicious Choices: The New Politics of Supreme Court Confirmations*. New York: Norton.

Simmons, Wendy. 1999. "The Social Construction of Target Populations and State TANF Policy." Paper presented at the annual meeting of the American Political Science Association, 1–5 September, Atlanta, Georgia.

Sinesio, Ronald. 1998. "Prosecution of Female as Principal for Rape." 67 *American Law Reports* 1127.

Singer, Judith, and John Willett. 1993. "It's About Time: Using Discrete-Time Survival Analysis to Study Duration and Timing of Events." *Journal of Educational Statistics* 18: 155–195.

Smith, Anna Marie. 1994. *New Right Discourse of Race and Sexuality: Britain, 1968–1990*. New York: Cambridge University Press.

Smith, Dan. 1993. "2 Sex Victims Ask State for Tougher Law." *The Press-Enterprise* [Riverside, CA], July 7.

Smith, Dinitia. 1998. "Wanted: Victim or Vixen at $7 an Hour." *New York Times*, 8 August.

Smith, John Donald. 1999. "Chickens and Eggs: Judicial and Legislative Innovation in the American States." Paper presented at the annual meeting of the American Political Science Association, 1–5 September, Atlanta, Georgia.

Smith, Kevin B. 1997. "Explaining Variation in State-Level Homicide Rates: Does Crime Policy Pay?" *Journal of Politics* 59, no. 2 (May): 350–367.

————. 2001. "Clean Thoughts and Dirty Minds: The Politics of Porn." In *The Public Clash of Private Values: The Politics of Morality Policy*, edited by Christopher Z. Mooney, 187–200. New York: Chatham House.

Smith, Richard. 1995. "Interest Group Influence in the U.S. Congress." *Legislative Studies Quarterly* 20: 89–139.

Smith, Tom. 1987. "That Which We Call Welfare by Any Other Name Would Smell Sweeter: An Analysis of the Impact of Question Wording on Response Patterns." *Public Opinion Quarterly* 51: 75–83.

Smith, Tom. 1990. "The Polls—A Report: The Sexual Revolution." *Public Opinion Quarterly* 54: 415–435.

Smith-Rosenberg, Carroll. 1985. *Disorderly Conduct: Visions of Gender in Victorian America.* New York: Oxford University Press.

Snyder, Howard. 2000. "Sexual Assault of Young Children as Reported to Law Enforcement." Bureau of Justice Statistics Bulletin (July). Washington, DC: U.S. Department of Justice.

Solinger, Rickie. 1992. *Wake Up Little Susie: Single Pregnancy and Race Before Roe v. Wade.* New York: Routledge.

Spohn, Cassia, and Julie Horney. 1992. *Rape Law Reform: A Grassroots Revolution and Its Impact.* New York: Plenum.

Spriggs, James F. II, Forrest Maltzman, and Paul Wahlbeck. 1999. "Bargaining on the U.S. Supreme Court: Justices' Responses to Majority Opinion Drafts." *Journal of Politics* 61, no. 2 (May): 485–506.

Stadler, Matthew. 1998. "Statutory Rape: A Love Story." *Spin* (June): 114–125.

Stanfield, Frank. 1998. "Sex Charge Dropped When Teen Vanishes." *Orlando Sentinel*, 27 March.

Stansell, Christine. 1987. *City of Women: Sex and Class in New York, 1789–1860.* Urbana: University of Illinois Press.

Stashenko, Joel. 1998. "Welfare to Include Addictions Testing." *Albany (NY) Times Union*, 28 June.

State Capitols Report. 1996a. "Issue Spotlight, vol. 4, no. 9 [Marriage, Family, and Children]." Information for Public Affairs State Capitols Report, 1 March.

———. 1996b. "Once Around the Statehouse Lightly, vol. 4, no. 19 (Florida)." Information for Public Affairs State Capitols Report, 10 May.

———. 1996c. "Session Recaps, vol 4, no. 19 (Florida)." Information for Public Affairs State Capitols Report, 10 May.

———. 1996d. "Session Recaps, vol 4, no. 20 (Tennessee)." Information for Public Affairs State Capitols Report, 17 May.

———. 1998. "Hot Issues of the Week, vol. 6, no. 18 (Delaware)." Information for Public Affairs State Capitols Report, 4 May.

"Statutory Rape." *First Cut.* KRON–TV (San Francisco).

"Statutory Rape Is Charged." 1998. *East Hampton (NY) Star*, 16 April.

Stevens, Darlene Gavron. 1998. "When Older Women Take Teen Partners; If Law Isn't Broken, Moral Issues Fuzzier." *Chicago Tribune*, 1 March.

Stephens, Sharon. 1995. "Children and the Politics of Culture in Late Capitalism." In *Children and the Politics of Culture*, edited by Sharon Stephens, 3–49. Princeton, NJ: Princeton University Press.

Stimson, James. 1991. *Public Opinion in America.* Boulder, CO: Westview.

Stolberg, Sheryl Gay. 1999. "U.S. Birth Rate at New Low as Teenage Pregnancy Falls." *New York Times*, 29 April.

Stoler, Ann Laura. 1995. *Race and the Education of Desire: Foucault's History of Sexuality and the Colonial Order of Things.* Durham, NC: Duke University Press.

Stonecash, Jeffrey. 1996. "The State Politics Literature: Moving beyond Covariation Studies and Pursuing Politics." *Polity* 28, no. 4 (summer): 559–579.

Stream, Christopher. 1999. "Health Reform in the States: A Model of State Small Group Health Insurance Market Forms." *Political Research Quarterly* 52, no. 3 (September): 499–525.

Streif, Tilman. 1998. "LeTourneau Case Raises Issue of Double Standard for Female Criminals." *Deutsche Presse-Agentur*, 5 February.

Strom, Stephanie. 1999. "Japan's Legislators Tighten Ban on Under-Age Sex." *New York Times*, 19 May.

Studlar, Donley. 2001. "What Constitutes Morality Policy? A Cross-National Analysis." In *The Public Clash of Private Values: The Politics of Morality Policy*, edited by Christopher Z. Mooney, 37–51. New York: Chatham House.

Survey Research Consultants International. Various Years. *Index to International Public Opinion.*

Tatalovich, Raymond, and Byron Daynes. 1981. *The Politics of Abortion: A Study of Community Conflict in Public Policy Making.* New York: Praeger.

Tatalovich, Raymond, and Byron Daynes, eds. 1998. *Moral Controversies and American Politics: Cases in Social Regulatory Policy.* Armonk, NY: M. E. Sharpe.

Tatalovich, Raymond, Alexander Smith, and Michael Bobic. 1994. "Moral Conflict and the Policy Process." *Policy Currents* 4, no. 4 (November): 1–7.

"The Teen Pregnancy Epidemic." 1995. *Sacramento Bee*, 31 March.

"Teens Talk About Peer Pressure: Round Table Members Discuss School, Sex, Drugs, and Smoking." 1998. *Detroit News*, 3 September.

Tennen, Ken. 1997. "Wake Up Maggie: Gender Neutral Statutory Rape Laws, Third-Party Infant Blood Extraction, and the Conclusive Presumption of Legitimacy." *Journal of Juvenile Law* 18: 1–33.

Terry, Don. 1998. "Fewer Teen-Age Mothers? Maybe." *New York Times*, 5 May.

Thompson, Kenneth. 1998. *Moral Panics*. New York: Routledge.

Thompson, Sharon. 1995. *Going All the Way: Teenage Girls' Tales of Sex, Romance, and Pregnancy*. New York: Hill and Wang.

Tong, Rosemary. 1989. *Feminist Thought: A Comprehensive Introduction*. Boulder, CO: Westview.

Trenkner, Thomas. 1998. "Constitutionality of Rape Laws Limited to Protection of Females Only." 99 *American Law Reports* 129, August 1998 (suppl.): [n.p.].

Tsang, Daniel. 1981. Introduction. In *The Age Taboo: Gay Male Sexuality, Power, and Consent*, edited by Daniel Tsang, 7–12. Boston: Alyson.

———, ed. 1981. *The Age Taboo: Gay Male Sexuality, Power, and Consent*. Boston: Alyson.

Tyler, Tom. 1990. *Why People Obey the Law*. New Haven, CT: Yale University Press.

UPI. 1982. "Schweiker Defends Proposal for Teen-age Chastity Rule." *New York Times*, 10 February.

———. 1984. "Charges Dropped in Six-Year Old Case [Michael M.]" *UPI Wire Services*, 17 October.

———. 1992. "Man Charged with Corrupting His Wife." *UPI Wire Services*, 6 March.

———. 1996. "Law Goes after Statutory Rapists." *UPI Wire Services*, 23 September.

Urban Institute. 1997. "Tougher Statutory Rape Laws Expected to Have Limited Impact on Teen Childbearing." Press Release, 15 April.

U.S. Census Bureau. 1998. *Marital Status and Living Arrangements, March 1998*. Update, P20-514. Unpublished tables. Available at http://www.census.gov.

Usdansky, Margaret. 1996. "Single Motherhood: Stereotypes vs. Statistics." *New York Times*, 11 February.

Vance, Carole, ed. 1993. *Pleasure and Danger: Exploring Female Sexuality*. 2d ed. London: Pandora/HarperCollins.

Ventura, S. J., T. J. Matthews, and P. E. Hamilton. 2001. "Births to Teenagers in the United States, 1940–2000." *National Vital Statistics Report* 49, no. 10. Hyattsville, MD: National Center for Health Statistics.

Verba, Sidney, and Norman Nie. 1972. *Participation in America: Political Democracy and Social Equality*. Chicago: University of Chicago Press.

Vergari, Sandra. 2001. "Morality Politics and the Implementation of Abstinence-only Sex Education: A Case of Policy Compromise." In *The Public Clash of Private Values: The Politics of Morality Policy*, edited by Christopher Z. Mooney, 201–210. New York: Chatham House.

Volpp, Leti. 2000. "Blaming Culture for Bad Behavior." *Yale Journal of Law and the Humanities* 12: 89–116.

Waldron, Martin. 1979a. "NJ Legislature Maintains 16 as Age of Sexual Consent." *New York Times*, 13 May.

———. 1979b. "Jersey State Assembly Votes 71 to 2 to Keep 16 as Age of Consent." *New York Times*, 4 May.

———. 1979c. "New Jersey Journal." *New York Times*, 29 April.

Walker, Alice. 1973. "You Can't Keep a Good Woman Down: Advancing Luna and Ida B. Wells." In *Revolutionary Petunias*. New York: Harcourt, 85–104.

Walker, Jack L. 1969. "The Diffusion of Innovations among the American States." *American Political Science Review* 63, no. 3 (September): 880–899.

———. 1973. "Comment: Problems in Research on the Diffusion of Policy Innovations." *American Political Science Review* 67, no. 4 (December): 1186–1191.

———. 1991. *Mobilizing Interest Groups in America*. Ann Arbor: University of Michigan.

Walkowitz, Judith. 1980. *Prostitution and Victorian Society: Women, Class, and the State*. New York: Cambridge University Press.

———. 1992. *City of Dreadful Delight: Narratives of Sexual Danger in Late Victorian London*. Chicago: University of Chicago Press.

Waters, Lou, and Susan Reed. 1998. "LeTourneau Lands Back in Jail." *CNN Today*, 6 February.

Wattenberg, Martin. 1991. *The Rise of Candidate Centered Politics*. Cambridge: Harvard University Press.

———. 1996. *The Decline of American Political Parties*. Cambridge: Harvard University Press.

Weaver, Nancy. 1995. "Grim Look at Efforts on Behalf of Children." *Sacramento Bee*, 16 March.

Weeks, Jeffrey. 1989. *Sex, Politics, and Society: The Regulation of Sexuality since 1800*. 2d ed. London: Longman.

Wells-Barnett, Ida B. 2002. *On Lynchings*. Amherst, NY: Prometheus Books.

Weston, Bonnie. 1995. "Adult Men Are Fathering Most Teen Girls' Babies; Experts See Jail, Fines as Options." *Orange County Register*, 18 June.

Wharton, David. 1992. "Sex and Section 261.5. California's Statutory Rape Law Applies Only to Female Victims. For Underage Males, There Is Less Legal Protection." *Los Angeles Times*, 30 April.

Whitmire, Richard. 1997. "Enforcing Statutory Rape Laws Brings Unintended Results." *Gannett News Service*, 24 July.

Wiggins, Charles W., Keith E. Hamm, and Charles G. Bell. 1992. "Interest Group and Party Influence Agents in the Legislative Process: A Comparative State Analysis." *Journal of Politics*. 54:82-100.

Wilchins, Riki Anne, Nancy Nangeroni, Lynn Walker, and JoAnn Roberts. 1996. "Trans-people as Child Molesters?" *Oasis.* Retrieved from http://www.oasismag.com on 15 August 1999.

Wilkie, Dana. 1995. "Governor's Meeting Focuses on Fatherless." *San Diego Union-Tribune* (June 14).

Wilson, James Q. 1973. *Political Organizations.* New York: Basic Books.

Wilson, William Julius. 1987. *The Truly Disadvantaged: The Inner City, the Underclass, and Public Policy.* Chicago: University of Chicago Press.

Wolfinger, Raymond, and Steven Rosenstone. 1980. *Who Votes?* New Haven, CT: Yale University Press.

"Woman Charged with Rape, Endangering 15-Year-Old." *Albany (NY) Times Union,* 7 July.

Zaller, John. 1992. *The Nature and Origins of Mass Opinion.* New York: Cambridge University Press.

Cases

Acosta v. State (Del Sup) 417 A2d 373 (1980).

American Academy of Pediatrics v. Lundgren, 16 Cal.4th 307 (1997).

B.B. v. State of Florida, 659 So2d 256, (1995).

Barnes v. Glen Theater, 501 US 560 (1991).

Barnes v. State 244 Ga 302, 260 SE2d 40 (1979).

Baynes v. State (Ala App) 423 So 2d 307 (1982).

Bowers v Hardwick, 478 US 186 (1986)

Constancio v. State (Nev) 639 P2d 547 (1982).

Craig v Boren, 429 US 190 (1976)

Curtis v. State (Tex Crim) 640 SW2d 615 (1982).

Ex parte Groves (Tex Crim) 571 SW2d 888 (1978).

Ferris v. Santa Clara County (9th Cir) F2d 715 (1989).

Frontiero v Richardson, 411 US 677 (1973)

Griffin v. Warden, C. C. I. 277 SC 288, 286 SE2d 145 (1982).

Hall v. State (Ala App) 365 So 2d 1249 (1978).

Hall v. McKenzie (4th Cir, W Va) 537 F2d 1232 (1976).

Hernandez v. State of Texas, 764 S.W. 2d 321, Tex. Ct. App. (1988).

Hill v. National Collegiate Athletic Association, 7 Cal.4th 1 (1994).

In Re Frederick, 622 N.E.2d 762 Ohio Ct. App (1993).

In Re Gladys R., 1 Cal.3d 855 (1970).

In Re James P., 115 Cal App. 3d 681 (1981).

In Re Jessie C., 565 NYS 2d 941, N.Y. App. Div. (1991).

In Re Meagan R., 42 Cal. App. 4th 17 (1996).

In Re Paul C., 221 Cal. App. 3d 43 (1990).

In Re Roger S., 19 Cal 3d 921 (1977).

In Re T.A.J., a person coming under the juvenile court law [People v. T.A.J], 62 Cal. App. 4th 1350 (1998).

In the Interest of B.L.S., a child, 264 Ga. 643, 449 SE 2d 823, 94 Fulton Cty DR 3737 (1994).

In the Interest of G. (Mo) 498 SW2d 786 (1973).

Jones. v. State of Florida, Rodriguez et al. v. State of Florida, 640 So. 2d 1084 (1994).

Jory v. State of Florida, 647 So. 2d 152 (1994).

Ledbetter v. State of Tennessee, 199 S.W. 2d (1947).

Meloon v Helgemoe (1977, CA1 NH) 564 F2d 602, cert. denied 436 US 950, 56 L Ed 2d 793, 98 S Ct 2858

Matter of C. Children, 5/26/94 NYLJ 31 [Vol. 211, No. 101] (1994).

May v. State of Texas, 919 S.W. 2d 422 (1996).

Mercer County Dept. of Social Services, O/B/O Imogene T. v. Alf M, 10/30/92 NYLJ 35 [Vol. 208, No. 85] (1992).

Michael M. v Superior Court, 25 Cal 3d 608, 601 P2d 572 (1979)

Michael M. v. Superior Court of Sonoma County, 450 US 464–502 (1981).

Moore v. McKenzie (WVa) 236 SE2d 342 (1977).

Navedo v Preisser (1980, CA8 Iowa) 630 F2d 636

Olson v. State (Nev) 588 P2d 1018 (1979).

Orr v Orr, 440 US 268 (1979).

People v. Davoli, 95 Misc 2d 402, 407 NYS2d 432 (1978).

People v. Fauntleroy, 94 Misc 2d 606, 405 NYS2d 931 (1978).

People v. Green, 183 Colo 25, 514 P2d 769 (1973).

People v Hernandez, 61 Cal 2d 529, 393 P2d 673, 39 Cal Rptr 361 (1964)

People v Liberta, 64 NY2d 152, 474 NE2d 567, 485 NYS2d 207 (1984)

People v. M.K.R. 6/7/95 NYLJ 31 [Vol. 213, No. 108] (1995).

People v. Mackey, (4th Dist) 46 Cal App 3d 755, 120 Cal Rptr 157 (1975), cert. denied, 423 US 951 (1975).

People v. McKellar (2d Dist) 81 Cal App 3d 367, 146 Cal Rptr 327 (1978).

People v. Mndandge-Pfupfu, 97 Misc 2d 496, 411 NYS2d 1000 (1978).

People v. Prainito, 97 Misc 2d 66, 410 NYS2d 772 (1978).

People v. Salinas, 191 Colo 171, 551 P2d 703 (1976).

People v. Scott, 9 Cal 4th 331 (1994).

People v. Smith, 97 Misc 2d 115, 411 NYS2d 146 (1978).

People v Verdegreen, 106 Cal 211, 39 P 607 (1895)

People v. Weidiger, 96 Misc 2d 978, 410 NYS2d 209 (1978).

People v. Whidden, (3d Dept) 71 App Div 2d 367, 423 NYS2d 512 (1979).

People v. Whidden, 51 NY2d 457, 434 NYS2d 936, 415 NE2d 927 (1980).

Planned Parenthood Affiliates of California et al. v. John K. Van De Kamp, 181 Cal. App. 3d 245 (1986).

Powell v State of Georgia, 510 SE2d 18 (1998)

Reed v Reed, 404 US 71 (1973)

Roe v Wade 410 US 113 (1973)

State ex. Rel Hermesmann v Seyer, 847 P2d 1273 (1993, Kansas)

State of Florida v Jory, 647 So.2d 152 (1994)

State of Florida v. J.A.S., a child, and J.L.R., a child, 686 So. 2d 1366 (1997).

State of Missouri v. Snow, 252 S.W. 629, Mo (1923).

State of Tennessee v. Hood, 868 S.W. 2d 744 (1993).

State v. Bell (La) 377 So 2d 303 (1979).

State v. Brothers (Del) 384 A2d 402 (1978).

State v. Drake (Iowa) 219 NW2d 492 (1974).

State v. Elmore, 24 Or App 651, 546 P2d 1117 (1976).

State v Gray, 122 Ariz 445, 595 P2d 990 (1979)

State v. Hill, 170 NJ Super 485, 406 A2d 1334 (1979).

State v. Housekeeper (Utah) 588 P2d 139 (1978).

State v. La Mere, 103 Idaho 839, 655 P2d 46 (1982).

State v. Meloon, 116 NH 669, 366 A2d 1176 (1976).

State v Navedo, 281 NW2d 34 (1978, Iowa)

State v. Rundlett (Me) 391 A2d 815 (1978).

State v. Thompson, 162 NJ Super 302, 392 A2d 678 (1978).

State v. Ware (RI) 418 A2d 1 (1980).

State v. Wilson, 296 NC 298, 250 SE2d 621, 99 ALR3d 115 (1979).

US v Hicks (1980 CA9 Ariz) 625 F2d 216

Weinberger v Weisenfeld, 420 US 636 (1975)

Laws

18 Eliz., ch. 7 §4 (1576)

18 Pa. Cons. Stat. Ann. §§3102, 3121, 3122.1, 3123, 3125, 3126, 3127, 4510; 23 Pa. Cons. Stat. Ann. §1304.

18 USC Sec. 2252A.

18 U.S.C.A §§2243 (a), 2241, 2243, 2244.

Ala. Code §§13A-6-62 through 13A-6-67; 30-1-4, 30-1-5.

Alaska Stat. §§11.41.434, 11.41.436, 11.41.438, 11.41.440, 11.41.445, 11.41.460, 11.61.110, 25.05.111, 25.05.171.

Ariz. Rev. Stat. Ann. §§13-1404, 13-1405, 13-1410, 25-102.

Ark. Code Ann. §§5-14-102 through 5-14-110, 9-11-102, 9-11-103, 106-16-20.

Cal. AB 327, Reg Sess., chap. 83. An Act to Amend Section 11165.1 of the Penal Code, 1997.

Cal. AB 1490, Reg Sess., chap. 789. Teenage Pregnancy Prevention Act of 1995.

Cal. Family Code §§301, 302.

Cal. Penal Code §§261.5, 288a, 289, 290, 294.

Colo. Rev. Stat. Ann. §§18-3-403, 18-3-404, 18-3-405, 14-2-106, 14-2-108.

Conn. Gen. Stat. Ann. §§53a-70, 53a-71, 53a-73a, 46b-30.

Del. Code Ann Tit 11, §§762, 768, 770, 773, 775, 1103, 1108; Tit. 13, §123.

D.C. Code Ann. §§22-1408, 22-1409, 22-2801, 22-3501, 22-4110, 30-103, 30-111.

Fla. Stat. Ann. §§775.082, 794.05, 794.011, 800.04, 827.04, 741.0405.

Ga. Code Ann. §§16-6-3, 16-6-4, 16-6-5, 19-3-2, 19-3-37, 19-7-5, 49-5-50, 49-5-251.

Haw. Rev. Stat. §§707-730, 707-732, 572-1, 572-2.

Idaho Code §§18-1506, 18-1508, 18-1508a, 18-6101, 32-202.

Ill. Ann. Stat., ch. 720, paras. 5/11-6, 5/11-9.1, 5/12-13, 5/12-14.1, 5/12-15, 5/12-16, 5/12-17, 5/11-6, 5/12-17; ch. 750, paras. 5/203, 5/208.

Ind. Code Ann. §16-1 to 16-28.

Ind. Code Ann. §§35-42-4-3, 35-42-4-5, 35-42-4-6, 35-42-4-9, 31-7-1-5, 31-7-1-6, 31-7-2-2, 31-7-2-3.

Iowa Code Ann. §§702.17, 709.1, 709.3, 709.4, 709.8, 709.12, 595.2.

Kan. Stat. Ann. §§21-3502, 21-3503, 21-3504, 21-3506, 21-3510, 23-106.

Ky. Rev. Stat. Ann. §§510.020 through 510-140, 402-020.

La. Rev. Stat. Ann.. §§14:43.1, 14:43.3, 14:80, 14:81, 14:106; art. 1545.

Me. Rev. Stat. Ann. Tit. 17A, §§253-258; tit. 19, §62.

Md. Crim. Law Code Ann. Tit. 27 §§463, 464A, 464B, 464C, 2-301.

Mass. Gen. Laws, ch. 265, §23, §35a; ch. 272, §35A; ch. 207, §§7, 25.

Mich. Comp. Laws. Ann. §§750.520b, 750.520c, 750.520d, 750.520e, 750.520f, 750.13, 750.145a, 551.103.

Minn. Stat. Ann. §§609.342 through 609.345, 609.352, 517.02.

Miss. Code Ann. §§97-3-65, 97-3-67, 97-5-21, 97-5-23, 93-1-5.

Mo. Ann. Stat. §§566.020, 566.032, 566.034, 566.062, 566.064, 566.067, 566.068, 566.140, 451.090.

Mont. Code Ann. §§45-5-501, 45-5-502, 45-5-503, 45-5-511.

Neb. Rev. Stat. §§28-319, 28-320.01, 42-102, 42-105.

Nev. Rev. Stat. §§200-364, 200-368, 201.230, 122.020, 122.025.

N.H. Rev. Stat. Ann. §§632-A:3, 645:1, 457:4, 457:5, 457:6.

N.J. Stat. Ann. §§2c:14-2, 2c:14-3, 37:1-6.

N.M. Stat. Ann. §§30-9-1, 30-9-11, 30-9-13, 40-1-5, 40-1-6.

N.Y. Dom. Rel. Law §§7, 15a.

N.Y. Penal Law §§130.05, 130.25, 130.30, 130.35, 130.40, 130.45, 130.50, 130.55, 130.60, 130.65.

New York State Counsel to the Governor Legislative Bill and Veto Jackets. 1987. Series #12590-87. A.58976 (King); S.4931-B (Kehoe). Chapter 510.

N.C. Gen. Stat. §§14-27.2, 14-27.4, 14-27-7a, 14-202.1, 51-2.

N.D. Cent. Code §§12.1-20-01, 12.1-20-03, 12.1-20-03.1, 12.1-20-05, 12.1-20-07, 14-03-02.

Ohio Rev. Code Ann. §§2907.02, 2907.04 through 2907.07, 3105.01.

Okla. Stat. Ann. Tit. 21, §§1111, 1112, 1114, 1123; tit. 43, §3.

Or. Rev. Stat. §§163.315, 163.345, 163.355, 163.365, 163.375, 163.385, 163.395, 163.408, 163.411, 163.415, 163.427, 163.435, 163-445, 106.010, 106.060.

PA Act no. 1994-151 HB No. 1001, "Child Abuse Reporting, Protective Service, Schools."

P.L. 104-193, "Personal Responsibility and Work Opportunity Reconciliation Act of 1996." Title I Temporary Assistance to Needy Families, 22 August 1996.

P.L. 105-314 "Protection of Children from Sexual Predators Act of 1998."

R.I. Gen. Laws §§11-37-6, 11-37-8.1, 11-37-8.3, 15-2-11.

S.C. Code Ann. §§16-3-655, 16-3-659, 16-15-140, 20-1-250.

S.D. Codified Laws Ann. §§22-22-1, 22-22-1.2, 22-22-1.3, 22-22-1.4, 22-22-7, 22-22-7.3, 25-1-9.

Statute of Westminster I, 3 Edw., c 13 (1275).

Statute of Westminster II, 13 Edw., c. 34 (1285).

Tenn. Code Ann. §§38-1-301 through 306, 39-13-506, 39-13-522, 36-3-105, 36-3-107.

Tennessee 1996 Session Laws, 99th General Assembly, Pub. Ch. 842, HB #2342, "Prevention and Detection of Crime—Statutory Rape—Reports by Health Care Providers or Department of Human Resources, Immunity."

Tennessee Bill Text, Senate Bill 1654 (Fowler), House Bill 1885 (DeBerry), Introduced 22 February 1999, "An Act to Amend Tennessee Code Annotated, Title 37, Title 38, and Title 39, relative to sexual offenses committed against children."

Tex. Family Code Ann. §§1.51, 1.52, 1.53.

Tex. Penal Code Ann. §§21.11, 261.101.

Utah Code Ann. §§76-2-304.5, 76-5-401, 76-5-401.2, 76-5-402.1, 76-5-402.3, 76-5-403.1, 76-5-404.1, 76-5-406, 76-5-406.5, 30-102, 30-1-9.

Va. Code Ann. §§18.2-61, 18.2-63, 18.2-66, 18.2-67.2, 18.2-67.3, 18.2-67.5, 18.2-370, 20-45.1, 20-48.

Vt. Stat. Ann. Tit. 13, §§3252, 3253; tit. 18, §5142.

Wash. Rev. Code Ann §§9A.44.010, 9A.44.073, 9A.44.100, 9A.44.076, 9A.44.079, 9A.44.083, 9A.44.086, 9A.44.089, 26.04.010.

W.Va. Code §§61-8B-2, 61-8B-3, 61-8B-5, 61-8B-7, 61-8B-9, 61-8B-12, 48-1-1.

Wis. Stat. Ann. §§940.225, 948.01, 948.02, 948.05, 948.07, 948.09, 948.10, 765.02.

Wis. Act 280, AB 876 "Statutory Rape Pilot Program; Nursing Home Forfeiture." 1997.

Wyo. Stat. §§6-2-303, 6-2-304, 6-2-306, 6-2-308, 14-3-105, 20-1-102.

Index